JOANNE LIPMAN
and
MELANIE KUPCHYNSKY

STRINGS ATTACHED

One Tough Teacher and the
Art of Perfection

SIMON &
SCHUSTER

London · New York · Sydney · Toronto · New Delhi

A CBS COMPANY

First published in Great Britain by Simon & Schuster UK Ltd, 2013
A CBS COMPANY

13 5 7 9 10 8 6 4 2

Simon & Schuster UK Ltd
1st Floor
222 Gray's Inn Road
London WC1X 8HB

www.simonandschuster.co.uk

Simon & Schuster Australia, Sydney
Simon & Schuster India, New Delhi

Conversations have been reconstructed from memory and from interviews
with participants. Some events have been compressed.

Design by Brooke Koven

A CIP catalogue record for this book is available from the British Library

Hardback ISBN: 978-1-47110-198-4
Trade Paperback ISBN: 978-1-47110-199-1
eBook ISBN: 978-1-47112-576-8

Printed and bound by CPI Group (UK) Ltd Croydon, CR0 4YY

To Tom, Rebecca, Andrew, and Mom,
and in memory of my dad, Burton E. Lipman

—J.L.

To Ed, who will always remember,
and to Nick, Greg, and Laura,
so you will never forget

—M.K.

———————————

Some people come into our lives, leave footprints on our hearts, and we are never the same.

—FRANZ PETER SCHUBERT

———————————

CONTENTS

STRINGS
ATTACHED

FOREWORD

Everybody has that one teacher who changes his or her life forever. And it seemed like we heard from all of them after Joanne wrote about Jerry Kupchynsky, the toughest teacher in the world, in the *New York Times.*

Even before the print newspaper landed on people's doorsteps, e-mail messages began pouring in from readers reminiscing about the English professor, the soccer coach, the bandleader who pushed them beyond their limits. They spoke of that one person in their childhood who forced them to achieve more than seemed possible, whom they cussed and whined about back then—and whom they wished, more than anything, they could thank now. They lovingly described the tyrant who once put them through living hell.

"My wife and I choked up over breakfast this morning. It got me thinking about every teacher, coach, even parents of friends, who connected with me when I was growing up," wrote a Boston lawyer. "It's funny how the ones who were the biggest pains at the time are the ones I recall most vividly all these decades later."

For an elderly retiree, Mr. K's story evoked "a journalism professor I had at Iowa and Kansas." For a prominent attorney, it was "my tough-as-nails soccer coach at Stanford." For a New York woman it was her son's ninety-seven-year-old cello teacher, who "often brings Eli to tears, but no one inspires him more." As a New Jersey woman who sent the piece to all three of her college-age children wrote, "They may not have realized it yet, but we are all influenced and touched by some teacher in our lives."

The outpouring following the *Times* piece surprised us both. And then it hit us: Everybody needs a Mr. K. Especially today— when it isn't just kids but grown-ups who have been raised on a steady diet of praise and trophies—a little toughness goes an awfully long way. Those who have endured a Mr. K of their own can handle just about anything. They're tougher, more resilient; they laugh just a little bit more. If ever there was a living, breathing, yelling embodiment of the old adage, "Whatever doesn't kill you makes you stronger," that would be Mr. K.

And this was the impetus behind our journey to write *Strings Attached*. We feel uniquely privileged to be able to tell Mr. K's story. We grew up together. Melanie, Mr. K's daughter, was a child violinist who began performing at the age of four; Joanne was a violist whom Mr. K plucked out of the beginner class and groomed to be a worthy enough musician to play with his own daughters. We spent much of our childhood performing together in a quartet that also included Melanie's younger sister, Stephanie.

As musicians who rehearsed together constantly, we learned to play in sync, to read each other's nuances and body language, and to trade melodies seamlessly from one to the other and back again. We went our separate ways after high school. Melanie became a violinist with the Chicago Symphony Orchestra, while Joanne became a journalist and magazine editor in chief. But we were reunited more than two decades later at Mr. K's memorial concert, and found ourselves right back in sync, right back in that familiar rhythm—not just on the concert stage, but long afterward, in our very distinct reminiscences about Melanie's father. This book is, in effect, a duet.

If Mr. K wasn't a real-life character, somebody would have had to invent him. A Ukrainian-born taskmaster, he yelled and stomped and screamed. But he also pushed us to dream bigger and to achieve more than we ever imagined. What's remarkable is that he did all this while enduring a life of almost unimaginable tragedy.

His is an unforgettable story about the power of a great teacher, but also about resilience, excellence, and tough love. Mr. K's subject, of course, was music. But the lessons he taught his students are universal.

It's hard to imagine a Mr. K in today's world. Parents would be outraged; administrators would be pressured to fire him. Yet he was remarkably effective. His methods raise the big issues we grapple with now ourselves, as parents. Are we too soft on our kids? How do we best balance discipline with praise? How hard do we really want our kids' teachers to push them? And if our kids do complain, how do we know when—or if—to interfere?

The latest research on kids and motivation, it turns out, comes down in Mr. K's corner. Recent studies have turned conventional wisdom on its head, concluding that overpraising kids makes them *less* confident and *less* motivated. Psychologist Carol Dweck, for instance, found that fifth graders praised for being "smart" became less confident, while those told they were "hard workers" became more confident and performed better.

Similar findings have transformed our understanding of business success. In his 2008 book *Outliers*, Malcolm Gladwell popularized the notion that true expertise requires 10,000 hours of practice.

He cited examples—Microsoft founder Bill Gates, for one—and credited the work of the Swedish psychologist K. Anders Ericsson. Perhaps it shouldn't be surprising that Ericsson's initial work was based on a study he did not of executives—but of violinists.

Ericsson expanded his research to the business world with a 2007 *Harvard Business Review* article, "The Making of an Expert." He and his coauthors identified three key steps that all experts take, including those 10,000 hours as well as deliberate practice with a teacher. Perhaps most significant was the third step:

> The development of expertise requires coaches who are capable of giving constructive, even painful, feedback. Real experts... deliberately picked unsentimental coaches who would challenge them and drive them to higher levels of performance.

In other words, real experts don't want soft teachers: They want tough ones. Unsentimental ones. Ones who give them "painful" feedback.

We couldn't imagine a more accurate description of Mr. K.

That research helped us to answer a key question: What was it that made Mr. K so effective? But, as we were writing, a business executive asked us what turned out to be an even more important question: What did Mr. K do that made his *students* effective?

"Any kid can be pushed to excel," said the executive, the CEO of a big U.S. company. "What I want to know is, what happens when the teacher isn't there any longer to push them?"

Too often, he said, he hired applicants with sterling résumés who turned out to be poor performers. They were incapable of taking initiative on their own. How, he wanted to know, do you raise kids to be self-starters?

The CEO got it right, we realized. That was the key to Mr. K's success. It wasn't about what happened in his classroom. It's what happened once his students *left* the classroom. Whether his students became musicians or doctors or lawyers, they shared one trait in common: They pushed themselves. They didn't need anybody else to do it for them. It dawned on us that perhaps it was no mistake that one of Mr. K's most frequent admonitions was "Discipline *yourself*!" His students, whether consciously or not, took him at his word.

"Discipline. Self-confidence. Resilience. These are lifelong lessons," as one of his old students told us. "Whether we stuck with the music or not, it stuck with us."

Mr. K was without a doubt the toughest teacher we ever met. But his legacy is proof that one person can make all the difference. And that legacy endures. Its power was clear when, after his death, forty years' worth of former students flew in from every corner of the country, old instruments in tow. They were inspired to take leave of their busy lives because they never forgot the lessons he taught them. And they were determined to thank him in the best way they knew how: by playing one last concert together, this time for Mr. K.

The outpouring of emotion—from students, colleagues, and those who read about his story afterward—made us understand how universal is the appeal of that tough teacher who can set us straight on what matters in life. Mr. K may be gone, but with *Strings Attached*, we hope his lessons will live on.

—JOANNE LIPMAN
New York City

—MELANIE KUPCHYNSKY
Chicago

Prologue

MELANIE

JUNE 1991

*W*e are walking hand in hand through a beautiful, sun-drenched meadow. In the distance, a line of shady trees marks the edge of a forest. As we approach a small hill, she lets go of my hand and climbs ahead. Seconds later, I reach the top, but she has disappeared. At first I think she has slipped into the forest, but she is nowhere to be seen. I look and look, and call her name, but she is simply gone.

When I wake up I am trembling, drowning in the deepest sadness I have ever known. In the early summer dawn, I can see the shadows of boxes littering the bedroom floor, awaiting the movers who will take them to our new house just outside of Chicago. I grab my sleeping husband and shake him awake.

"Ed! Ed!" I half-sob, half-whisper. "I dreamed I lost my sister."

1

JOANNE

AUGUST 1991

The phone rang while I was on deadline. I grabbed it without looking up from my keyboard. I didn't have time for interruptions. My daily column was going to be late—again. But at least I had a scoop to show for it, if I could only finish the damn thing without distractions. Around me were the familiar sounds of the newsroom—Kevin in the cubicle next to mine, on the phone with a source: "You better not be fucking with me. It's going in the paper tomorrow." Our boss, Laura, tapping a stiletto heel and yelling for copy, *where the hell is everybody's copy?* Dennis, complaining loudly about the editor recently promoted from our bullpen of reporters: "Didn't take him long to become an *asshole!*"

The phone cord knocked a pile of magazines onto the floor. My desk was a disaster, a firetrap of newspapers, discarded drafts of articles, photos of my infant daughter, dead flowers still in the vase, scrawled reminders for the babysitter. It was barely controlled, comfortable chaos, just the way I liked it. Unless this caller had something I could use for tomorrow's paper, this would be a very short conversation.

"It's Jerr . . . ," the caller began, tentatively.

"Yes?" I was ready to slam the phone down.

Pause. "It's your Mr. K."

I froze.

I turned away from the keyboard. *Mr. K?* I hadn't seen my childhood music teacher, Jerry Kupchynsky, in a decade, maybe longer. Once, he had been the most towering figure in my life, other than my parents. His voice, a *booming, yelling* voice with a thick Ukrainian accent that never mellowed, was embedded in my brain. I could still hear him from all those years ago: "Playing sounds like cheeken plocking! Wrist back! Elbow out! Again!"

But that was a long time ago. Now I was a columnist for the *Wall Street Journal* and lived with my husband and my new baby and a live-in nanny in a Manhattan apartment. I was on a first-name basis with chief executives and politicians and billionaires. I hadn't thought about my old music teacher back in New Jersey, much less picked up my viola, in years. Yet here I was, suddenly feeling like I was twelve years old again. "Your Mr. K" realized it even before I did: he would always be Mr. K, never plain "Jerry," to me.

This wasn't a social call. "Stephanie is missing," he said, his words spilling out quickly. Stephanie, the younger of his two daughters, was, like him, a violin teacher. She had just moved to a new job in upstate New York, he was telling me. When she didn't show up for lessons a few weeks back, the police searched her apartment. Her groceries were still on the floor, waiting to be put away. But she was nowhere to be found. No note, no sign of struggle . . . and no trace of where she went. It was as if she just disappeared.

She is simply gone, Mr. K told me. *I lost her.*

I had grown up with Mr. K's daughters. The older one, Melanie, was my age. Named for the saintly sidekick to Scarlett O'Hara in *Gone with the Wind*, she was just about as perfect: a violin prodigy, brilliant student, conservatory graduate, violinist with the Chicago Symphony. Stephanie, just a few years behind us, was the fun one: a gifted violinist with a mischievous streak, the kind of girl who laughed good-naturedly when she hit a wrong note and who listened to Pink Floyd when her father thought she was practicing Mozart.

And now she was missing.

Could I possibly help get media coverage of her case? Mr. K was asking. Perhaps if others heard about her disappearance, some stranger out there might provide some clues. Maybe she had fallen and hit her head and gotten amnesia, he said. If her story made the news, surely someone would recognize her. Maybe she needed a break and wanted to clear her head alone, away from the phone, for a few days, he said. His voice was pleading.

I forgot about the deadline. And the column. I pulled Kevin in from the next cubicle—he covered the television business and had almost every TV news producer in town on speed dial.

It was unfathomable that fun-loving Stephanie would simply disappear. Mr. K knew that better than anyone. With a new daughter at home myself, I couldn't even begin to ponder the horror of simply . . . losing a child. It was too awful to contemplate. Nor could I reconcile this vulnerable, frightened old man on the phone with the invincible, intimidating figure from my childhood.

But I knew what I *could* do. For the first time in my life, I was the one giving instructions to my old teacher. "Tell me everything, from the start," I commanded him, flipping open a fresh reporter's notebook. "Tell me your story."

PART I

*To play without passion is
inexcusable!*

—LUDWIG VAN BEETHOVEN

1

The Debut

JOANNE

The meanest man I ever met came into my life when I was five years old. I first saw him from behind. Shoulders hunched, he was flailing his arms wildly, straining the seams of his black suit jacket so ferociously that I feared it might rip right apart. He looked like the villains I had seen in my big sisters' comic books: any moment now he would burst out of his civilized shell, shredding the clothes that restrained him, and terrorize the high school auditorium.

I shrank into my seat, squirming in my hand-me-down party dress and the ugly Mary Janes that pinched my toes. My feet didn't quite touch the concrete floor beneath the fold-down seats. Next to me, my mother shot me a look that silently commanded: "Be still!"

Onstage, the terrifying man still had his back turned to us. He was gesticulating even more maniacally now, looking as if he might career right off the raised wooden platform where he loomed, impossibly large and menacing. One hand had a death grip on a pointy stick that he waved frantically to and fro. I could swear I could hear him grunting. In front of him sat several dozen kids—big kids, these were, at least nine or ten years old—each fumbling with a musical instrument and each looking up at him in abject horror. One of them was my big sister.

He was conducting the East Brunswick Beginner String Orchestra.

They were playing "Twinkle, Twinkle, Little Star."

The man's arms waved faster and more wildly, as if he were straining to extract each note by brute force. Then he made one last furious swing with his pointy stick and the orchestra—almost in unison, save a few stragglers—struck the last chord. As they did, he stretched out his arms and held them wide. The music stopped. The kids froze. Their instruments remained motionless in the air, their bows still poised on the strings, their eyes unblinking as they looked fearfully toward the man.

The auditorium erupted into applause. The scary man slowly lowered his arms and turned around. I winced. His face was fierce, even more frightening than I had imagined. He had narrow black eyes and a thin mustache perched over an unsmiling mouth that seemed cast in plaster into a rigid, straight line. Though my big sister was now standing with the rest of the orchestra, proudly clutching the neck of her rented three-quarter-size violin, I paid no attention to her. I couldn't look away from that fearsome, mesmerizing presence.

And then it happened. It was just a flicker, and it disappeared in an instant.

But years later I remember that moment: as the applause

swelled, a glimmer of a smile, with the faintest hint of mischief, passed over Jerry Kupchynsky's face.

A man like Jerry Kupchynsky had no business being in a place like East Brunswick, New Jersey. It was one of those featureless suburbs that sprouted out of dairy pastures and chicken farms, a muddy expanse of new developments with streets named "Tall Oaks" and "Evergreen," after the trees that had been plowed into oblivion to make way for cookie-cutter houses with new-sod lawns. The town's local highway—home to the International House of Pancakes and the drive-in McDonald's boasting OVER 1 BILLION SERVED—roared with the sound of teenagers gunning their Mustangs and Camaros. There was no real center of town in East Brunswick, no quaint shop-lined streets. The height of local culture was the drive-in movie theater.

Some families, the leftover farm families, had been there for years. But most had moved in more recently, like my parents, who bought our brand-new house because it was near my dad's first job. Their college friends back in Queens had laughed at them for settling in "the sticks," and it's true that when you stood in our front yard, you could hear the gunshots from the cattle slaughterhouse down the road. But my parents didn't mind. The neighborhood was new, the families were young. Like my dad, the other men in our neighborhood were up before the sun, commuting to bigger towns or taking the bus to New York City. The kids—three or more to each family—spilled out into the streets, roller-skating or playing curbside basketball when the weather was good, huddling at the corner school bus stop when it wasn't.

East Brunswick barely had a music program back when the foreign teacher with the impenetrable accent and the funny last name came to town. The school board had figured he could whip up a marching band to cheer on the football team or maybe pull together a glee club. Instead, he ordered up storerooms full of violins, violas, and cellos and began drilling his students on the finer points of Mozart and Bach. By the time my big sister started the violin a decade later, his program was giving lessons to five hundred kids.

Mr. K ruled with an iron will at East Brunswick High School, an inelegant complex of low-slung brick buildings situated atop a hill, with a steep driveway and a sloping lawn perfect for sledding down on cafeteria trays in the winter. There, in the cavernous practice room, where the dust of violin rosin was so thick you could see it swirling in the sunlight slanting through the grimy windows, his voice would echo clear into the disinfectant-scented corridors. He was so loud that the football players running laps around the outside of the building would catch snippets of his shouted commands every time they passed.

"Who eez *deaf* in first violins?" you'd hear him yell.

If you peeked through the door into the rehearsal room, you'd see him putting the orchestra through its paces at almost any time of day. Standing atop his little box, waving his big stick wildly, he'd lurch forward like he was set to grab the kids, his tie flying, his sleeves pushed up past his elbows, his mouth wide open, spit flying right into the students' faces. When somebody played a wrong note, he'd stop the whole lot of them, glare at everyone in turn, and snarl, "Who eez *slob* who play wrong note?"

The kids weren't even sure what he wanted half the time, what with the Boris Badenov cartoon-villain accent that made him sound like he was plotting to foil Rocky and Bullwinkle. "Cellos sound like hippopotamus rising from mud at bottom of *reever!*" he screamed at the players fumbling in the back of the section when they drowned out the better players in the front. Backstage, he yelled at the students waiting to go on for acting like *mahnyiaks*. After much consternation and speculation—was a *mahnyiak* some kind of strange Ukrainian marsupial?—one of the violinists finally screwed up her courage to step forward and ask him.

"*Idyot!*" he replied. "Everybody knows what *mahnyiak* eez. A crazy person. *M-a-n-i-a-c. MAHNYIAK!*"

Every spring, he corralled all the kids into a big concert, attended faithfully by the families that liked to think themselves the more cultured residents of town. The performance began with the beginner orchestra and culminated in a performance by his showcase high school orchestra.

That's why we were here, with me squirming in my seat as my parents proudly watched my sister Michele take her place in the second violins. To my great annoyance, Michele, the oldest of the three Lipman girls, was pretty and smart and so impeccably behaved that she charmed every grown-up we knew. Of course, the adults weren't there to see when she picked me up by the armpits and dangled me over the upstairs banister, teasing and threatening to throw me down the stairs.

But that day, up onstage, Michele was the one who looked terrorized. She was peering at Mr. K through frightened saucer eyes. It seemed as if she weren't breathing. I knew she sometimes came home from orchestra rehearsals in tears, and that she dreaded that the conductor might pick on her. I knew she was even more of a perfectionist than usual when it came to practicing her violin. I finally understood why.

Not far from Michele onstage sat a tiny girl no bigger than me. She was wearing a pretty pinafore with a big bow in her short red hair, and holding the smallest violin I had ever seen. It looked like a toy. Her legs didn't reach the floor. The "Twinkle" triumph finished, Mr. K was now waving her over to the front of the stage. She hopped off her chair and walked toward him. Remarkably, she didn't seem afraid. As he helped her climb up onto the podium, I could see she was smiling right at him.

The year before, my parents had taken us all the way to Philadelphia to see *The Sound of Music*. The movie was long and we were wearing our most uncomfortable fancy dresses, but the three of us—aged three, six, and eight—loved it so much we sat through it twice in a row. Now, up on the podium, the tiny girl with the tinier violin began to play. And out from her hands came a remarkable sound: the strains of "Edelweiss."

As the audience murmured in astonishment, my mother leaned down to whisper in my ear. "That girl is just about your age," she said. "Her name is Melanie. She's Mr. K's daughter."

MELANIE

"*Melanie! Time to play violin! Let's go!*" I can hear my dad yelling. Looking back to the very beginning, to when I first learned "Edelweiss" and my family was still whole, that is what I remember. He is downstairs in his basement studio, calling for me to start my lesson. I am upstairs on the floor of my bedroom, playing with my Barbie dolls. My dad has been teaching me the violin for a few months now, since I turned four years old, though he disguises my lessons as a game we play together in his studio every night after dinner.

I never used to be allowed in his studio, with its teetering stacks of music, jumble of stereo equipment, and string instruments and cases of every size, spilling out across the couch and floor. But now every night I enter the inner sanctum, just like the big kids who parade through our house every weeknight from six until ten P.M., bumping up and down the stairs and scratching the walls with their cases as the strains of Vivaldi and Mozart fill the air. I like playing the violin, but I love getting to spend time with my dad and having his attention all to myself.

"Eez time for windshield wiper game," he says, positioning my right hand on the violin bow. "Pinky curved on top. Now sweep the bow back and forth een the air, like windshield wiper. Here we go, one, two, one, two, back and forth, back and forth."

"My pinky hurts, Daddy!"

"Just a few more, back and forth, back and forth...Eet weel make your pinky stronger! Keep going! *Keep going!* Okay...There, you're done. Good girl!"

The pain is worth it. I live for those last two words.

"*Melanie!*" Daddy is calling again, impatient for my lesson to begin. I can still hear him, all these years later, his words echoing from the basement while my Barbie dolls stare up at me from the pink carpet. He's anxious because we are preparing for my first solo performance, when I will play "Edelweiss," my favorite song, at the annual spring concert. He says it that way—"first"—as if there will, of course, be many more. My mother has arranged the music herself, penciling the notes on manuscript paper and composing a piano part, too, so that she can accompany me on the stage. Sometimes my mom and I practice together, with me on my one-quarter-size violin that we nicknamed Violet, and she on her beloved big black grand piano that seems to swallow up the whole living room.

Carefully, I put my Barbie dolls in their place on my bookshelf and slide the little black violin case from under the bed. I flip open the latches, gently grasp Violet by the neck, and unhitch the bow from its felt-lined clasp. That's when I hear the thud. And then crying. Feet come pounding up the stairs, and at first I think that Daddy is mad at me for not coming right away when he called me. His favorite expression is "When I say jump, on the way up ask how high!" But the feet stop at the end of the hallway, at my parents' bedroom.

Now I can hear my mother sobbing and my father trying to calm her down. His voice sounds different than usual. My father never talks like other kids' dads. He's loud, has a thick Ukrainian accent, and gives orders that make me, my mom, and my little sister, Stephanie, snap to attention. People always turn to stare when they hear him, which I figure is because he is important, though Mom says it's just because they can't understand a word he is saying. But now, his voice sounds . . . shaky. I have never heard him like this before. I creep down the darkened hallway, my feet soundless on the thick brown carpeting, and stop outside their door. It is open a crack, and I peer inside.

At first I can't understand what I'm seeing. There is a shoe, an elegant high-heeled pump, lying on its side on the floor. And a pair of legs crumpled nearby. One foot is still wearing the other shoe.

Mommy and Daddy fight a lot about how much money my mother spends on her wardrobe. Her closets are filled to bursting with brightly colored dresses, funny-shaped boxes holding hats that have little nets and veils hanging from them, and stacks and stacks of shoes. Sometimes she lets me play dress-up and I wobble around the room on something called a Cuban heel, which has an exotically curved heel set almost in the center of the sole. Lord only knows how anyone can walk on those things.

She loves costume jewelry, too. She says it is important to always look nice, which is a corollary to her other rule: "Always be a lady!" Before I was born, when she was a school music teacher, she prided herself on never letting her class see her wear the same thing twice. And she made sure to shop for dresses with interesting backs. When she conducted her chorus, she always said, the audience deserved to have something nice to look at other than her behind. Daddy never stops fretting and fuming about how much she spends, so usually I close my bedroom door and pull out my Barbie dolls when the screaming and door slamming start.

But now I am puzzled. Why isn't my mother getting up? Is she hurt? Daddy can fix anything. Why isn't he fixing this? Something is wrong, but I'm not brave enough to push open the door to find out what.

Later, I will learn that this wasn't her first fall. When she was pregnant with my little sister, Stephanie, she lost her balance as she and Daddy were leaving the house and tumbled down the four concrete steps to our driveway. My father rushed to her side and scooped her up in his arms, cursing and berating her for being a clumsy fool. It was only after they were both safely in the car that my mother noticed his hands shaking uncontrollably as he attempted to put the key in the ignition, while tears ran down his cheeks. Daddy has never been a crier. But he is a man of strong emotions—quick to anger, fiercely protective. And he must have known then that for all his cussing and yelling, this was no ordinary fall. It would be a long time before he admitted it, but something was deeply wrong.

But on that day, the day I hear the thud while waiting to practice with my dad for my first solo performance, I know none of that. As I stand on the worn brown carpet peeking through the crack in my parents' bedroom door and hear my mother sobbing while Daddy tries in vain to comfort her, all I can see are my mother's legs, one shoe still on and the other lying on the floor nearby. My mother will never walk on her own again.

May 3, 1967, SENTINEL, SPOKESMAN...Page 22

Scheduled this Friday in East Brunswick:
the concert that is more than a concert

By LOUISE SAUL

For 180 young musicians, their teachers and the East Brunswick schools music department this Friday's performance is more than just another concert.

"In a sense," Music Supervisor Jerry Kupchynsky explains, "such a concert is 'project survival.' Here in East Brunswick we have the community and the administration behind us. We want to keep it that way. But you just can't teach children an instrument and then hide them in a hole. Music involves the composer, the performer, and the listener. Besides enjoying the music, the listener can judge what is being done in his schools in music only by these performances."

What is being done in East Brunswick is considerable.

In the All State Orchestra -- for which competition is particularly keen, East Brunswick children outnumber those from any other school system. In the Central Jersey regional orchestra string section, East Brunswick students number 18 out of 55.

Kupchynsky believes the East Brunswick program has been successful because of the stability of the music department.

"In the instrumental program, especially, we have good people who have remained with us a long time, giving continuity and stability. It may seem hard to believe today, but there was a time-- years ago -- when the superintendent of schools laughed in my face when I suggested we have orchestra rehearsal on school time. Now, of course, we teach instrumental music and have rehearsals during school. Between the band and the orchestras we work with 500 students. The results are obvious and gratifying."

Instrumental music is started in fifth grade level, with music aptitude tests given a year earlier. "These tests," Kupchynsky said, "are to identify talent but never to deprive anyone of lessons who wants them -- even if the tests show zero aptitude. They can be wrong, you know."

For Kupchynsky, who came to East Brunswick in 1956 with a bachelors and masters degree from Murray State University and a masters from Rutgers, this year's concert has added meaning. First, it is the first orchestra concert since his appointment last September as East Brunswick's supervisor of music. Second, it will mark the debut of his five-year-old daughter, Melanie.

Perhaps it is only natural that a child who is the daughter of two music teachers should show an early interest in the violin. "At first I was

THE KUPCHYNSKYS - Jerry and Melanie

hesitant about starting her,' Kupchynsky said, "but when she continued to show interest, we began, but without setting any goals. We worked 20 to 40 minutes a day -- always together, so that she wouldn't pick up any bad habits on her own. Almost before I knew it -- certainly before she could read words -- she was reading music."

When he thought Melanie was ready for the Beginners Orchestra, Kupchynsky had her play for the fifth grade group. "I wanted them to know she could really play and hold her own so they would accept her."

Friday night's concert will begin early -- at 7:30 -- to accomodate not only the High School String and Symphony Orchestra, but also the Intermediate and Beginner's Orchestras.

"It is important for the younger children to feel the satisfaction of performing," Kupchynsky said, "the sooner they feel the dedication of giving of themselves, of working together on a high project, the greater their determination to continue with their music.'

Getting ready for her solo debut, five-year-old Melanie and her father practice "Edelweiss" together. "At first I was worried about starting her," Mr. K says in the article, but "almost before I knew it—certainly before she could read words—she was reading music."

2

The Rehearsal

JOANNE

My parents had a firm rule: Teacher is always right. If your teacher tells you to jump off a cliff, that's what you do.

Once, in kindergarten at Memorial Elementary School over on Innes Road, my teacher sent me to the corner of the cloakroom for talking out of turn during story time. "Don't come out until I tell you," she said, and then promptly forgot about me. You couldn't blame her. I was abundantly forgettable: quiet and shy and perpetually drifting through life in a fog. So I sat silently in the little wooden chair pushed up against the hospital-blue-painted coat cubbies. I stared at the *Lost in Space* lunch boxes and *Bonanza* Thermoses tucked inside the cubbies, wondering how long my sentence would last, even as the fire bell started clanging and everybody in class pushed back their chairs with a clatter and—*single file,*

17

everyone!—lined up to leave. The teacher turned out the lights as she shut the door behind her.

I waited for the teacher to come back to fetch me. She didn't.

I could hear all the other classes emptying out. Footsteps hurried down the hall. The kids were whispering to one another as they filed out quickly through the fire doors into the parking lot. Their voices floated back to my darkened corner of the cloakroom, hanging in the air around me. Then the corridors were empty. I heard the heavy fire doors swing closed, the loud click of the latch echoing through the abandoned halls. The classroom was silent. I stayed in my seat.

This must be the punishment for speaking without raising my hand, I thought. *Death by fire.*

I sat still, imagining my fate in gory detail. Was the fire outside the door yet? When would I see the flames? What would it feel like? I strained to listen for fire engines, but none came. *I guess this is how it will all end.* I was prepared to accept the consequences: Teacher clearly knew what she was doing. So I was puzzled and more than a little surprised when the students started to file back in. Not as surprised, however, as the teacher was when she found me, still cowering in my chair. It was only afterward that I learned that there was such a thing as a fire *drill*.

The teacher apologized to my parents, but they didn't pass the apology along to me. They didn't see any need to. It didn't matter to them that I actually believed I was going to *die*. You don't question a teacher. You just follow orders.

Maybe that explains why my parents didn't seem nearly so scared of Mr. K as I was. After my first sight of him at my big sister's concert, I did everything I could to steer clear of him. When I tagged along with my mom for orchestra carpool duty, I hid in back of her, poking my head out from behind her waist when I thought nobody was looking.

It was hard to avoid Mr. K if you were anywhere in his vicinity. For starters, he must have been the biggest man you ever saw—and the loudest. He didn't walk like normal people, either. He *stomped*.

He stomped onto the stage, every step sounding like an angry ballerina slamming the floor with wooden pointe shoes. He stomped off the stage, so loud you could still hear him when he disappeared into the wings. He stomped up the steps to rehearsals, pounding his feet so that the whole staircase shook. The clamor of his stomping matched the volume of his voice, which apparently was permanently stuck on HOLLER.

"Orchestra eez not democracy," he would yell. "Eez benign dictatorship."

I watched from the back of the rehearsal room one afternoon as he stomped up on the box in front of the orchestra, then down again. The box was called a *podium*, my mother told me. It was made of scuffed, worn-out tan wood. It was hollow on the inside, so when he clomped up on it, it made a great, echoing wallop of a sound that boomed like a firecracker and bounced off all the walls of the big room and made everybody sit up like they'd just been smacked.

With his black suit jacket off and the tendons in his neck bulging from the top of his collar, he stomped up on that podium, and all the kids snapped to attention, with violins propped on kneecaps. When he clomped off, they scrambled to tuck their instruments back under the crooks of their arms. On he stomped, then off again. The kids would whip their instruments up, then down, then up, then down. All the while, he yelled.

"Snap to attention!" He stomped on the podium.

The kids bolted up straight in their seats, instruments propped up on their knees.

"Rest!" He stomped down, and the kids scrambled to get the instruments under an arm again.

"Attention!" He clomped up again.

"Rest!" Down he went.

"Attention!" Up again.

"Rest!" Down once more.

"Again!" Up he went.

"Fiddles up!" Standing on the podium, he held his arms up high.

The kids whipped those instruments up to their chins, bows on strings, trying not to move or make a sound, as if they were playing a giant game of "Mother, May I?"

"Fiddles down!" He lowered his arms. Instruments came flying down onto laps, tucked under arms.

"Fiddles up!" More scrambling.

"Fiddles down!"

Mr. K's booming voice bounced off the walls and made the panes of glass in the doorway shake. Why he had to bellow like that was a mystery to me, because other than his stomping and his screaming, the room was absolutely silent. The kids were far too terrified to speak.

"*Oh. My. God.*"

Apparently, somebody had messed up.

Mr. K let his arms drop and slowly shook his head from side to side. "You are most *un-DEEZ-eeplined* group I haf ever seen."

Later, when we sat down for dinner, my sister Michele was still smarting. "Why does he have to be so nasty?" she said to no one in particular. My mom was clearing away our appetizer of canned fruit cocktail. She set out the main course of flank steak with Hawaiian Medley frozen vegetables, which Michele promptly sneaked under the table to our dog, Skippy, the family mutt who was the color of peanut butter. All of us kids secretly fed our vegetables to Skippy: the frozen peas with little squares of carrots, the canned corn, the dreaded brussels sprouts. Skippy must have been the healthiest dog in all of New Jersey.

Michele had never met anybody like Mr. K. Our own parents didn't often scream, or stomp, or call us names. Ours were sensible parents, the kind who carpooled in a faux-wood-paneled station wagon, and who played bridge with their friends on Saturday nights, and who didn't believe in spanking children. My dad's harshest threat when I misbehaved was to tease, "I'm going to put ice cream in your face!" One time he actually did it, though he stopped when I broke out in great heaving sobs because I thought it was an actual punishment given to terrible children.

Mr. K, on the other hand, was brutal even to his own kids. On the first day of Michele's beginner orchestra rehearsals, he ordered his daughter Melanie, who like me was in kindergarten, to the front of the room. "Melanie has been playing violin as long as the rest of you," he said as she climbed up onto the podium, clutching her tiny violin in one hand. "But to prove she eez not just here because she eez my daughter, she weel demonstrate."

Melanie played a few songs from memory, Mr. K looking on in stony silence. After she was done, she quietly retreated to her seat, and he instructed the orchestra to pull out the music for "Reuben and Rachel." That was one of the easier pieces; it required only about half a dozen notes, and even the worst beginners could usually handle it. But when he raised his baton, somebody burst out crying in the back of the room. Mr. K halted the orchestra, surveyed the group, and fixed an angry gaze on the culprit: his daughter.

"Melanie, what eez the matter weeth you?" he roared, his voice ricocheting off the walls and making the kids in the orchestra shrink into the backs of their metal folding chairs. "Why aren't you playing? I brought you here to play, so play!"

"I can't f-f-find it, Daddy!"

She could read notes—but not words. Apparently, that was not a sufficient excuse for Mr. K.

Tales of Mr. K's tirades were passed from one generation of students to the next. He was an equal-opportunity terror. When he first began teaching in East Brunswick a decade earlier, a violin student named Darlene Morrow was so nervous that she broke down in tears at her first orchestra concert, right on the stage. Mr. K came striding over, a smile on his face, and bent down to whisper in her ear as the audience looked on. What the audience didn't know was what he was whispering:

"You leesen to me, seester," he was spitting, the smile for the benefit of the spectators never leaving his face. "You *shot up* you crying right now. You going to put your bow on thees string and you going to play best concert you ever played een your life. And you going to love eet."

She did as she was told.

Whenever I heard stories like that about Mr. K, I just hoped he would never be *my* teacher. But my dad just shook his head and smiled. "Nobody ever said life is fair," he told us.

That was one of his favorite sayings, and really, it fit almost any situation. Bad grade on a test? Neighborhood kids saying mean things about you behind your back? Picked last for volleyball? Whatever injustice had been visited upon us that day, "Nobody ever said life is fair" pretty much covered the waterfront, usually delivered with a genial shrug and a laugh.

Almost all the parents we knew felt that way. They didn't care much if Mr. K was tough and unbending: he got results. So what if he used Old Country tactics? Whatever he was doing, it worked. The nuns at the Catholic school still thwacked their students for misbehaving. Mr. K got way better results, and all he did was holler.

Nor did anyone—the parents or their kids—display the slightest curiosity about his life outside the music room. They knew he was Ukrainian, but nobody thought to ask how he ended up in our unremarkable New Jersey suburb, or when, or why.

Music to East Brunswick

String Concert Tomorrow

1961

A unique high school musical organization will perform tomorrow evening in East Brunswick.

It's the local high school's String Orchestra which will be featured in the last of three spring concerts by musical groups at the high school. The concert will begin at 7:30 o'clock in the auditorium.

Tomorrow's concert will also feature the Symphonette and the Choir. Tickets are 50 cents for adults and 25 cents for children.

"NOT MANY SCHOOLS IN New Jersey have string orchestras capable of performing original works by great composers," Conductor Jerry Kupchynsky said.

The String orchestra will present: "Serenade" by Mozart, ":Concerto for Cello and Orchestra" by Handl featuring Richard Sher as soloist, "Concerto Grosso No. 6" by Correlli featuring William Criswell, Neil Schuster and Robert Kady, and "Suite for Strings" based on American folk songs by Freckenpohl.

Fifteen members of the String Orchestra passed the tryouts and

GET THE POINT?—Leader Jerry Kupchynsky puts all he has into directing the high school orchestra

A 1961 article captures Mr. K in action.
"Get the point?" the caption says. The students got it.

MELANIE

My mother comes home in a wheelchair. Neither she nor Daddy explains why. After my mom's fall in their bedroom, I end up performing "Edelweiss" in the big auditorium without her. She doesn't have the strength to accompany me. When we get home after the concert, her piano stands silent, untouched. Up until now, the big black grand piano had been her greatest happiness, the place where Stephanie and I would find her if we were looking for an afternoon snack or a kiss for a skinned knee. The house was always filled with the strains of her practicing Beethoven and Chopin or accompanying Daddy's most advanced violin students on Mozart or Bach.

Now, Daddy pushes her in the wheelchair to their bedroom, doing his best not to bump into the hallway walls along the way. She eats dinner there on a tray. "Mommy is tired," our father says, shooing us out of the way and closing the door behind him. He doesn't mention the wheelchair then, or the next day, or the day after that. But that night Daddy gives us our baths and tucks us into bed, and over the next few nights he starts taking over Mommy's other duties as well.

Before long, we settle into a new routine. At bath time, Daddy teaches us the names of our body parts in singsong Ukrainian: "*Day ruku, day nohy*" he says, and we lift our hands and feet to be washed. At bedtime, he reads us "Medovy Tolasik," a Ukrainian version of "The Gingerbread Man," and sings us Ukrainian folk songs. For breakfast he makes us scrambled eggs and toast—one of his specialties, another being Black Russians, a drink that is most certainly not for little children.

When our hair needs cutting, he does it himself, chopping our bangs clear up to our hairlines in a hopeless attempt to make them straight. At dinner, after Steph and I carry our plates to the sink, he dashes around the kitchen, cleaning up in a frenzy so he can be ready for the private students who begin letting themselves in through the unlocked front door early every evening.

A few days after the wheelchair makes its first appearance, my mom maneuvers herself onto the piano bench. But when she starts to play, she stumbles over the keys, and I hear her cry out. Soon she is hardly touching the instrument at all. My parents used to talk about how my mother was going to teach Steph piano one day, how they were just waiting until her tiny hands got a bit bigger. They looked forward to the day Steph and I would perform together, she accompanying me on the piano. But when Steph turns three years old—the age she is supposed to start lessons—nobody says a word.

Not long afterward, I wake up screaming, torn from sleep by a nightmare: the Communists have come for Daddy. In my dream, soldiers in red uniforms invade our house. They storm up the front staircase, rush past the kitchen, muscle through the bedroom hallway with its Pepto-Bismol-pink-and-blue bathroom, and grab my daddy. They pull him away from me as he struggles mightily to break free. I reach out for him, straining to grab him, but the soldiers are too strong. I call out to him—"Daddy! Daddy!"—and realize I am still shouting for him as I wake up. I hear his feet hit the floor with a thump as he comes running into my room.

"Shh! Lastivko, I'm here!" My father is at my bedside, whispering in my ear.

Lastivko is Ukrainian for "little bird," the first word of my favorite lullaby. When I was a toddler, the tune was so effective that I would protest, "No 'Lastivko,' Daddy! Please, no 'Lastivko'!" because I knew I could never keep my eyes open once he started singing that soothing song.

I'm not actually sure who or what Communists are. All I know is that they're evil and that Daddy escaped from them when he was a boy, back in Ukraine. I once heard him tell my mother, over one of his end-of-the-day Black Russians, that they murdered his father and want him dead, too. What upsets me most is how scared my fearless father seems when he mentions them.

"Always tell the truth," he lectures Stephanie and me. "Unless the Communists come looking for me and I'm hiding under the bed. Then it's okay to lie."

My night terrors will continue for years. I fall asleep easily in my bed with the pink fuzzy bedspread, but in the dead of night I jolt awake screaming—instinctively calling for Daddy, not Mommy. He always comes running as soon as he hears me crying out for him, always with the same comforting whispers, assuring his Lastivko that everything will be all right. The world is a bleak and frightening place in the dark of night, perhaps for my dad as much as for me. But no matter how exhausted my father is, he's never mad or impatient with me then.

During the day is a different story.

"Okay, sis, now let's do it again. But put more *life* into eet!" Daddy is yelling as I practice with him in his studio. "Use some energy, move a leetle, flex your fingers! Lift your bow *up* in the air!"

Since my successful debut performance of "Edelweiss," my daily dose of violin has gradually increased. Every night after dinner, I unpack Violet and head downstairs to Daddy's studio. He'll be waiting for me, on the edge of his chair, one hand clutching a conductor's baton that he uses to poke me when my left wrist comes up or my right wrist goes down. A crooked bow gets an instant whack with the baton, as does a straight right pinky that should be gently curved instead. As I play, he bangs the baton on the music stand to keep the beat, like some kind of agitated human metronome. Tonight he is especially manic, pounding so hard with his baton that little slivers of wood break off and go flying through the air.

"Okay, sis, *again*!" I hate when he calls me "sis"—his interpretation of American slang, which comes out sounding like *Sease!* when he says it—but I just wince and try to concentrate harder.

"Don't stand there *dead*, weeth fingers hanging like sausages on the bow!" He practically spits out the words.

I take in a sharp breath but will myself not to cry. Daddy won't stand for it. "Discipline yourself," he says, when he sees me fighting back tears.

My mother's illness is wearing on us both. Daddy charged through the door a few hours earlier in a mad dash back from work so that he could drive the after-school babysitter home, then stop at McDonald's to grab some dinner for everyone. Steph and I both hate fast food, but Daddy loves it. There is something about its sheer abundance—the row upon row of prepackaged hamburgers at the ready under warming lights, the fryer baskets filled to the top with French fries—that he finds irresistible.

At least it's better than the TV dinners we more regularly eat these days. On those nights, Steph and I sit glumly at the table, shooting each other glances as Daddy unveils our meals from the foil coverings. We survey the compartments, which have inevitably all spilled into one another, leaving us with peas covered in apple-sauce and gravy, all of it congealing in a lump as Daddy yells at us to eat it anyway.

"Seet down! You haf not been excused! Eef you won't eat them, I weel feed them to you myself." My dad scoops up a forkful of peas and tries to shovel it into Steph's mouth while she lunges for her glass of milk, missing it and sending it flying. My mother shrieks, Stephanie gags through tears, and my father jumps up, cursing, to get the paper towels. I run down the hallway and dive onto my bed, covering my head with my pink blanket and squeezing my eyes tightly shut, hoping it will all just go away.

We miss Mommy's cooking. Before she got sick, she loved to make elaborate dinners of ham studded with cloves and pineapple slices, potatoes au gratin, and fancy desserts. She learned from her mom, Grandma Brown, who was the sort of hostess who served cold cuts on silver platters and ketchup in china bowls. My mom comes from pretty fancy stock, Grandma Brown always reminds us. She grew up in a New Jersey village in a proper Protestant home, playing the church organ from the time she was big enough to reach the pedals. According to family lore, she can trace her roots back to both Civil War general William Tecumseh Sherman and Richard Stockton, one of the signers of the Declaration of Independence and a close friend of George Washington.

My parents met while they were music graduate students at Rutgers University in New Brunswick. She was an all-American girl with piercing blue eyes, a gorgeous singing voice, and a taste for high heels. He was "a dashing Ukrainian man with a funny accent," or at least that's how she describes him. He had landed in the United States just a few years before, attending college in rural Kentucky, and "he had learned his English with a Kentucky twang. I thought it sounded hilarious."

Compact and muscular, with a hairline that was already receding, my dad was an avid hiker who stayed in shape by doing sit-ups every night. He was a romantic who wrote poetry but also a prankster who laughed at his own off-color jokes. His stern brow was set over eyes that sometimes seemed somber and haunted by private thoughts that she couldn't decipher. But when he smiled his face was transformed. The years melted away, and he was suddenly a delighted, impish boy, with an expression that one of his students would later call "a mixture of glee and victory."

They went on dates to concerts, my mother towering over him in her heels. After he returned to a teaching job in Illinois, they courted long distance for a year. Their plaintive love letters flew back and forth over the thousand miles between them, until at last he found a teaching post in East Brunswick so that they could be together. "I am overjoyed about the job!" she wrote to him in the spring of 1958. They married a few months later, and she was hired to teach in East Brunswick, too. Their students promptly dubbed them "Lucy and Ricky," after the *I Love Lucy* television show.

When my mother became pregnant, they asked their classes to

vote on potential names. I will be forever relieved that "Olga" didn't win. When my little sister came along two years later, the orchestra named her, fittingly, Stephanie Joy. An old newspaper clipping shows a photo of my dad conducting the high school orchestra while my mother accompanies the group on piano, with me in a playpen between them. "All our babysitters are in the orchestra," my mother explains in the caption.

But the marriage has frayed since then. My mom spends too much, cooks too many side dishes, is simply too excessive in every way for my dad. He was born in 1928, right into the teeth of Ukraine's Holodomor, a great famine when millions of Ukrainians starved to death. Growing up, he used to sneak into the workmen's quarters at his grandfather's farm at mealtime, bringing his own spoon to eat out of their communal pot. After he and his mother arrived in the United States as refugees, his mother's "good" dishes were promotional giveaways from the local supermarket, and her glassware sported the logo of their neighborhood gas station. The ketchup bottle sitting on the table at every meal was diluted with water.

One morning at breakfast, I reach over to my dad's bowl of Life cereal to try to grab a few pieces, as I often do. This time, he slaps my hand away. That's when I notice that as he is eating, he is picking little black pellets off his spoon and gingerly placing them on a napkin. A mouse had gotten into the cupboard, but he doesn't want to waste perfectly good food just because of some droppings. My mother is horrified, but my father just shrugs: "I'll eat around eet."

Not long afterward, I reach into my sock drawer, but it's empty. The laundry is piling up. The pink wicker hamper in the bathroom is overflowing. My mom can't manage the stairs to the basement laundry machines, and my dad is too busy at work to do it himself.

"I've got a new game for you," my mom says.

At five years old, I am up for a new game. But this one doesn't sound so fun. My mom tells me to carry the pink plastic laundry basket downstairs, load up the washing machine, and turn it on. The laundry room is near my dad's studio. The big blue furnace is in there, too, and the water heater, both of which make frightening noises when they kick on and off without warning.

"Oh, Ste-eph," I sing out to my three-year-old sister. "We have to do the wash."

From then on, we play our game each week with Mommy. Down the stairs we go, me with the overflowing laundry basket while Steph trots along behind, picking up stray socks. I can't reach the controls on the washing machine, and I am still just learning to read. So I jump on top of the machine, sit on my knees, and stuff the clothes inside, while Mom shouts out letters for me to find: "*W!*" when she wants the wash cycle; "*C!*" when she wants cold.

From her wheelchair, my mom teaches me how to cook, clean, and do the Irish jig. She teaches me to cross the street by watching from the big bay window upstairs and giving me a thumbs-up when the coast is clear. Her hands are too tired to play the piano most days, but she teaches Steph and me how to sing melody and harmony for what seems like every show tune ever composed.

At mealtime, Steph and I follow her as she rolls into the kitchen, and she shows us how to make dinners of baked beans covered in bacon strips and hot dog slices, or macaroni and cheese. After we help her mix up the ingredients, she wheels herself across the room, holding the casserole dish on her lap. I stand on a chair so I can reach the wall oven, and she hands the dish up to me with a warning: "Careful! It's heavy!" I practice my numbers by listening to her directions about where to turn the temperature dial.

"Someday, I'm going to write a book: 'How to Cook without Really,'" my mom says with satisfaction when dinner is in the oven.

"Really what?" I ask.

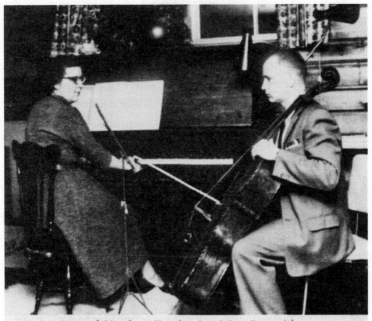

Mr. and Mrs. Jerry Kupchynsky of East Brunswick.

Jean and Jerry Kupchynsky pictured in the March 1960 *Town Crier* magazine. The article describes young Mr. K as a "muscular, sandy-haired young man who easily could have passed for the local high school football coach, instead of director of its string orchestra."

She laughs. "Really cooking. It will be about cooking from a wheelchair."

She sighs and plants a kiss on Stephanie, who cuddles on her lap in the wheelchair, a thumb in her mouth.

In the coming years, my mother will miss every parent-teacher conference and mother-daughter event. She will never see an in-school pageant, play, birthday celebration, or musical performance. She will depend upon the kindness of acquaintances—she doesn't have the opportunity to make many friends—to pick me up when it rains or snows. Even a working mom can often adjust her schedule to be there for her kids at least some of the time. We never discuss it. Mommy can't, and that is that.

On the day a tow truck comes to take away my mother's '57 Chevy, I watch from my bedroom window in confusion. She tells me that someday she might get another one, but then I hear her crying when she thinks I am out of earshot. I have no recollection of the grand piano's disappearance. One day, it is simply gone.

At home, cut off from the other moms and the suburban strip malls where everybody else congregates and does their shopping, my mother becomes a connoisseur of every service that delivers, mails, or shows up at your door. Dittman's Food and Meat Market brings groceries, and Schwartz Taub Pharmacy delivers medicines and toiletries. The Sears catalog supplies us with clothing, and my father is left to handle all the bills.

"We're going to lose the house!" he yells at her one night.

How do you lose a house? I wonder. *Who is going to take it? The Communists?* I imagine being forced to leave my pink bedroom, being marched outside by the angry men in red uniforms, and having to live outside, not just in summer but in the rain and snow and cold.

I will grow up believing my father's dire predictions that at any moment our house can be taken away. Of course, the money issues are tangible, which makes them easier to argue about. The underlying fear and desperation about my mother's health and the uncertainty of our own future are too terrible to speak aloud.

No matter how difficult their days are, the one thing my parents always agree on is music. I practice seven days a week, with no days off *ever*.

My progress is quick. Once Daddy closes the door to his studio and we get to work, all the other distractions—the unpalatable dinners, my mom's frustrations—melt away. I quickly make my way through the beginner books. Daddy pastes star stickers on the pieces I master, or writes the word *AGAIN* in angry red capital letters when my efforts fall short. He signs and dates the last page of each lesson book I complete, then pulls out a fresh, crisp new book for us to start.

One night, Daddy hands me a new piece of music: Bach's Concerto in A Minor. I am excited; this is a *real* concerto, just as the German composer wrote it in 1748, and the first piece Daddy has ever given me that isn't simplified for students. I have been listening to the big kids play it all of my life. I can hear in my head exactly what it should sound like. Tentatively, I start to play. It doesn't sound quite right, not at all like when my dad's best students do it.

"Sharp!" Daddy yells, insistently banging the offending note on the piano over and over again.

I try again. "Now you're flat!" More banging the note on the piano. "Make sure hand eez een position *before* you start to play!"

I gulp in a breath, hold it, and dig into the strings again. This time the notes are right, but the sound is tinny and small. It is never easy to get a big sound out of the tiny violin I am playing, but still, the sound doesn't match the music I hear so clearly in my imagination.

"Lift you bow *up* een the air after first note and *again* after second note. Let the sound *ring*!" Dad is talking louder and faster now.

I try one more time, this time while attacking the strings with my bow just as my father showed me. Success! This is a new feeling: the first time I realize I can pluck a sound from inside my head and make it real with my violin. With astonishment I plunge ahead, from one phrase of the piece to the next. And the next. And . . .

. . . I stumble.

I stop, lowering my violin and tentatively stealing a glance at my dad.

"That's eet!" he is yelling, his head bobbing up and down. "Not *bad*!"

I would have hugged him, but Daddy always says there is a time and place for everything. Lessons are strictly business. Hugs will come afterward.

My father turns back to his piano. That's where he always sits, for hours every night, in the dress shirt and tie he wore to work that day with an old cardigan sweater thrown over it. His brow is furrowed again with concentration. With a single finger, he begins jabbing at a note I hadn't gotten quite right, banging out the tone over and over and over, as loud as he can play it. The whole piano shakes with the force of his one finger. Then he turns back to me.

"Again," my father says.

3

The Students

JOANNE

In our green-shingled house, in our neighborhood of identical Colonials and split-levels so new that the saplings in the yards provided no shade, the piano had pride of place in the living room. The instrument's upholstered bench was never empty, always occupied by one of my older sisters. The rest of the room was strictly off-limits. With its tailored couch and floor-length drapes, the room was immaculate, never a knickknack out of place, and nobody ever sat in there except on holidays. Nonetheless, my mom vacuumed the sofa cushions, moved the overstuffed armchair to clean underneath it, and dusted the sideboards in that room every Wednesday morning.

This is the room where I realized that I had no talent.

Both of my sisters were becoming accomplished musicians.

Michele, having graduated from Mr. K's beginner orchestra, was progressing rapidly on the violin, while Ronni would soon take up the flute. Both took piano lessons. At any hour of the day, somebody was playing an instrument somewhere, and often two different melodies would be coming at you in uncoordinated stereo. The two of them were always singing together, too, harmonizing during car rides in the big maroon Oldsmobile and telling me to shut up if I tried to join in.

My dad, an energetic amateur photographer, was there to capture it all on film. One sister would happily take her place at the piano bench, while the other would pose with her instrument. And I...I had nothing. "Try holding up your arms like you're a ballerina," my father would coach me helpfully when he photographed the three of us grouped around the piano, so there would be some display of artistry demonstrated by the apparently ability-free little sister. Except I didn't take ballet, and my attempts at dance usually ended with me banging into a wall.

"I want to play an instrument, too," I announced one day, as my dad, having rearranged our photographic tableau around the piano yet again, stepped back and fiddled with the camera viewfinder.

"You're too young," my mom yelled back from the kitchen.

I tugged at my jumper, an uncomfortable concoction of stiff embroidered cotton with a matching white blouse and scratchy elastic cuffs that left indentations on my arms.

"Why can't I take piano lessons?" I ventured again.

"Because I said so." From the kitchen again.

Of course no is a familiar word to any youngest child. As in, "No new clothes—your sisters' hand-me-downs are perfectly fine." And "No long hair like your sisters—your pixie cut will do"—that would be the sheared-sheep look that compelled strangers to pat me on the head and call me a sweet little boy. "No music lessons" was just another indignity to add to the list.

The truth is, I was always a half step behind my chatty, quick-witted sisters. When I was three, my mother had attempted to enroll me in a nursery school run by the home economics class at East Brunswick High School. I cried so hard that the teachers gave up and sent me home, to the great glee of my sisters who would forever taunt me for flunking out of preschool. After that, my teachers kept telling my parents that I was far too timid. I never fought back, they told my parents with concern, even when the girl I considered my best friend nicknamed me "Dodo," as in the television cartoon *Dodo, the Kid from Outer Space*.

I didn't mind the teasing. My parents always figured me for the easygoing one: with two precocious older daughters, they were happy to have the littlest one be good-natured, if not terribly bright. Anyway, even if I had tried to protest, chances are nobody would have noticed.

The piano in our living room had been my dad's idea. Not that he knew how to play it. He was born in Oakland, California, in 1931 to a Romanian immigrant mother and a father who grew up as an orphan, shuttled from one impoverished relative to another. His parents named him Burton but called him Boots, to rhyme with his older brother Sydney's nickname, Scoots. When Dad was a toddler, my grandmother was hauled in by the Oakland police because he bore such a strong resemblance to the missing Lindbergh baby, the aviator Charles Lindbergh's kidnapped son who would soon turn up murdered. My grandmother had to produce her son's birth certificate before the cops let her go, prompting a local newspaper to print side-by-side photos of the two toddlers above the headline "Lindbergh Baby's Double Gives His Family Trouble."

Money was always tight on my grandfather's wages as a traveling X-ray technician. The family moved frequently, hopscotching across the country to St. Louis and Brooklyn before landing in

Queens, New York, where Boots entered his fifth elementary school in five years. He slept in the galley kitchen of the family's one-bedroom apartment, cramming his lanky frame—he grew to be six feet three inches—into a narrow bed. When he joined the Boy Scouts, he was humiliated by having to wear his much older brother's outdated Scout knickers years after the uniform switched to long pants. To help make ends meet, he went to work starting at age nine, first selling *Liberty* magazine subscriptions, then the *Saturday Evening Post*, then running errands for a butcher and delivering laundry for a dry cleaner during World War II, when there was a steel shortage and he had to wait by the door for customers to return their metal clothes hangers.

My father was what they euphemistically called a "slow starter"—he was held back a year and sat in the back row cracking jokes until an astute teacher figured out the problem was he had such horrendous eyesight that he couldn't see the blackboard. By the time he hit high school he had become a standout student. At a Boy Scout party one night, he met my mother. She had dark brown hair, flirtatious dark eyes, and long black eyelashes, and she attended the same gifted high school program that he did. She was fourteen years old. He was smitten.

He courted her through high school and while working his way through Columbia University, commuting from home by subway three hours a day to save money and working in the university's atomic physics laboratory, helping tend to the atom-splitting cyclotron in the basement of Pupin Hall. During the summers, he popped salt pills to keep from getting dehydrated while packing boxes in a Garment District sweatshop, earning enough money to buy a diamond engagement ring. "I married your father because he was the only man I could find who was smarter than me," my mother would say.

My father's interest in music grew out of a peculiar hobby: the theremin, a strange electronic instrument that was the forerunner of the synthesizer. He had learned to play the theremin from my grandfather, an inveterate electronic tinkerer who built several of them from scratch, assembling them inside empty wooden radio cabinets out of spare radio parts and glass tubes. The instrument made a satisfyingly eerie whine, and my grandfather had earned a few extra bucks creating sound effects for television sound tracks. He even made a 1962 appearance on the TV game show *I've Got a Secret*, a surprisingly dapper figure who stumped panelists Bill Cullen and Henry Morgan with his mystery contraption before performing his rendition of the Rodgers and Hart classic "Lover." Such was my father's sentimental attachment to it that it was the only possession he brought with him to my parents' marriage. But my father always regretted that he couldn't read music and was resentful that his parents refused him a proper music education.

Dad was determined to provide for his kids what his own parents had not. So after my mother's parents threw them a properly extravagant Manhattan wedding in the penthouse of the St. Moritz hotel overlooking Central Park, they moved to the burgeoning suburbs of New Jersey, where he began his management trainee job. He had been working his way up the corporate ladder since then. By the time the third girl in five years was born (they were so sure I would finally be a boy that they had already picked out the name "Jeff"), they had moved from their little garden apartment behind the Korvettes department store into our four-bedroom house in a new subdivision.

On weekends, my dad would take the three of us girls on "nature walks" through the backyard or on field trips to nearby farms. He ordered science kits from the Edmund Scientific catalog that arrived each month and that we would put together in our fluorescent-lit basement, delighting in the whiff of danger surrounding our experiments with magnets and iron filings and chemistry sets and telescope lenses.

My dad was the one who insisted that my parents buy the piano that now stood in our living room. He had hoped to take lessons himself. But once my sisters got their hands on it, he never had a chance.

My mother took it from there. She was the one who made sure we found our way to Mr. K. She didn't have much use for the piano herself. I never saw her so much as touch it, other than to dust it. As the only child of a prosperous ladies' clothing store owner, she had grown up in an attached house in the shadow of the old Forest Hills Tennis Stadium and Clubhouse that hosted the U.S. Open tennis tournament each year, though she never went because Jews weren't allowed to join. Her parents, striving first-generation Americans whose families had escaped Czarist Russia, had insisted that she take six full years of piano lessons, during which she learned only that she was tone-deaf. Her singing voice was so god-awful that as a toddler Michele, who had an excellent ear, faithfully learned to sing off-key.

But Mom did know that anyone who showed any musical talent in East Brunswick studied with Mr. K. And she was determined that her daughters would, too.

Mr. K's reputation preceded him. His arrival in East Brunswick had coincided with my parents' own. Not long after he started, he made headlines for creating a school orchestra, a rarity in a town better known for its 4-H livestock exhibitions at the county fair held each August down on Fern Road.

There hadn't been enough musicians at first, not enough even to field a baseball team, much less an orchestra. To make sure they showed up, on concert days he tooled around in his big white Pontiac, collecting students along the way. His car was a familiar sight in the older section of town, where the homes were a little bit smaller and the driveways were empty. Passing the Colonial Diner and Two Guys on Route 18, Mr. K would turn off the highway and go house to house, honking, as screen doors banged open and students with instrument cases came flying across the lawns. When he'd gotten everyone, sometimes he'd stop off at his house and treat the whole lot of them to dinner with his own kids. Mostly, the students just toyed with the glutinous red borscht that, disconcertingly, always seemed to be on the menu.

He invited the best of them to study privately with him on school nights in his basement studio, where he sat on a piano bench with his tie unknotted and a ratty cardigan sweater thrown over his dress shirt, banging out notes on the keyboard.

His music program attracted a lot of attention—even more so after the concert where we watched his daughter Melanie play a solo. The newspaper that landed on our driveway every morning sometimes ran photographs of him with his daughter and her violin. I was intrigued by the little girl my age whom I'd never met and never heard speak, but who I had watched perform on the stage.

One of those articles showed a photograph of Mr. K with "Little Melanie, aged 5," and "already a gifted young violinist," as he helped her practice. The article said Mr. K had made East Brunswick into "a hot-house for young string players," and that more of his students were accepted into New Jersey's competitive student orchestras— All-County, All-Region, All-State—than any other town in the state. The article was headlined "Mr. Music" and it said Mr. K was called "the Santa Claus of Strings."

I didn't think Mr. K looked at all like Santa Claus. I had never heard the older kids call him that, either. I heard them call him other names—none that my parents would allow me to repeat—but

Santa Claus was not among them. I thought, instead, he looked like one of the bad guys in the movie *The Russians Are Coming! The Russians Are Coming!* My parents had taken us to see it in a double feature with *Bambi* at the Turnpike Drive-In Theater out on Route 18, where I was allowed to play on the swings in my pajamas and fall asleep in the back of our station wagon.

Sometimes the newspapers printed the pictures of Mr. K's conquering students, posing with their unblinking, unsmiling teacher in his dark suit and severe little mustache. He looked old to me— maybe even thirty—and when you peered at his face, an involuntary "Yes, sir" just popped right out of your mouth. Some of the students were shown mid-performance, their violins held high. Each one had the same ramrod straight posture, the left wrist held back smoothly, the right bow arm precisely angled, and the right wrist moving so fluidly that the bow seemed to glide back and forth like nature intended it that way.

You could see that my sister Michele, after playing for barely more than a year, already had the same elegant form. Her straight posture and firm wrist made her look just like the kids in the newspaper pictures with Mr. K. Someday Michele hoped she could get private lessons with him, too, not just the group lessons offered for free at school. My mom had already asked, but there was a year-long waiting list for a spot on his roster. And besides, he seemed unusually preoccupied these days.

I, meanwhile, was resigned to pretending to be a ballerina.

"Why can't I play an instrument?" I asked my dad once again, as I lifted up my arms clumsily in a thoroughly unconvincing port de bras.

"Have patience," he said, smiling. "Maybe next year."

Left to right: Joanne, Ronni, and Michele Lipman at ages five, eight, and ten. Their dad, Burton Lipman, an avid photographer, was behind the camera.

MELANIE

"Get your *keesters* into the car!" Daddy yells at Steph and me. He is often impatient these days. I grab Stephanie by the hand, pulling her away from the half-eaten ham sandwich on her plate. Down the steps toward the garage we go, with a quick stop so I can pull an old towel from the linen closet in case she gets carsick.

On weekends like this one, my parents go hunting for a cure for my mom. They have found a doctor, hours away in Delaware, with an experimental treatment they hope will make her better, or at least prevent her from getting worse.

My mother had gone to lots of doctors before one of them finally figured out a diagnosis: multiple sclerosis, which, the doctor bluntly told her, had no treatment and no cure. She had to be wheeled out of the office the day he gave her the news, though she had entered it on her own power.

My parents don't believe that there is no cure. There has to be. My mother is always trying a new vitamin or some crazy diet that she read about. When I ask her how she can bear to give up tomatoes or eat liver all the time, she just shrugs and tells me she would eat far worse things if they would help her get better.

"Even rattlesnake juice? Even dog poop?" I ask, trying to make a joke.

"Yes, anything," is her solemn reply.

The physical therapist who comes to our house teaches me how to help with her exercises. I rotate her legs, pushing them back and forth like giant rolling pins. To stretch her hamstrings, I stand on the bed where she lies, propping up one of her heels on my shoulder and slowly walking toward her, pushing my hands down on her knee to keep it straight, while she moans in pain. But the therapy doesn't seem to help.

The Delaware doctor offers the most promising treatment yet. I watch as Daddy hoists my mom over his shoulder, then carries her down the stairs to the garage. I run to open the door for them, Daddy huffing as he lumbers past, my mom's legs flopping heavily against his stomach. In a few hours' time, the Delaware doctor will greet them, ready with an injection for my mother's spine. She'll have to go for spinal shots every few weeks for the treatment to work.

I hear my mother whispering with my dad as he settles her into the front seat. The shots hurt terribly, she says. "It weel be worth eet," he grunts, trying to maneuver her legs into position in the big white Pontiac.

On the road, my job is to keep Stephanie entertained and, above all, quiet. But no sooner has Daddy started the car than we hear, "I feel sick."

Steph looks terrible. Her face has a greenish tinge. She has a sensitive stomach and hates almost every food except for hot dogs and peanut butter. She is three years old and barely eats anything, but somehow, whenever we get into the car, whatever she did manage to get down comes right back up.

Now she is wedged in the backseat, her little legs pressed tightly against mine, looking queasy even before Daddy pulls the car out of our driveway. Guiding the car down our street, he puts his foot on the gas and we lurch forward. Then he slams on the brakes and we jerk to a stop. He steps on the gas again, then stomps on the brake once more. The seats squeak as we stagger along like that while our necks whip back and forth, smacking the backs of our heads against the seat cushions. This is the way it always is. Daddy has never quite gotten the hang of American driving.

"I'm going to be sick!" Stephanie cries again, as we turn from our development onto the highway, lurching and screeching along the way. I try rubbing her back, telling her to think of flower gardens, her dolls, things that she loves, but I can feel her muscles tightening through her shirt. I already have the bath towel spread across my lap.

At almost six years old, I am a surrogate mother to my little sister. When Steph needs a Band-Aid pulled off, her temperature taken, or her hair combed out of a snarl, she turns to me. We were born twenty-seven months apart, and my earliest memory is of watching my breath make clouds on our living room window, my head barely clearing the windowsill, as I waited for my mother to bring Steph home from the hospital.

My excitement was tempered when Steph arrived, colicky and crying and monopolizing all of my parents' attention. I tolerated it when my mom took care of her, but for the life of me I couldn't figure out why Daddy should have anything to do with her. I was hurt and miserable when, after being sent to bed, I heard him sitting up with her, rocking her and singing to her. In the morning, I'd grab his legs when he was on his way out the door to work, begging him to stay and play with me. I wouldn't let go until he pulled Pez candy from his breast pocket to distract me.

In the car, I look over at my sister, now clutching her stomach. She is everything I am not: dark-haired, dark-eyed, a mass of whirling arms and legs that seem to happily be everywhere except where they are supposed to be.

Steph's clothes are perpetually disheveled, her toys always in disrepair. Her bright yellow bedroom is like a scene from a disaster movie: her floor is invisible beneath a kaleidoscope of crayons, colored paper scraps, plastic teacups, doll clothes, art projects, dirty laundry, and the strands of polyester hair she cut off from her dolls' heads. "I need it all, Daddy!" she says when he tries to make her throw anything away. The top of her dresser is crammed with an infirmary of bald dolls with imaginary ailments whose symptoms are a lot like our mom's. Steph lovingly bandages their legs and arms and heads with casts made out of Kleenex.

Most nights, Steph sneaks downstairs after dinner to the room outside my father's studio to draw crayon pictures for his waiting students, or to entertain them with funny stories she invents about girls with long hair from normal families without foreign fathers or mothers in wheelchairs. Her tales are elaborately detailed, and she lingers over descriptions of birthday parties with pink layer cakes topped by princess crowns and gifts wrapped with satin bows. Daddy inevitably hears her giggling and opens his studio door to shout, "Stephanie! Get your *keester* upstairs!" Later, giving in to Stephanie's pleas for a pet, he brings home a parakeet as a reward for cleaning her room. She promptly names it "Keester."

People are always drawn to Stephanie. Harried parents rushing in to collect their students at night find themselves stopping to visit with her, and I hear them both laughing as if at some private joke. During my grandmother's weekly phone calls, while I deliver

dutiful responses of "Yes, Nanny. No, Nanny. Thank you, Nanny,"
Steph flops down on the couch, props up her feet, and gushes,
"Okay, Nanny darling, let's *chat!*" Though she has ferocious temper
tantrums—her little feet once kicked a hole in the living room
wall—her tears are over in a flash, and soon she is giggling again,
living up to her middle name, Joy.

I envy how easily Stephanie climbs up on Daddy's lap, makes
him laugh, and smothers him with kisses. How she draws pictures
for him that he saves in his sock drawer. How she can get away with
teasing him, something I wouldn't dare try. When he is sick with a
fever in bed for a few days while our mom is in the hospital, I set us
up with picture books and sit quietly on the floor outside of his
room. Steph brushes past me, impatiently bursts into his bedroom,
climbs on top of him, and rubs her little finger along his unshaven
chin, making up songs:

> *Meow goes the mustache*
> *Woof woof goes the beard*
> *I love my Daddy*
> *Even though he's weird.*

Steph can't hold anything in—not laughter, not love, not
anger—and, at the moment, in the car, not her lunch, either.

"I've got to throw up!"

Daddy glares back at us, then tunes the radio to the classical
music station and turns up the volume.

Sometimes the music helps Steph take her mind off her stomach. My parents are always playing recordings of the classics for
us, though between my mother's health and the expense, we can't
afford to go to live concerts. Daddy started us off with kid-friendly
pieces like *Tubby the Tuba* and Saint-Saëns's *The Carnival of the
Animals* and then moved on to my mother's favorite choral works

that she used to conduct, excerpts from Haydn's *The Creation* and Brahms's *Requiem*. My mother especially loves Mendelssohn and Mozart. She always talks about the day I will play Mendelssohn's Violin Concerto in E Minor, her all-time favorite and apparently some kind of milestone for budding violin soloists.

The only thing our parents won't let us listen to is rock and roll. Anything but "that popular crap that eez called music, like the Bittles with their 'Yeah, Yeah, Yeah,'" my father grumbles.

On the car radio, a Wagner opera fills the air.

"That makes me feel worse!" Steph wails, as an overwrought soprano reverberates through the backseat. Steph hates opera, even more than Daddy hates the Beatles.

And with a sudden lurch, Steph heaves into the towel spread across my lap. Daddy pulls the car to the side of the road and fumbles for the plastic bag we always have on hand just in case, and I deposit the dirty towel that I'll wash with the rest of poor Stephanie's sour-smelling laundry when we get home.

I crack open the car window as Steph gasps for air. Her face is already turning from green to its usual pink, her breath is steadying, her muscles relaxing.

It will all be worth it, of course, if the shots work.

But months later, my mother's condition has only gotten worse. That is the last she sees of the Delaware doctor.

Kids hardly ever come over to our house to play. So when I'm not practicing violin, Steph and I make up games to play with each other. We imagine that we're babies, crying for our imaginary mother to come running to take care of us. Our imaginary older sister is a doctor who gives us shots. The pretend shots are painful, like the ones our mom gets from the doctor in Delaware, but they will cure us from ills like growing up and dying.

One afternoon, after the daytime babysitter has left but before the evening sitter has arrived, Steph and I are deep into our game in the living room. I have just gotten my imaginary never-grow-up shot when my mother cries out from the upstairs bathroom. Steph and I run in to find her sprawled on the floor where she had fallen, between the sky-blue bathtub and toilet, her head jammed up against the bright pink tile. She is trying desperately to pull herself up, but there is nothing to grab on to.

Lots of times she gets stuck on her way into or out of the bathtub and has to call me to help lift her leg up and over the side. In fact, the only times I see my mother in an upright position are when I help her in the bathroom or to get out of the car. Later on, when I think of my mother, I always imagine her at seated height. I will grow up with no memory of how tall she actually is.

But this time is different. Steph and I are terrified to see our mother sprawled out helplessly on the floor. We try as hard as we can to lift her up, but her legs are just too weak. Her condition has deteriorated.

"Girls, I need you to run across the street to get help. Go, quick!"

Steph and I look at each other, a single thought shared between us both: *No way. Uh-uh.*

Not only are we scared to death of Missy, our neighbor's vicious biting dog, but the family's three boys have never missed an opportunity to tease and torment us. We certainly aren't going to tell them our mother is at this moment trapped on the floor beside the toilet. We would die of embarrassment, and those kids would never let us forget it.

"Grab an arm," I order Stephanie.

She takes one, I take another, and we pull with all our might. No luck.

"Try her legs!"

We try again, and when that doesn't work, we tug her by the armpits. But my mother is wedged tighter than ever between the toilet and the tub.

There is no way we can get her into a standing position.

We have no choice. Steph circles her little arms around one of my mother's legs and tugs, while I hug the other to my chest and pull, and we drag my mother by the ankles out of the bathroom. Across the worn brown carpeting we go, my mom crying and laughing at once, as we strain and pull her down the hall and finally into her bedroom, where she grabs the bedsheets and hoists herself on top of the bed. That's where we all collapse in a heap until Daddy comes home and finds us.

My mother heads back to the hospital after that. "Just for a few days," she tells us before she leaves. After the car pulls away, our babysitter shoos Steph and me out to the sandbox. It is a sunny June day, and we can smell freshly cut grass. My throat is tight and my breath catching as I sit, letting the sand run through my fingers.

"Hey, Steph," I say, looking up from the pile accumulating at my feet. "Let's make a surprise for Mommy!"

"Okay, what will we make?" Steph turns her little face up to me.

"Let's make a sand castle, and write 'Welcome Home' in the sand so she can see it when she comes back."

By the time she gets home it is winter. Eight months have passed. Our sand castle is long gone, and the sandbox is covered with snow.

Every August, almost all of my dad's older students go to the music camp he runs at Douglass College, just down the highway from our house. The American String Teachers Association, or ASTA for short, holds a weeklong conference of orchestra and chamber music during the day and concerts and recitals at night. Students stay in bunk beds in the Katzenbach Hall dormitory and eat at the cafeteria where you can get as many bowls of wobbly Jell-O cubes as you want. At seven years old, I am years younger than most of the other campers. But with my mother in the hospital, Daddy ships Stephanie off to stay with Grandma Brown and takes me with him.

My roommate, a thirteen-year-old viola player named Jeannie, lets me tag along with her to rehearsals and meals so I don't get lost. On the first night, she brings me with her to the "get acquainted" dance, where girls in short dresses and patent leather

"Dance!" Mr. K commanded his students at the New Jersey ASTA Conference get-acquainted party. Here, he takes matters into his own hands, circa 1969.

sandals stand on one side of the room, while boys with shaggy hair drink punch on the other. The high school jazz band is playing "Take the 'A' Train."

My dad strides in, his white socks flashing underneath his dark suit. I hear tittering all around. I can't figure out why. Then I see: He has marched over to the boys' side and is dragging one boy by the hand to a girl across the room. He puts their two hands together and commands: "Dance!"

They don't dare disobey.

Now he is back on the girls' side, grabbing the hand of a quiet brown-haired girl in a sleeveless lace dress and dragging her out to the dance floor himself: "Let's show them how eet eez done!"

My dad loves to dance. I've never seen anyone else move like him. He jerks his legs and kicks up his feet like a drunken Cossack dancer. His movements don't seem to relate in any way to the music, not to the speed or the beat or anything else. The kids scream in laughter and applaud. My dad kicks up his feet even higher. His toes trace awkward angles in the air. I'm glad he hasn't dragged me onto that dance floor. But I can't help thinking he looks happier than I've seen him in a long time.

At ASTA, I have my first audition. I play my solo and scales in front of a couple of music-teacher judges in a classroom. Later, they post the results on a sheet of paper in the hallway. The other kids run to the wall and madly search for their names, jumping up and down to get a look over other people's heads, then screaming in excitement if they've done well or slinking away angrily if they haven't.

I don't care. I have yet to learn that the world of student orchestras is one of hierarchies on top of hierarchies. There are tryouts to get in, then placement in either first or second violin sections, then rankings from first chair to last. If you are seated in the front near the conductor you must be good; if you are seated in the back you must be plain awful. The stigma attached to being placed in the rear of the section is devastating.

It will take years before I understand the gravity of the seating chart. That summer, I place into the intermediate orchestra, in the middle of the violin section. I am too short to see the conductor, blocked by a thirteen-year-old boy in front of me.

"Hey, Gordon. Switch seats with Melanie," the conductor calls over to him casually. "She can't see over you."

Gordon looks stricken. "Everyone will think she *beat* me in the audition!" he erupts. During the break, I hear him tell his friends: "I'm going to challenge her. Then the conductor will have to give me my seat back."

The dreaded challenge. I've never heard of it, but it doesn't take long for Gordon to explain it to me. We will both perform an excerpt from the orchestra music, alone in front of the group. Whoever plays it better wins. The conductor agrees, and the challenge is on, scheduled for the following day.

After the rehearsal, seeing my dad across the room, I run up to him and fling myself into his arms.

"Daddy! A boy challenged me! I have to learn a part of the orchestra music and play it alone tomorrow!"

"What? Calm down, now. Who challenged you?"

"Th-th-that boy over there!" I point. Gordon is standing across the room, laughing with his friends.

I wait for the warmth of Dad's sympathetic hug. I wait for him to tell me that this isn't fair, that he won't let some boy pick on me. Daddy will fix it, I'm sure.

Instead, he grabs a music stand, sets it up right there in the corner of the room, and tells me to start practicing.

For fifteen minutes, my dad watches over my shoulder as I work on the piece, barking orders. "More bow!" "Intonation!" "Watch your rhythm!" Then he dispatches me: "There, now you just go out there and play like that. And may the best man win."

Melanie's first chamber music performance at age seven, standing on a podium. Michele Lipman plays the violin across from her, in partial profile.

Maybe I should have expected as much. When we play checkers or Parcheesi, my dad always wins. He says if he eased up and let me win, that would be cheating. It's one of the first lessons I remember from my father: Work hard, but don't whine if you lose. And if you do lose, pick yourself up and try harder next time.

In the end, Gordon backs off from the challenge when he figures out I'm Mr. K's daughter. My dad solves the problem anyway, placing my chair on a box so I am tall enough to see over Gordon's head.

I stand on boxes a lot these days. My first ASTA chamber music performance is in a violin quartet with three teenage girls. One of them is a pretty thirteen-year-old violinist with straight brown hair named Michele. She's from East Brunswick, too. She wears little denim cutoff shorts during the day and white Mary Janes and lacy minidresses when we have to dress up for concerts. That afternoon, I'm wearing a Sears catalog dress my mom ordered from her hospital room, and my dad has made a mess of cutting my bangs.

While my dad searches for a podium for me to stand on, Michele eagerly scans the audience, pointing out her parents, who sit waving in the front. Alongside them sit her two sisters, the smaller one a girl about my age named Joanne, who has a book in one hand and looks bored.

I am the first violinist, which means I'm supposed to lead the group. As we begin our piece, I look up at the others every once in a while to make sure we're all playing together. Each time, Michele smiles reassuringly back at me. When we finish, the audience applauds enthusiastically, Michele's family loudest of all. I can see my father in the wings. He isn't clapping, but he looks satisfied.

I gaze out from the stage, the last chords of the piece still in my head. My mom isn't here—nothing can change that—but so many other familiar faces are, smiling back up at me. It's a wonderful feeling, like an embrace, and relief and happiness. And belonging. There is no better feeling in the world. I want it to last forever.

4

The Concertino

JOANNE

I glared silently at my parents who were dragging me into Hickman Hall at Douglass College to go watch Michele play in her dumb summer music program. My mother pulled me by one hand. In the other, I gripped my paperback copy of *Harriet the Spy*, which I was reading for the third time in a row.

Seriously. It was summer vacation. What were we doing here?

All I wanted to do was go to the county fair, which we were missing right this very second. My mom never let me go on the good rides—the upside-down Ferris wheel or the roller coaster—because she was convinced that I would be thrown out and die, splattered across the fairgrounds. She never let us go on rides when we went to the boardwalk on the Jersey Shore, either, because they were rickety and run by convicts. But at least at the county fair, held just a short bike ride from our house, I knew she'd offer up a consolation prize like frozen custard or fried dough.

Instead, here we were at Mr. K's ASTA conference, to watch my thirteen-year-old sister, Michele, perform chamber music. I lagged behind my parents as they pushed through the doors into the bracingly cold, over-air-conditioned auditorium. A shiver went through me as my mother prodded me to keep up.

"I'm cold," I said, but I knew it was useless to protest, because my mother would just tell me it was hot outside and you weren't supposed to wear long sleeves in the summer anyway.

"It's going to be hot later. You don't need a sweater now," she said, as if this logic made perfect sense.

I wrapped my arms around myself as we settled into the scratchy pull-down seats with the nubby upholstery. Around us, teenagers were sitting in groups whispering and giggling. Up on the stage—a wide, low-slung expanse with a green curtain drawn against the back wall—Mr. K was talking loudly about how important it was to be quiet during the performance.

I yawned and fidgeted in my seat as the first few groups played, daydreaming about frozen custard and Ferris wheels. But I was jolted back to reality by a commotion on the stage. Mr. K was clomping across the floor—my, could he do *anything* without making a racket?—looking for something. I watched as he noisily dragged over a podium to the center of the stage.

Michele's quartet drifted out from the wings: three teenage girls and Melanie, Mr. K's daughter. Melanie was wearing a smock dress and shiny black shoes with ankle socks. I silently thanked heaven that I didn't have to wear clothes like that anymore. In my second grade class, I had signed a petition so girls could wear pants to school. Melanie's red hair was even shorter than mine, and her jagged bangs looked the way mine did that time I got hold of my mother's scissors and started snipping away. I couldn't reach the mirror while I cut and figured no one would notice anyway. When my mom got a look at me, she tried to yell, but she was laughing too hard.

Melanie was tiny, so it was a good thing she had the podium to stand on. Hauling herself up the two big steps and positioning herself on the top of the box, she lifted her little violin with a theatrical flourish. The other violinists looked toward her expectantly. Michele, who so easily lorded her authority and wisdom over me at home, was gazing at this little girl with respect.

I sat up in my seat as they began to play, watching with equal parts curiosity and envy. You could see that Melanie was better than any of them. She led them through the piece, through to its grand, galloping finale, and all four girls ended with their bows high in the air. My parents clapped madly. Mr. K, visible in the wings, didn't clap at all. He gave a barely perceptible nod.

"Can I read my book now?" I asked my mother. On the cover, Harriet the Spy wore a red hooded sweatshirt and big horn-rimmed glasses. She carried a marbled composition notebook under one arm. I had convinced my mom to buy me a notebook just like it, so I could go write observations about people the way that Harriet did. I was going to be a spy, too.

I pulled the book onto my lap and starting searching for the page.

"No," my mother said.

The truth is, while it was fun to see a girl my age play the violin, the music itself left me cold. At home, we never listened to classical music like that.

Instead, whenever one of my sisters wasn't practicing an instrument—before school or right afterward, when we grabbed a snack of Yodels at the kitchen table—we would crank up the scratchy transistor radio. It was perpetually tuned to WABC AM Top 40, blaring the Beatles and Three Dog Night. My big sisters had their favorite songs—there was "Michelle" by the Beatles that Michele loved and "Help Me, Rhonda" by the Beach Boys that spoke to Ronni. Later there would be David Bowie and the Allman Brothers and Yes and Led Zeppelin. The first time I ever heard about sex and drugs had been the year before, when I wandered into Michele's red-, white-, and blue-flowered bedroom and she helpfully tried to explain the lyrics to the song playing on her portable radio, "Hey, Jude."

"What does 'let it out and let it in' mean?" I asked, as she sang along.

"Let me try explaining again," she said, sighing.

Our parents were strict in lots of ways, but music wasn't one of them. We gathered on the green family room couch to watch the Who smash their instruments on *The Smothers Brothers Comedy Hour* and the Doors infuriate their host on *The Ed Sullivan Show* after Jim Morrison sang "Light My Fire" and refused to change the line "girl, we couldn't get much higher." My dad listened to the Beatles' "Yesterday" on his hi-fi stereo, a massive contraption encased in a wooden cabinet that dominated our family room. Later, my parents would take us to see *Hair* on a vacation in London, with a bunch of naked actors running around onstage.

When the rock opera *Jesus Christ Superstar* opened on Broadway not long afterward, Mr. K chaperoned a music-class trip to see it. My sisters, who both went, were ecstatic. He was repulsed. His face contorted in disgust as the overture began to play. He got more agitated when he peered into the orchestra pit and saw the electronic synthesizers that mimicked the sound of violins. "Where are the strings?" he sputtered. "Electronic music eez taking over real music!"

He would never warm to rock and roll. He once described it to a reporter as "A bunch of wild savages running around a campfire and howling like a bunch of wild hounds." Mr. K was on a crusade, one that anybody could tell you was crazy. He wasn't going to let his students turn into "wild savages" who listened to god-awful music. He would teach them discipline, even if it killed him.

Mr. K clearly lived in some other world than the one we inhabited. On our street, the boys were all growing their hair long. They worried about the Vietnam War and the draft. There was a rumor that the older brother of a neighborhood boy had died in the jungles over there. Some of the girls started showing up at school wearing silver POW and MIA bracelets with names of strangers etched into them. Our parents were arguing about the new president, Richard Nixon. The teenagers on our road tuned out the grown-ups with psychedelic music and tried to one-up each other as they bragged about how many people they knew who went to Woodstock. Every time we saw a rock band on television, I would say, mimicking the older kids, "That guy's on drugs!"

Mr. K's world, meanwhile, was populated by clean-cut girls with Patty Duke flips and sensible shoes. His rule inside his music room was autocratic; his enforcement unyielding. He regulated his students' speech (no talking); their dress ("No mini mini mini and no maxi maxi maxi!"); their fingernails (he chopped off nails that grew too long with the clipper he carried in his pocket). Still, he groused to a reporter that "the children today are not disciplined enough." When his orchestra was invited to play in Washington, D.C., in early 1969, he seemed a world away from the race riots that had rocked the city in the aftermath of Martin Luther King Jr.'s assassination the year before. "I told them they'd work 'til they sweat," he told a reporter about his students. "I put it to the students squarely, telling them to search their soul to make sure they really were ready to put in the extra work necessary for the concert."

Perhaps there was another reason Mr. K was so maniacal about maintaining control of the world inside his rehearsal room: he had so little control outside of it. The chaos of war protests and love-ins and drugs was crashing into the shoals of our little suburb. The fallout would ultimately threaten even his own younger daughter, who at that moment was barely a toddler. The accent and mien that so effectively intimidated his students inside his music room didn't always translate outside of it.

On his way to a music-teachers convention in Chicago in the late 1960s, as his plane idled on the tarmac at Newark Metropolitan Airport, he chatted up a stewardess, cracking what he thought was a mild joke: "I hope thees plane eezn't going to Cuba."

A couple of minutes later, the pilot and two burly passengers escorted him off the jet and into a holding room, where the police questioned him for an hour. What they saw: a swarthy foreigner in a tight black suit with a little mustache and a sinister accent—a potential hijacker. What they got: a frightened immigrant. The closest thing he had to a weapon was the clipper he always carried in his breast pocket to cut his students' nails. The cops let him go when he showed them something else he never left home without: his discharge letter from the U.S. Army.

I wouldn't realize it until much later, but he had reason to try to keep reality at bay.

Back at school that fall, a letter from Mr. K arrived at our house. Every year, he gave a music aptitude test to fourth graders. The children who got the highest scores got personal letters from him, recommending that they play a string instrument. He invited their families to a meeting at the elementary school, to hear about instrument lessons kids could get in school for free starting in fifth grade.

Michele had been the first one in my family to get the letter from Mr. K, and when it arrived, she was so happy that she screamed and danced around in circles with the envelope. Now Ronni got one of the letters, too. Our family went to the meeting, sitting on folding chairs in the cafeteria while Mr. K spoke from the stage. Near him, a man from the local music store set out a display of violins and cellos and flutes and bassoons, alongside a stack of rental forms.

"A low score does not necessarily mean that the child has no musical aptitude," Mr. K was saying. "However, eef your child performs well on the test, that eez no accident. That does not happen by chance. You cannot be genius and *idyot* at the same time."

Music teachers circulated as he spoke, peeking inside students' mouths to look at teeth. Apparently kids who were going to need braces shouldn't take up the oboe. Ronni was looking longingly at the wind instruments; she had already decided to play the flute. Meanwhile, Mr. K stood in front of the room, going on about music education, and discipline, and how important music is to civilized society. He was getting wound up now, talking as if music were crucial to survival itself.

"Your child weel be pulled out of class to take a lesson," he was saying. "Every effort weel be made not to take your child from a class they are struggling weeth. But let me say that een all my years of teaching I haf never seen music lessons bring about an academic collapse! Our music students excel at their classes. Eet instills wonderful discipline."

That's when the room got real still. Mr. K had gotten to the part of his speech where he was telling the parents that if they sent their kids to him, he wouldn't let them become wild savages listening to rock and roll and howling like wild hounds. They would learn to discipline themselves.

"There eez a saying," he said with a meaningful look at the hushed crowd of parents. "No keed who blows a horn weel ever blow a safe."

MELANIE

I'm sick of you wanting to have fuuunnn," Daddy sneers one day when I complain about practicing while my friends are going to the movies. "The only *fun* that lasts, the only fun that means anything, eez the happiness you can achieve through hard work!"

I sigh and go back to practicing.

The problem is, I can remember a time when our family *did* do fun things together, at least once in a while. I still think about the last time our family went to the movies: a double feature of *The Russians Are Coming! The Russians Are Coming!* and *Bambi* at the Turnpike Drive-In, when I was five years old, right around the time my mom got sick. My dad laughed louder than I'd ever heard him laugh before at the fumbling Russian Communists in the first movie. But *Bambi* proved an unfortunate choice.

"Mommy? What's going to happen to Bambi? Where is his mama? Who's going to take care of him now?" Steph asked as Bambi ran searching through the snow, calling out for his mother.

My mom reached for my dad's hand, which was resting on the steering wheel.

"It's okay," she said softly. "He still has his daddy, honey."

Now, at eight years old, I envy the kids whose families go to the movies or the bowling alley on weekends, or spend hot summer afternoons swimming at Dallenbach's lake, or take vacations to exotic places like Florida.

We don't even go to the Jersey Shore anymore. It's too difficult to travel with my mom. She can't go anywhere, and there's no money to pay for it if she could.

"Daddy? How come we never go away?" I know the answer, but I ask the question anyway.

"Eef you want to travel, then practice," he erupts. "Your violin weel take you where you want to go someday."

I turn back to my music stand.

The violin is slowly taking over my life. It isn't like I have a choice. I can't have friends over to play, and I'm too embarrassed to expose my home life anyway. Being the youngest in my grade, one of the "brainy" kids, and clueless about sports—nobody in my family could tell you what the NFL or the NBA is, much less tell them apart—compounds the humiliation. Put it all together, and it's clear that a perfect storm of conditions is brewing that will ensure years of discomfort as a social outcast.

I used to make friends easily. When I was three years old, before my mom got sick, she took me to the nursery school run by the high school home economics class. I still remember that first day, running to greet all the other children, and feeling sorry for another girl who was wailing and crying and refusing to let go of her mother. I would find out later that the girl was Joanne, though we didn't meet then because she was so hysterical that the teachers sent her home. But now things have changed for me, too. By the end of second grade, painful shyness creeps in, the kind that keeps me from raising my hand in class ever, even if I'm sure of the answer. My teachers complain that I need to contribute more. I have become a quiet kid.

Meanwhile, the violin comes easily to me. All my teachers know my dad, and they all know that I play. Every year my dad has me perform for my classmates, and I like the attention from kids who usually ignore me. There's always lots of oohing and aahing over my little violin, and the other kids think it's cool that I can do something special that they can't.

The day I play for my second grade class, one of the girls lingers to examine my violin. Miriam Simon is plump and bookish and has thick brown braids that reach all the way down her back. We've occasionally been thrown together before: in the top reading group, sitting with the other social nobodies at lunch, or pretending not to care when we're among the last to be picked for teams in gym class. She gets teased for wearing flood pants that she's long outgrown, and I'm at the mercy of whatever is on sale in the Sears catalog, which accounts for my lime-green-plaid stretch bell-bottoms. I wouldn't have been allowed to wear pants to school at all, except that they're required for phys ed. And blue jeans are out of the question, being what my father calls "dungarees—what farmers wear to *fling dung*!"

Miriam and I are soon spending recess together and picking each other first when it's our turn to be team captain. A few times she invites me to her house after school. Her home is a wonderfully chaotic place full of noise and laughter, the TV always blaring some sports event or other, dog barking, brothers bickering. Her mom is frantically busy with six kids under the age of nine—a seventh will be on its way soon—yet she can always make room for one more around their giant dinner table. "That Melanie, I've never met such a loud, noisy girl!" her dad teases me as I sit silently, taking it all in.

It takes a long time, but I finally screw up my courage enough to invite Miriam to my own house. It's a Saturday afternoon, and Daddy is home.

"Ahhh! So thees eez Miriam! Such a lovely creature! She has braids like the girls back een Ukraine. Oh, and cello hands...she has cello hands!" He holds up her hands to the light streaming in from the front window to examine them.

"What's a cello?" Miriam asks as we head upstairs to my room.

"A big violin. It sits on the floor when you play it," I begin, when suddenly Miriam freezes, her eyes fixed above my shoulder. I turn and follow her gaze. My mother is struggling toward us, attempting to walk, wearing leg braces and leaning on her bulky metal walker.

Miriam looks pale, as if she wishes she were anywhere but here. I wait for her to make her excuses, to say it is time to go home and to call her mom in her noisy, boisterous, *normal* house.

"Hello, girls," my mom greets us as she sinks into her parked wheelchair. "You must be Miriam. I've heard so much about you!" She smiles warmly as she grasps Miriam's trembling hand. As quickly as we can escape, we hurry off to my room and get out my Barbie dolls.

To my surprise and relief, Miriam doesn't run home. Within a year, she is taking cello lessons with my father. In time, every one of her six younger siblings will take music lessons with him, too.

As I advance, practice sessions with Daddy are sometimes stormy. He runs me through bowing and vibrato exercises until my brain is numb with boredom and my hands burn with pain. He yells constantly.

"Bow away from you!"

"Violin up!"

"Are you *deaf*?"

To correct me as I play, he smacks at my wrists and elbows with one of his conducting batons.

Crooked bow? *Whack.*

Straight pinky on my bow hand? *Slap.*

Elbow in the wrong position? *Jab.*

Lately, no matter how hard I try, I never stand up straight enough for Daddy while I play. So one day when I come down to the studio for my lesson, he takes my music stand and sets it on top of a box. It's so tall, my music now perched so far above my head, I have to lean over backward, my spine arching like a gymnast's and my violin pointing almost straight up to the ceiling, to read the notes.

"Better," he says.

The music stand stays on the box for months. It hurts my back and strains my eyes, but my posture is perfect.

Rhythm reading—figuring out complicated combinations of beats—is another trouble spot. It isn't my strongest suit, and my dad's sense of rhythm is even worse. As an orchestra conductor, he stomps and waves his baton so wildly that no one can figure out what the beat is anyway. Substitute a fly swatter for the oversize baton he favors, and there wouldn't be an insect left alive for miles.

In his studio, I can tell he's all wrong when he counts out the rhythm, even if I'm not sure what is right. At times I learn a new rhythm through some inner intuition of my own, powered by the sheer force of Daddy's frustrated, unhelpful shouting.

"What's the matter weeth you? Can't you count to three?!"

Intonation poses another whole set of problems. Daddy sits at his piano banging the offending note with a single finger, over and over again, shouting "Sharp!" or "Flat!" Then he sings what I'm supposed to play, but his singing is awful and out of tune and makes things even worse. I say nothing, just try harder.

"You'll thank me later," he says.

I rarely fight him, and I'm usually fairly quick to learn something new. Sometimes that is enough. Often it isn't. But nothing I go through in a practice session can compare with Stephanie's struggles.

Steph is five years old when Daddy decides she's ready for lessons, too. Creative and smart, sensitive and affectionate, Steph is a natural performer—just not on the violin. Nobody can top her when it comes to taking a bow at the end of a performance. At her beginner orchestra concert, misunderstanding my dad's instructions, she alone stands up after each piece, bowing with a grand flourish each time my father turns to the audience to acknowledge the applause. I am mortified as I watch from my seat in the front row, but the audience loves her, laughing and clapping.

But Steph is neither detail oriented nor coordinated. She has inherited my dad's lack of rhythm, along with his fierce stubborn streak. During her lessons it is always a challenge for her to remember which way to curve what finger or wrist, all while trying to learn to read notes and listen to what she is doing. Nothing about the actual technique of violin playing comes easily to her, from creating a sound to sight-reading new music to simply standing still long enough to practice. She is miserable as Daddy shouts and screams through her practice sessions.

Unlike me, Steph can be reduced to tears instantly, though that carries no weight with Daddy.

"Sorry, Daddy!" she cries during her lesson one night. I try not to listen, but their voices are so loud that I can't help but hear my father's yelling and Steph's muffled sobs through the closed studio door. "Stand steel and focus!" Daddy is shouting.

The door slams. My dad comes stomping up the stairs holding a broken violin bow in his hand. His usual baton hasn't been aggressive enough to prod her into doing as he demanded. He used the violin bow instead. Then he whacked her so hard with it that it splintered.

I can hear Steph wailing downstairs, but my dad isn't paying any attention to her.

"Goddamn cheap bow," he mutters as he clomps up the stairs. "They don't make them like they used to."

Of course there are times when I don't want to practice, even want to quit. On one or two occasions I mention this to my father.

"Melanie, time to practice!" Why does this always happen right in the middle of my favorite TV show, or when I reach the best part in the book I'm reading?

"I don't want to do it now, Daddy!" I venture.

"Come on, eet's time."

"Do I have to? Why do I have to?"

"You haf to practice so you'll get better. You want to be good at the violin, don't you?"

"Daddy, I don't think I want to play the violin anymore." My words fall like a bomb into our living room.

Silence. Long silence.

"Well then, eef you don't want to do the things I want you to do, don't expect me to do the things you want me to do!"

What things? I wonder. I soon find out. My father does not speak to me for two days. The longest two days of my life. The pain of those days is worse than any spanking I ever receive.

I get it. I play the violin.

As I begin to practice on my own I develop some coping strategies. Like memorizing my entire lesson quickly and putting a book up on the stand where my music should be. When I hear Daddy's footsteps in the hallway, I grab my Nancy Drew mystery and throw it under my bed, then start playing again furiously. I am amazed he never seems to catch on or to question the loud *thwack* of my book hitting against the wall as he approaches my room.

Different techniques are tried to get me to practice more, and more effectively. Setting the kitchen timer is one of the first tactics my parents use. Of course, I try the old move-the-timer-ahead trick, reducing my sentence from forty-five minutes to maybe ten. Mission accomplished. I'm lounging in the dining room on the bright plastic seesaw Stephanie got for Christmas—that season's hot item, the "swervy curvy topsy turvy tipsy skipsy doodle. The all-day toy!" as the ads call it—when my father bursts in.

"What are you doing?" he demands angrily. "Why aren't you practicing?"

"I'm done. The timer rang." Technically not a lie, though I had helped it along quite a bit.

"You just started. How could eet ring? Deed you touch eet?"

Caught! My brain freezes. I'm afraid to lie and afraid to tell the truth. A spanking is now unavoidable.

One August evening when I am eight years old, Daddy takes me on a trip to Princeton, New Jersey, to meet Dr. Philip Gordon, a composer friend of his. Dr. Gordon had written a piece called Three Preludes for String Orchestra for the high school string ensemble, which it had performed with great success a few years back at the Music Educators National Conference in Washington, D.C. Now my dad has asked him to write a piece especially for me.

In order to write music for an eight-year-old, Dr. Gordon has requested that I come to his house and play for him so he can see for himself what I am able to do. According to Dr. Gordon, who was interviewed for the *Home News* newspaper in February 1971, he faced the task with some trepidation because "what do you write for such a little girl? Her emotional scope must be limited, and she plays on a half-size violin that's not big enough to produce any volume." But he said that when I met him, "she threw her arms around me and kissed me," and that my performance as a musician won his respect. "Oh, I was so impressed with that little girl. She plays with such a flair, tosses her bow up," he said.

My childish recollection of the evening is slightly different. Of course we get lost several times on the way to Princeton. As Daddy has promised me repeatedly, Dr. Philip Gordon is not the kind of doctor who gives shots. He's a soft-spoken, older gentleman, sweet-tempered and not at all scary. His wife, Julie, who has a handicap that impairs her walking and reminds me of my mom, gives me cookies and milk after I play, while my father and Dr. Gordon confer. Daddy is pleased with the whole endeavor, and within a few weeks there is a new piece of music for me to learn. A very challenging piece.

For the next several months I am immersed in my Concertino. At first, my progress is painfully slow. The tonalities are much more modern than anything I have ever played before, and it's hard to figure out how the piece is supposed to sound, since there aren't any recordings for me to listen to. My dad seeks help from his longtime friend and colleague Chris Cornell, a gentle violin teacher who I know as "Uncle Chris," to coach me. He brings in one of his advanced students, Stephanie Haun, who is already one of my favorite babysitters, to help, too. My mom spends a lot of time banging out notes on the piano with one finger to help me find the pitches. Even when I practice alone in my room she's listening, always ready to correct my intonation from her wheelchair, screaming out across the house "Sharp!" or "Flat!" as the case may be.

As the performance draws near, my practice sessions increase to upward of two hours a day. Not only do I have to master the musical and technical challenges and memorize the piece, but I also have to learn how to fit it all together with its orchestral accompaniment. That's the most difficult part. Playing alone in my room is much easier than stopping and starting and having to count the rests—the beats when I'm not playing but the orchestra is—and then figuring out when to start in again at the right time.

My parents argue constantly. There is no way my mother will be able to attend the concert, all the way in Atlantic City, at a national music educators' conference. I'll be performing with the junior high school orchestra; the beginner orchestra, of which Steph is a member, will play, too. My dad is conducting both, of course, plus giving a lecture demonstration beforehand. He's too preoccupied to even think about transporting my mom in her wheelchair.

"Jerry, I can't miss seeing my babies perform in Atlantic City. I'm their mother!" she pleads one night at dinner. But my dad remains firm—it's simply too big an ordeal to get her there—until she lashes out in anger: "If I can't go to the concert, then I won't let them go, either!" It's an empty threat, but the fact that this causes such tension and pain between my parents is not lost on me. Along with my own feelings of excitement and fear, a hefty dose of guilt is mixed in, a cocktail of emotions that will become my companion for life.

The morning of the concert dawns with a snowstorm and freezing winds whistling down the streets. My parents insist that Steph and I wear snow boots; we can change into our concert dress shoes later. I put mine on along with my Sears-best yellow polyester dress with lace sleeves and lace stockings. Somehow in the confusion of our departure, Stephanie's brand-new Mary Janes are left behind. In the sea of scrubbed faces, suits and ties, hair bows and frilly dresses, poor Steph's muddy brown clodhoppers stick out across the cavernous room. Daddy is mad, and Steph cries, but there is nothing to be done about it. The show must go on.

At the hotel ballroom, every seat is taken. I stand onstage, looking out at the grown-ups in their metal folding chairs, with overcoats and hats piled on their laps, stomping the snow from their feet. The carpet is a garish riot of big diamonds and stripes and starbursts that makes me dizzy if I look at it too hard. I focus on my dad instead.

He's standing on the podium, speaking directly to the audience. He describes how difficult it was to teach me the music and even tells the audience about Hoppy. Hoppy is my good luck charm—a tiny frog made of seashells that I had gotten at the beach one summer, when my mother could still travel. The frog usually sits on the piano in Daddy's studio. But now Daddy turns toward me and pulls Hoppy from his pocket, placing him reassuringly on the edge of the stage, where I can see him.

I just want it to be over, so that all the tension in my house will go away, too. But being onstage is not uncomfortable for me, and I don't have enough experience yet to know you're supposed to be nervous when you perform. Besides, I'm as ready as I can be. It seems as if I have done nothing but practice this piece for weeks, and I know it so well that I barely have to think anymore when I play it. To be honest, I'm getting a little tired of my Concertino.

Daddy likes to say that you have to strive for perfection in order to achieve excellence, and he may have gone overboard this time. Still, as I play before the crowd, I'm glad he did. Before the last chord has stopped ringing, my senses are flooded with the swell of applause, a glimpse of my dad glowing with pride, and an overwhelming feeling of relief mixed with satisfaction, a brand-new emotion that makes my head feel light. On the stage, through the applause, I hear his words replaying inside my head: *True happiness can only be achieved through hard work.* I'm starting to think I understand what he means.

PART II

I did my work slowly, drop by drop. I tore it out of me by pieces.

—MAURICE RAVEL

5

The Viola

JOANNE

Nobody had any reason to have any faith in my musical ability. At ten years old, my track record was awful. I had already given music lessons a try once. After epic bouts of whining and begging, my parents finally gave in, and when I was seven years old they allowed me to take piano lessons with Mrs. Hubbard, who came every Tuesday to teach my sisters. She was exotic, Mrs. Hubbard, with unruly dark red hair swept back into a disheveled ponytail, dark red lipstick, and armfuls of bracelets that jangled while we plunked out our scales. She dressed in flamboyant gypsy skirts in bright colors, and when you sat next to her on the piano bench and looked up at her face, you'd see the light catch on the downy trace of whiskers on her chin. Her clothes and her scent and her manner all spoke of bohemian living and Greenwich Village jazz clubs and unfiltered cigarettes smoked at dim café tables during poetry jams.

She always caused a frisson of excitement when she walked in for our piano lessons, the screen door banging behind her. We were a no-frills family. We didn't go for lots of jewelry or flashy clothes or perfume. Our house was functional and orderly and spare; we hadn't yet given in, as we would in the coming years, to the siren song of lime-green shag carpeting and metallic wallpaper. I was still wearing my sisters' hand-me-down dresses—did I ever hate that brown jumper with the ugly felt gingerbread appliqué—and the sight of Mrs. Hubbard in her flowing riot of colors never ceased to fascinate.

For all her loud jewelry and gaudy colors and wafting perfume, Mrs. Hubbard was unfailingly gentle. She never yelled or called us "*idyot!*" or asked if we were "deaf!" She never told us we sounded terrible or disciplined us for not being prepared. She never banged a stick to keep time. She never even insisted that we practice. My parents didn't remind us to practice, either—they figured that was up to us.

Perhaps that's why, a year after I started lessons, I was so surprised when my parents suddenly told me I was done. No more piano for me.

"You never practice," my mother said. "We aren't paying for lessons."

"But I want lessons!"

"Then you should have practiced."

"You didn't remind me!"

"I shouldn't have to."

My dad, interjecting: "Nobody ever told you life was fair."

And that was that. No piano. No talking back. No discussion.

After a year of lessons, I still couldn't read a note.

Jarema at about age three, in his hometown of Stryj in 1931. His town would be occupied by the Soviet Union and then by Germany within a decade.

Jarema with his mother, whom Melanie called Baba, and his stepfather, Walter DeBaylo, around the time they emigrated to the United States in 1946.

Jarema, who Americanized his name to Jerry, takes up the cello under music professor Roman Prydatkevitch at Murray State University in Kentucky. His senior recital, circa 1951.

Jean Brown, soon to become Jerry's wife, in the fashionable dress and high heels she favored, at the piano in 1956, before she became ill.

Mr. K began teaching at East Brunswick High School when it opened in 1958.

"Now DANCE!" Mr. K takes charge at a "get acquainted" dance at the ASTA summer music conference.

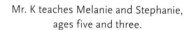

Mr. K teaches Melanie and Stephanie,
ages five and three.

Stephanie multitasking at about age five.

Mr. K helps Stephanie, age three, with her bow stroke.

Burton Lipman developed an interest in music as a teenager, playing a theremin that was built by his father, Paul. He demonstrated the instrument at a high school performance, circa 1948.

Diane Lipman, far right, loads up the station wagon in the driveway of the family's home with, left to right, Michele, Joanne, and Ronni, ages about eight, three, and six.

Diane Lipman and daughters Michele (ten years old), Ronni (eight years old), and Joanne (five years old), on a family vacation to Florida. Michele was a beginning violin player.

Melanie plays for composer Philip Gordon in his Princeton, New Jersey, home so he can hear for himself what an eight-year-old violinist can do. After the meeting, he composed Concertino for her.

Melanie performs Concertino by Philip Gordon, accompanied by the East Brunswick Junior High School Orchestra in Atlantic City, New Jersey, February 1971.

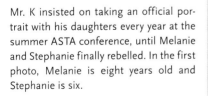

Mr. K insisted on taking an official portrait with his daughters every year at the summer ASTA conference, until Melanie and Stephanie finally rebelled. In the first photo, Melanie is eight years old and Stephanie is six.

Joanne, age twelve, leads the viola section in the Central Jersey Region II-Intermediate Orchestra. In the background, far right, Miriam Simon plays cello; next to Miriam is John Stine, whose music-teacher mother was a close friend of Mr. K's.

The *Sentinel* newspaper reports on the quartet's first national appearance, at the Music Educators National Conference in Philadelphia in April 1975. Left to right: Melanie, Stephanie, Mr. K, Miriam, Joanne.

*   *   *

So there were no great expectations when, in fourth grade, the letter from Mr. K arrived. I had scored well on the school-wide music aptitude test, it said. I should consider taking up a string instrument the next school year, when I could get lessons in school for free. My parents were skeptical—that test must have been pretty easy, they shrugged—but they agreed to let me give another instrument a try.

We decided on viola pretty quickly. I liked the sound of the instrument, and it was appealingly unpopular in a neglected runt-of-the-litter kind of way. More to the point, I didn't have a choice. I wasn't allowed to play violin because there was no way I could compete with Michele, who was not only five years older but also demonstrably talented. Neither of the other two instruments Mr. K taught—the cello and bass—would fit in the trunk of my mother's green Plymouth Duster. Viola it would be.

A viola is sort of like a violin but bigger. And lower pitched. And clumsier. And more embarrassing. You've probably heard of famous violin players like Itzhak Perlman and Isaac Stern and Jascha Heifetz. You've probably never heard of any violists. Violinists play the melody in great symphonies. Violists play the background notes, if they're playing at all. Student violinists get kicked around by every kid above them in the social pecking order. Violists get kicked around by violinists.

Q: What's the difference between a violin and a viola?
A: The viola burns longer.
Q: How do you get a dozen violists to play in tune?
A: Shoot eleven of them.
Q: What is the definition of "perfect pitch"?
A: Throwing a viola into a Dumpster without hitting the rim.

The viola has been around in one form or another for more than five hundred years, dating back to the invention of the viola da braccio in sixteenth-century Italy. For most of that time, it's pretty much been a joke. Most charitably, it has been called the "salt in a meal: it's not the main ingredient, but it's indispensable." More frequently, it is referred to as "neglected," "ignored," "awkward," and "the butt of the orchestra." The viola is an underdog, the least prestigious instrument in the entire orchestral repertoire. A step above a monkey grinder. Maybe not even.

Q: Why did the violist marry the accordion player?
A: Upward mobility.

"The viola is often merely a source of anxiety to the composer," wrote British musicologist Cecil Forsyth in his 1914 book *Orchestration*. "We feel that he must have regarded its existence as something in the nature of a prehistoric survival. The instrument was there and had to be written for." As a result, the great classical composers wrote orchestral parts in which the viola "either did nothing or something which by the ingenuity of the composer was made to appear as much like nothing as possible."

Time has not mellowed that view. Type "famous violists" into Google, and until recently it would ask, "Do you mean famous *violinists*?" Type simply "violists," and the top result was "Viola Jokes (part 1)."

It doesn't help matters that the viola is ludicrously difficult to play. As with a violin, the instrument is held up not by your arm but by clenching it between your chin and neck. But because a viola is heavier than a violin, the strain of holding it up guarantees you a permanent backache, a throbbing between the shoulder blades that no spa day can soothe. The instrument is longer than a violin, too, which means you have to stretch your left arm far away from your body at an awkward angle to play it. It's confounding to move your left arm, hand, and fingers in any coordinated fashion deftly enough to produce notes quickly and accurately. Altogether, it's a lumbering, potentially graceless affair.

And yet when it is played well, there is no more beautiful instrument. Deep and mellow, the viola is the instrumental equivalent to an alto or a tenor voice in a choir. At its best, it conveys emotional depths and nuances that other instruments can't. For me, it was perfect. As far as I was concerned, my three favorite violists—Paul Doktor, Raphael Hillyer, and Walter Trampler, all of them gods among viola cognoscenti—left the actual Three Tenors in their dust. Some of the great composers were violists themselves, from Johann Sebastian Bach—who was said to prefer playing the instrument above all others—to Antonín Dvořák to Paul Hindemith. So was Jimi Hendrix, before he switched over to electric guitar.

Mr. K had a special affinity for the viola, too. "I'm romanteek slob," he often said, and he warmed to its soulful sound. It's fashionable among music savants to be disdainful of melodic, romantic music. People who really *know* music will roll their eyes over the melodramatic excess of popular classics like the *1812 Overture* by Russian composer Pyotr Ilich Tchaikovsky. They prefer instead the intellectually rigorous, often atonal, the-more-sterile-the-better challenge of contemporary music.

But Mr. K was unabashed. He programmed as many of the overwrought classic orchestral works as his kids could manage and often added in schmaltzy Ukrainian folk songs that he had written out and arranged himself. He would conduct them with great, grand sweeping gestures, throwing himself into the music with unapologetic abandon, stretching out one arm and shaking it as if to pull in more, bigger, sappier sound.

"Thees concert would not be complete," he would tell the audience, "without raw Slavic sentimentality."

As it turns out, if raw Slavic sentimentality is what you're after, then the viola is for you. I never once heard Mr. K tell a viola joke.

My first viola lessons, with a group of other ten-year-olds, were in the summer after fourth grade, taught by two of Mr. K's best violin students early each morning in the oppressively un-air-conditioned performance room at the high school. Each had a calloused, angry red welt under her chin, the badge of a violinist who practices hours each day. One had deep grooves etched permanently in the fingertips of her left hand, an imprint left by the strings of her violin.

Every morning, in shorts and a T-shirt, with my frizzy hair pulled into pigtails against the New Jersey humidity, I would laboriously fold my fingers into place as the teachers pushed my elbow out, my wrist back, my pinky up. One day, while practicing our bowing on the instrument's four open strings—drawing the bow across the A, D, G, and low C strings, one at a time—I could feel the energy of the room change. Before I even turned around to look at the door behind me, I knew he was there. I straightened in my chair, focused on moving the bow as smoothly as possible, and looked up at the anticipation reflected in my teenage teachers' eyes.

Mr. K strode into the room, wearing a white short-sleeved dress shirt with a tightly knotted tie despite the wilting heat. You could already see the muscles tensing in his forearms. With his trim mustache and fierce mien, he looked more like a union boss, or maybe an off-duty ironworker angling to pick a bar fight, than a violin teacher. He eyed us intently, unsmiling. Slowly, he walked over to the student to my right and jerked the boy's neck into the proper position over the chin rest. Then he approached the girl to my left and jabbed her elbow. Finally, he walked over to me. I could feel my breath catching in my throat as he bent over to examine both hands and arms.

Here goes.

He gave my left wrist a sharp nudge.

Yikes.

He gave my right elbow a rough yank.

Ow!

He straightened up and fixed his cold, remorseless gaze on me.

Crap.

And then he spoke his first words to me: "Not bad."

Clearly, Mr. K saw something the rest of us didn't. With an un-sharpened pencil in one hand, the better to poke and prod, he corrected me over and over again that summer, singling me out from the group. Then when my fingers were burning, he barked: "Again!"

When I look through my earliest music lesson books, they are filled with Mr. K's handwriting in big red capital letters. Mostly, what he wrote was "AGAIN!" If you were to count up all the words he ever uttered in his entire life, I have no doubt that *again* would come out at number one.

It quickly became apparent that to Mr. K, there was no such thing as an untalented kid—just a kid who didn't work hard enough. You *are* going to fix this problem, he said when he diagnosed whatever was wrong, and there was never any question. Of course you would. It was just a matter of trying and trying and trying some more. He yelled not because we'd never learn, but because he was absolutely certain that we would.

In the eternal debate over nature versus nurture, Mr. K came down unequivocally on the side of nurture. Admittedly, his students, including me, would have been hard-pressed to identify that quality in his particular brand of torture. But with the benefit of hindsight, it's clear he didn't care how much innate talent you had. He believed any kid could learn to play an instrument, even someone with a proven track record of failure like me.

"Now you listen to me, seester," he would bark when he got frustrated. And eventually, no matter how much or how little

God-given talent you started out with, you actually did get it right. You knew you did, because Mr. K would give you that highest compliment of all, the one that made you run home and practice even harder: "Not bad."

There was already too much coddling of kids in school, as far as Mr. K was concerned. The school reform movement that started in the late 1960s had finally, in the 1970s, taken hold in East Brunswick, too. The women's movement, the civil rights movement, and the era of progressive politics all fed into a new paradigm of teaching that emphasized building up children's self-esteem and that replaced discipline with praise. The teacher-led model of the classroom morphed into a student-centric model.

In East Brunswick, that translated into "open classrooms" presided over by sideburned teachers who wore Tom Jones–style shirts with tufts of chest hair peeking out and who you just knew spent their weekends at transcendental meditation retreats. The high school abandoned most of its rote learn-the-dates history courses in favor of fact-free seminars like "Racial and Cultural Minorities." Years later I would say, only half jokingly, that I became a *remedial* history major in college—I needed to load up on so many courses simply to catch up on the basics that I ended up fulfilling most of the requirements of the major.

Mr. K had nothing but contempt for it all, sticking to his formula of discipline, repetition, and hollering. His insults were cutting; he didn't care whose feelings he bruised. Once, when one of my classmates proudly displayed a Jackson Pollock–inspired abstract-art project on the rehearsal room floor, he called for the janitor, erupting, "What eez thees mess? Who let the dog een here?"

Yet there was something intoxicating about a teacher who had such absolute confidence—faith, really—in my ability to do better.

Whatever I managed to achieve, he expected more. All I had to do was work harder. It was a simple formula, really, and it seeped into my consciousness without me even realizing it. If I imagined a ceiling on my ability, he raised the roof higher and then shattered it altogether. How far could I go? He gave me no sense of limits, so I set none for myself.

Mr. K required beginners to keep track of daily practice time. My first official "practice report card," signed weekly by my father, documented my growing resolve: thirty minutes one day, sixty minutes the next, then ninety, then two hours. My determination was matched only by the patience of my parents, my sisters, and Skippy as I screeched and scratched my way through my exercises for hours at a time. Each time Mr. K doled out a criticism, I would go home and up my practice time by an extra half hour. A much more rare compliment, and I'd up it by an hour. I don't remember now what I was practicing, but I do remember what I learned: Never give up. Never give in. Trust that I can always do better.

I'd been playing for less than a year when Mr. K approached my parents. I was sufficiently motivated, he told them, to study privately with him.

The first private lesson I took with Mr. K, in the sixth grade, is the first time I remember being truly scared, that kind of belt-choking-your-gut jitteriness that prevents you from eating your dinner. I went with Michele, who was already his private student and knew the routine. Mr. K's house was on the other side of the highway. It was a plain house for such a grand personality: a slightly tired split-level with cement front steps leading into a small entrance hallway. Half a flight of stairs led up to the living quarters, where I caught a glimpse of Mr. K's daughter Melanie clearing the dishes in the kitchen—the first time I had ever seen her not onstage and not holding a violin. Half a flight down led to Mr. K's basement music studio. Both staircases were narrow, made narrower still by the chair lift that ran on a track attached to the wall, apparently for Mrs. K, whom I could hear doling out orders upstairs but could not see.

Michele had her lesson first. While I sat in the waiting room outside his studio, Mr. K's younger daughter, Stephanie, darted down the stairs to introduce herself. She was a tiny scrap of a kid, giggling, her stick-straight dark hair flying every which way, her delighted expression looking like somebody just offered her an ice-cream cone, and she was holding out a crayon picture she had drawn for me. She plopped herself down on the arm of my chair, put her arm around my neck, and peered down at the book I was reading.

The book was called *The Bog People*, and it was about corpses that had been unwittingly preserved for thousands of years in Danish peat bogs. It had sublimely graphic photos—most of the "bog people" died macabre deaths from stabbings, hangings, throat-slittings, mutilations, and an assortment of other atrocities before being dumped by their Iron Age murderers into the bogs— and the photos showed bodies that were basically pickled, with everything preserved from their skin to their clothes to the last meals in their stomachs. I began reading aloud, forgetting my nervousness as we icked and eewed and shrieked our way from one deliciously grotesque photo to the next.

We were so immersed that we didn't notice the studio door had opened, until Mr. K poked his head out.

"Stephanie, get your *keester* upstairs! You better practice, seester!"

"Sorry, Daddy!" She disappeared upstairs before he even finished yelling.

Clearly, this was a regular routine.

When my turn came, I was ushered into his studio, which turned out to be a small, cluttered room, overflowing with instrument cases and sheet music and metronomes and vinyl records pulled out of their sleeves, with no visible clear surface anywhere except the spot next to the battered upright piano where I was to stand. A rubber chicken dangled by its feet from one wall. When he rehearsed the high school orchestra, Mr. K regularly yelled at kids for plucking at their instruments' strings while he was speaking. "Stop that cheeken plocking!" he would scream. One day, when he started going on about "cheeken plocking," the rubber chicken came sailing toward him out of the percussion section. Mr. K had brought it home and strung it up like a hunting trophy.

Mr. K sat perched on his chair in front of the piano. One hand gripped a pencil, poised to jab at me as I played my lesson assignments. The other hand rarely strayed from the piano keyboard, where he would bang out notes to correct my pitch when I played out of tune.

I knew I didn't have much to offer. I only had to compare myself to my sisters, both of whom were far more advanced on their instruments than I was. Sometimes I listened to recordings of their concerts. I had purloined one of my favorites from Michele's room: a performance in Atlantic City a few years back, when Michele was playing with the junior high school orchestra and Mr. K's daughter Melanie had performed Concertino, a solo written just for her. It was a spectacularly showy and difficult piece, full of complicated runs and ridiculously high notes that Melanie played at heart-stopping speed.

Meanwhile, I was just starting book two of the *String Builder* beginner series, written by pedagogue Samuel Applebaum. It had songs that were two lines long. The songs had names like "The Fishy Scales" and "The Elephant Takes a Walk."

Mr. K sat coiled regardless, ready to strike as I played through the simple melodies. "Don't crush bow een to strings!" he would say, stopping me. Then, "Sweep the bow!" Then, "*Listen!*"

While I was sawing my way through "Little Brown Jug" for the umpteenth time, trying to play with "smooth bow!" he barked into an intercom on the wall, connected to the kitchen upstairs: "Melanie, bring me my tea!"

Moments later, his redheaded daughter quietly opened the door, china cup and saucer in hand, silently handing it to her father. We had never met, though I had watched her perform many times before. Everybody in school knew who Melanie was. Probably everybody in town knew who she was, because the newspapers always wrote about her concerts and printed her picture. She was a celebrity. She may as well have been one of those child actors you saw on TV—remote, unknowable, not quite real, a world apart from the kids I played kickball with on the playground every day. It was hard to conceive of her doing anything ordinary. If Ali Mac-Graw had stepped out of the movie *Love Story* to hand Mr. K his teacup, it wouldn't have been any more improbable.

I looked up awkwardly from "Little Brown Jug," suddenly and acutely aware that I was playing out of tune.

She glanced back at me through a fringe of eyelashes and whispered an almost inaudible "hello" as she ducked out, closing the door quickly behind her.

Mr. K turned back to me and said simply, "Again!"

In music, the phrase *double time* means you play a piece twice as fast as before. With Mr. K, double time could also describe the speed with which he pushed me along.

Two months—and untold man-hours of practice time, pencil pokes, and shouts of "Again!"—after I started private lessons with him, I had finished book two of the *String Builder* series. Within a few months after that, I had moved on to my first "real" concerto, Telemann's Viola Concerto in G Major.

I was named principal violist—the leader of the section—first of the beginner orchestra, then of the sixth grade orchestra. I would sometimes practice two hours or more a day. Every afternoon, I came home from school, raided the kitchen pantry, and wolfed down three or four packages of Yodels or Hostess cupcakes with a big glass of milk, stealing a glance at my mom while she scrubbed the potatoes for dinner, silently praying that she wouldn't notice how much I was snacking and complain that I was ruining my appetite. Then I would rush through my homework so that I could have more time to practice.

Perhaps it isn't surprising that the extra practice time affected my schoolwork. My teacher noted it the night my parents showed up for parent-teacher conferences that fall. Like all Lipman girls, I was expected to get good grades. This time around, my teacher wanted to talk about something else.

As my parents folded themselves into the wooden school desks, they waited for the usual set of adjectives teachers used to describe me. *Shy. Tentative.* I needed to become "more forceful," as my teacher the previous year had written on my fall progress report. But now, the teacher was using an entirely unfamiliar set of words like *confident* and *assertive*.

Maybe it was thanks to Ronni, who outfitted me in her cool hand-me-down bell-bottoms. Maybe it was because of Michele, who brought home her high school books so I could write reports on *Love Story* and *Animal Farm* instead of Hardy Boys mysteries. But just maybe the music had something to do with it.

I was still in elementary school, but Mr. K told my parents he was going to promote me into the high school orchestra.

Still, I wasn't prepared for what came next, when Mr. K somehow got it into his head that I was ready to play in a string quartet with his talented daughters.

MELANIE

Joanne comes flying into the rehearsal room in the shortest shorts I've ever seen, wearing wire-rimmed glasses and a pop-top shirt, her hair in pigtails. Miriam follows, laughing, easily carrying her cello in one hand, her long hair loose and falling past her waist. Steph and I are already waiting. Despite the August heat, we both have on long pants—not blue jeans, of course—and modest T-shirts with high necks. My dad doesn't approve of short shorts. He doesn't like skimpy shirts, either, and is always yelling at his teenage girl students, "Cover up you belly boot-ton!"

It is the first full day of ASTA summer music camp and the first day of rehearsal with our new string quartet. My dad came up with the idea. He says now that I'm eleven years old and Steph is nine, it's time to play with musicians our own age, instead of performing only with older kids. So he put together the quartet—two violins, a cello, and a viola—and chose two other girls in my grade to join us.

Steph and I will play the violin parts, of course. Miriam is a natural as our cellist. Besides officially being my best friend, she has been taking lessons with my father for more than three years. A gifted musician—she really does have strong, sturdy "cello hands," as my dad noticed the first time he met her—she has made quick progress on her instrument. We already spend as much time together as my parents will allow, and this will give us an excuse to spend more.

For the viola part, my dad chooses Joanne. I don't know her well. Among the four of us, she is the least advanced, having played for less than two years. She is from the other side of East Brunswick, where the homes are a little bigger, a little farther apart, a bit more luxurious than the houses on my street. Later, when she invites me over, I'll see that her house is as neat and beautifully decorated as I imagined it to be, with a living room that kids are not allowed in and curtains we are not permitted to touch when we look out the window to check if our ride home has arrived. In contrast, Miriam's house smells faintly of diapers and Clorox, and her living room couch is always covered with laundry from her five younger siblings. My house is orderly, but the walls are scratched from my mother's wheelchair, and the first thing you see when you walk in is her mechanical chairlift.

Joanne comes from what I think of enviously as a "normal" family. Her dad tells jokes and always has a camera in one hand; her mom is pretty and stylish. She has two older sisters, which to my mind is an amazing stroke of good fortune, the next best thing to having a healthy mom. I'd give anything to have someone to help shop for clothes and give advice about rock bands and boys. Sometimes I imagine what it would be like to go to a restaurant or a store with a family like Joanne's, without people stopping to stare at my dad when he talks, or at my mom in her wheelchair, shaking their heads with pity while shushing their preschoolers who point and ask, "What's wrong with that lady's legs?" No wonder Joanne is so worldly and confident, the opposite of me. If we weren't both studying music, it's not hard to imagine that our paths might never have crossed.

Our first quartet rehearsal at ASTA is in a basement room that is as cramped and airless and hot as a dungeon. It is intended as a practice room for one person, and most of the space is taken up by a baby grand piano. We're squeezed in tight. My dad is too busy to coach us and dispatches gentle old Mrs. Graffam, a teacher he has known for years, to instruct us instead.

Without him watching over us, we are free to giggle and joke. Mrs. Graffam—Miriam promptly dubs her "Mrs. Grandma"—hands

One of the quartet's earliest rehearsals. Left to right: Joanne Lipman, Miriam Simon, chamber music coach Katherine Graffam,
Melanie Kupchynsky, and Stephanie Kupchynsky.

us our first piece: Franz Joseph Haydn's "Emperor" Quartet no. 62
in C Major, second movement. The melody is familiar—it's the tune
used for the German national anthem—and the piece isn't difficult.
I give the other girls a beat, and we play through the opening
theme. I see Joanne and Miriam trading a look that is as pleased as
it is surprised. We try once more, but Stephanie starts laughing
at something Miriam says, and soon we have all dissolved in a fit of
giggles. By the time we're done with rehearsal it's lunchtime, and
we head off down the path to the cafeteria.

We find a table together at lunch, where we amuse ourselves by
trying to invent the most disgusting concoctions possible. Miriam
starts with a glass of milk, then adds ketchup; Joanne pours in orange juice and Coca-Cola; I contribute mustard and Russian dress-
ing with a dash of pepper and grated cheese. When we're done, we

have a foaming mess the color of pond scum that Joanne dares the cute boys at the next table to drink, while the rest of us look on, squealing with glee. Before the boys—John the cello player and Michael, Paul, and Jonathan, all violinists—have a chance to retaliate, we escape through the back doors of the cafeteria, running so fast and laughing so hard that we can hardly catch our breaths.

We sit together again at dinner, and at every meal after that, and at the concerts we are required to go to at night. For a whole week at ASTA, I forget about laundry and wheelchairs and feeling left out. I even forget that I am Mr. K's daughter. It's a relief to not be the only person carrying around a violin. I'm surprised at how much I have in common with girls like Joanne. During our free time we play pranks and make up nicknames for people. At night, after lights out, we whisper on walkie-talkies—me and Miriam on one, Joanne and her roommate on the other. For the first time since I can remember, I'm just like everybody else.

I am swimming up through a sea of sleep, fighting to break the surface. In my dream I hear an announcer giving the weather forecast, but his voice is distorted, the words barely recognizable.

I sit up abruptly, fully awake.

"Jerry!!!! Jer-ry!!!" My mother is calling for my dad, but he is not answering.

What time is it? Where is Daddy? The TV in my parents' bedroom is turned up all the way, the volume deafening. I look over toward my clock; it's almost midnight. I start to get up, to go see what she needs, when I hear feet pounding up the stairs. My father.

"What the hell eez going on? Turn down that *goddamned* television! You weel wake up the girls!"

"I turned it up because I got tired of yelling. Why didn't you answer me? I've been calling and calling you! I can't stand it when you ignore me."

"Jean, goddammit, eet's the end of a long day. Everyone wants something from me. Can't I have a moment of peace without you nagging..." The door slams, muffling the sound of their voices.

I lie down. If I cover my head with the pillow I can't hear anything. In the darkness, the door to my room opens and I feel Stephanie slide into my twin bed beside me. I scrunch over to make room for her, and wordlessly we fall asleep, our arms around each other.

For as long as I can remember, my mother has focused on what she *can* do as opposed to what she cannot. She taught me to read fluently before I entered first grade. When I was out of school for three weeks with bronchitis once, she homeschooled me so vigorously that I was well ahead of the class when I returned. She is a ruthless enforcer when it comes to practicing the violin.

But as time wears on, I notice that she is getting weaker. Her limited energy is increasingly consumed by her preoccupation with her disease. She has no reserves left and no energy to spare for mothering me, much less nine-year-old Stephanie. Steph will never stop craving love, attention, and nurturing, and searches for it from anyone who will give it to her. I'm just the opposite, shutting down that area of my heart and learning to make do with what I get from my dad, my sister, my violin, and myself.

My father isn't equipped to relate to Steph and me the way a mother could. One morning when I'm in seventh grade, a dreary winter unexpectedly turns to spring, the weather unseasonably warm and sunny. All the girls at school will be wearing shorts, and I decide that I will, too. I'm in a good mood as I serve my mother her usual breakfast of coffee and Special K on a tray in her bedroom, then clear the breakfast dishes in the kitchen.

"Daddy, hurry up! I'll get in trouble if I'm late again!"

My dad comes racing into the kitchen, buttoning up his suit jacket and knotting his tie, exuding a cloud of Aramis and hairspray. He grabs a cup of scalding hot instant coffee and begins to pour it from one cup to another to cool it, gulping it over the sink. We follow the same routine each morning, with my dad dropping me off at the junior high school on his way to work. I hate being late, having to walk in front of the whole class to my desk, wilting under the scrutiny of the pretty, disdainful girls already in their seats.

I suddenly feel my dad's accusing eyes on me.

"What are you wearing?"

"What do you mean?"

"Those shorts are too short. You can't wear them to school. Go change!"

"But, Daddy! They're not too short! And I'll be late ..."

"No daughter of mine weel go out of house wearing shorts like that, like a harlot. Go change!"

"No! I want to wear these!"

I rarely defy my father. But honestly, must I always be the class dork? All I want is to look like the other girls.

THWACK!

An angry, red, hand-shaped welt appears on the pale skin of my thigh, where my father has slapped me.

I look at him in shock. Sobbing, I run to my room and throw myself on the bed. My father follows a few minutes later. He has calmed down. But when he sees the telltale mark on my leg—all five fingers and a palm—he sits down next to me and rubs the spot until his handprint is obscured. Soon it's a shapeless patch of bright red spread out like a messy inkblot across my pallid skin.

I can tell he is ashamed of himself. He will never do it again. But he doesn't apologize. I do.

*   *   *

"I'm sorry, Daddy!" Steph cries.

On a Tuesday night not long afterward, our quartet is working on a new piece, Haydn's Quartet in D Major, op. 64, no. 5, better known as the "Lark." It's quite a bit trickier than the "Emperor" quartet movement we'd cut our teeth on last summer. But my dad still can't understand why Steph has such a hard time figuring out how to count rests—the part where a musician doesn't play.

"You dragging like dirty rag across rests!" he yells. He stomps from one foot to another for emphasis, to illustrate how her playing lags behind everybody else's. His heavy galumphing isn't helpful as she tries to navigate the delicate, prettily latticed music composed with eighteenth-century royal drawing rooms in mind, but I don't dare point that out.

We struggle even more when we move on to the hardest passage in the piece, a series of triplets all four of us have to play in unison. It seems just about impossible for us to get it right. Every time we try, it feels like we're jumping off a cliff: we start off linked together as if we're holding hands but quickly fly apart in midair before we crash-land in a heap.

"Violin and viola not together! Sounds like huge spot of mud on white dress!" my dad says. My dad often refers to Joanne only as "viola" and Miriam as "cello," as if that were actually their first names.

We try again, but the passage is still a muddy mess. You can see my dad's mouth moving as he searches for yet another way to explain himself. Finally, he looks squarely at Steph. "You steek to viola like flea to dog's tail!"

Time is running short. We have already played a few local concerts, with me performing a solo and the quartet running through a few simple tunes. Most are small events, at schools or at hospitals, where the patients are appreciative but in truth happier when we stop playing Haydn and perform what my dad calls slush music—easy, old-fashioned songs I enjoy, like "Begin the Beguine" and "Over the Rainbow." But now we're preparing for our major debut, at a national teachers' convention in Philadelphia.

When the day finally comes, and we pile into the van that my dad has arranged for us, we're so keyed up that we barely speak all the way there. At the Holiday Inn on Penn Square, just down the street from the Liberty Bell, teachers in suits and dresses are swarming through the lobby, some carrying instruments, a few looking bleary-eyed and hungover, all sizing each other up. The four of us set up nervously in the Thomas Eakins room, named for the Philadelphia-born realist painter, an ironic choice given the industrial-drab box we find ourselves in. The acoustic wall tiles are gray. The wall-to-wall carpet is of indeterminate color. There are no windows.

My dad sweeps in, directing us where to put our instrument cases and our coats, telling us to *go ask somebody else* where the ladies' room is, and ordering us to get our *keesters* into our seats for a quick rehearsal. He turns straight to the passage that has given us so much trouble during our practices. Some curious passersby in the hallway stop to listen, a few of them edging toward the seats.

"Remember," he says, turning to Stephanie. "*Like flea to dog's tail.*"

By the time we've finished warming up, every seat is taken. Someone has sent out for more chairs.

"Breathe, everybody," I whisper to the other girls. "This is going to be fun!" None of them smiles back.

Not long before, my dad had taken Steph and me to climb Mount Katahdin in Maine. Daddy loves mountain climbing almost as much as music. He spent weeks getting us ready—poring over maps, packing up the snakebite kit, and slathering water-proofing gel on his old Korean War boots and baking them in the oven overnight. But once we got to the trail, he took off ahead of us, practically running up steep ledges as Steph and I scrambled to keep up. "Daddy, wait for us!" we called. But he didn't.

"You can do eet yourselves!" he called over his shoulder. "No turning back now."

That's how I feel now, with my dad offstage and the other girls looking at me expectantly. We're ready; no turning back now. Nodding my head, I signal the start of the Haydn.

I can feel how nervous Steph is. She and Joanne play alone for the first few notes. Steph's bow is wobbling. I suck in my breath and hold it, trying to will her to be calm.

But my dad is right. We are ready, and after the first few measures we settle in to doing what we have done so many times before. The music flows. The audience seems to recede into its seats, and even my dad fades into the background. We stop thinking about the crowd and focus on the music and on one another. I only have to nod slightly, or glance up from the music to lock eyes for a millisecond with the other girls, and we all lean in to the music, or play softer or louder, or dig in to a passage together. We really are breathing together. We really do feel the music as if we share one brain. Picture a school of fish, or a flock of migrating birds all moving seemingly effortlessly in sync. Okay, it isn't exactly *effortless*. But it is at least as miraculous.

When we get to the end of the piece, we all exhale at once. This is something none of us has experienced before, a secret bond that we're sure nobody else can understand. The audience is cheering, but it barely matters to us. We've discovered something even better: the indescribable pleasure of playing together. For us, it is our earliest exposure to the magical feeling of interconnectedness that sometimes happens when musicians perform together, when everyone onstage becomes one not just with each other, but with the composer and his music, the audience, and transcendently beyond.

When it's all over, my dad hugs each one of us in turn. He plants a kiss on Stephanie's cheek. Then, before he heads off to his next meeting, he presses a twenty-dollar bill into my hand and points us toward the hotel restaurant. "Go celebrate," he says. "You earned it."

6

Academic Overture

JOANNE

Mr. K was always yelling at students for being *mahnyiaks*. But in seventh grade, I began to wonder if he was the one who was nuts.

I suggested as much at dinner one night. "He's gone off the deep end," I said. "Absolutely insane." My sisters just nodded. Mr. K had become a frequent topic of dinner conversation—and sometimes, as my sisters got older, of amusement as well. But this time he had gone too far.

We were wolfing down our meal because all three of us were rushing off to orchestra rehearsal. My mom had joined a gourmet-cooking group not long before, and the Hawaiian Medley frozen vegetables and canned fruit-cocktail appetizers were gone, replaced by exotic dishes like cheese fondue and teriyaki chicken with pineapple. The vegetables she cooked were fresh rather than frozen now, but Michele still couldn't stand them and still snuck them under the table to feed to Skippy.

We talked all at once as we ate, cutting each other off and plowing right over each other's sentences. Usually, just the girls talked—my mother and the three of us daughters. My dad couldn't get a word in edgewise. He had very little to add to our typical girl-world conversations, most of which made him squeamish. Every once in a while, he would interrupt us, saying, "Can't we get through *one* meal without discussing bodily fluids?"

That night, though, we had more important things to discuss: namely that Mr. K had pushed us way too far. It was one thing to set high expectations; it was another to expect the absolutely, completely, incontrovertibly impossible. I had been promoted to the high school orchestra just months before, along with the other girls in my quartet. Both of my sisters were already big shots in the group: Michele was co-concertmaster and Ronni the principal flute player, leading the section.

The problem was, the music Mr. K expected us to play was *insane*. At the first rehearsal of the year, he handed out mimeographed parts for Johannes Brahms's *Academic Festival Overture*. The music terrified me. I stared at the vaguely shiny sheets of the viola part, held together at the edge by translucent Scotch tape blotched by fingerprints. I may as well have been looking at hieroglyphics. There were strange notes, strange key changes, and unexpected rhythms. It was fiendishly difficult, well beyond the level of anything I had ever played before. Even for Michele, who had performed the piece with the All-State Orchestra, and Ronni, an All-State flute player, it was a challenge.

Mr. K had been making our quartet practice the piece together during our Tuesday night rehearsals, pushing our usual Haydn off the agenda while we diligently tried to perfect some of the trickier string entrances. *Academic Festival Overture* has a great booming melody—you'd know it from the antic parade scene in the movie *Animal House*—but underneath that big brass line there's a whole lot of mystifyingly difficult string playing darting in and out.

As we streamed into the high school practice room after dinner and took our places, I waved my bow in greeting to Melanie, Stephanie, and Miriam, who wiggled their bows back at me. In that first blush of adolescent friendship, each time we saw one another was a fresh thrill, even when we'd only been apart for a few hours. Then I settled into my seat in the back of the viola section, and the other girls sank out of view in the farthest reaches of their own sections. It was unfortunate that the four of us were so spread out that we couldn't even see each other, because Mr. K chose this moment to show us off to the older kids. The whole orchestra apparently had been screwing up the staggered entrances.

"Quartet weel demonstrate proper way to play," he announced. "Girls, you play."

The hair on my arms stood straight up. My heart dropped to somewhere in my bowels. I had never been singled out in front of older kids. I noticed that the other violists were now craning around in their seats to get a good look at me. Their faces betrayed a bit of curiosity, and a bit more of hope that the uppity young new kid would fall on her face.

The four of us timidly tried the passage. We were used to looking to Melanie to give us a nod to start, and then to each other as we played. But the other girls were nowhere in my line of sight. As we started to play, they sounded impossibly far away. This was so unlike our rehearsals in Mr. K's tiny waiting room, when we were within fingertip distance of one another. The notes came out all wrong, the timing out of sync. My heartbeat sounded louder to me than my own playing.

Mr. K scowled. "Again!"

Tentatively, we tried it once more. I was so nervous that my bow skittered along the strings. Melanie sounded louder, more insistent this time, as she tried to lead us—will us, really, or more like pull us—from the other side of the room. You could tell the rest of us were straining to follow.

"Again!"

I took a deep breath, mustered my courage and attacked. This time, the four of us cut through the silence in the rehearsal room with a precision I had no idea I was capable of. Mr. K glanced at the high schoolers arrayed in front of him with a look of satisfaction. "Like that," was all he said.

As the performance got closer, Mr. K upped our rehearsal schedule. Almost every day it seemed we were rushing off to the high school in the afternoons or after dinner. We practiced so frequently that my fingers almost bled. The marks that violin and viola players get on their necks from gripping their instruments—the aptly nicknamed "violin hickey"—grew raw and inflamed. Mine started oozing and I had to slather it with antibiotic ointment each night.

Mr. K didn't notice, or if he did, he didn't care. But it was a pointless exercise. The orchestra simply wasn't able to play the Brahms. I knew it. My sisters knew it. Mr. K was the only one who hadn't figured it out.

One night at rehearsals, Mr. K finally realized it, too.

"Who eez *idyot* who play wrong note?" he yelled, cutting off the orchestra with a dramatic "you're out!" crosswise sweep of his arms, looking like a crazed umpire in an undertaker's suit.

"You play eet!" He was pointing his baton square at Michele's face, as he sought to find the culprit in the first violin section. This was among the most dreaded of Mr. K's methods. He would single out the players, sometimes two at a time, sometimes all by themselves, and make them play in front of the whole orchestra.

Michele played the passage without any mistakes, then sat back with a visible sigh of relief.

"Now you!" The baton was shoved between the eyes of the violinist sitting next to her. This girl, too, dispatched the phrase without error.

"Now you!" he yelled, moving on to the next violinist.

"You play!"

"You play!"

And down the line of violinists he went, one after the other, in search of the culprit, the *idyot* who dared play a wrong note.

It was an excruciating moment. The violinists started to tremble when he got that diabolical look in his eye. You'd get heart palpitations just watching the kids with their sweaty palms and shaky fingers.

As he went down the line, toward the less advanced players in the back, each violinist played worse than the one before—their hands shaking, their arms cramping up, their notes sounding like painful screeches. More than one broke into a flop sweat. They wiped away the grimy drops trickling down their acne-covered faces with the backs of their bow hands. Sometimes they started tearing up.

Usually, when Mr. K finally did single out the *idyot* who played the wrong note, he forced the poor violinist to play over and over again alone, exposed, until he got it right. The unfortunate soul would miserably try to play while simultaneously trying to disappear, and you could see him physically shrinking down into his seat as he stared at the music and willed his fingers to move. Mr. K sang along for emphasis, his big coarse voice always off-key.

The problem now was there wasn't just one violinist who couldn't play the passage; almost the entire section was muffing it. It was just too damn hard. Mr. K's face was darkening. I saw something else there as well: defeat.

It's about time, I figured. We'll never get it. Mr. K's shoulders sagged and he lowered his arms. His conducting baton hung limply at his side. *Maybe he'll just send us home,* I thought.

But then you could just see it. He raised his head and looked out toward the back of the violin section.

"Melanie!" he barked. "You play."

She played the passage quietly but spotlessly. The other violinists leaned in to listen.

"Again!" Mr. K said. But this time, he pointed to one of the violinists having trouble, barking: "You play along with Melanie." The kid picked up his violin, furrowing his brow as he strained to mimic the correct notes she was playing. It was a noticeable improvement.

The gleam returned to Mr. K's eyes.

After that, Mr. K employed a new solution when somebody screwed up. He motioned Melanie to play along with whoever was having trouble, while he stood there clapping out the rhythm and singing along the notes. It worked surprisingly well, this method of the strong helping the weak.

The closer we got to the performance, the harder Mr. K drove us. At rehearsals, he waved his arms wildly from side to side and leaned so far forward that it looked like he would topple from the podium right into the second violin section.

His giant, exaggerated motions, accompanied by his ever-stomping feet, had an effect akin to putting a gorilla in a tutu on-stage in *Swan Lake*. I had played under a couple of other conductors by now, and my parents had taken me to see professional orchestras, and it never failed to surprise me how small those conductors' gestures were. It seemed that they barely moved; their baton motions were economical and precise. Mr. K used an oversized baton that only made his exaggerated waving that much more frenetic. He seemed certain that big sound required giant gyrations and that soft sound . . . well, that required giant gyrations, too.

One day, through the music, we suddenly noticed an odd sound. A distinctive *slap-clomp slap-clomp slap-clomp*. Up on the podium, Mr. K had stomped his feet so hard that his soles had separated right from his shoes. As he kept pounding out the beat, oblivious, the tips of the soles flapped open and smacked together with each step.

All around the orchestra, you could see the smiles on the faces of the kids as they furiously played the notes. Nobody dared tell Mr. K.

Michele was one of Mr. K's top violin students. Pretty and popular, she had a penchant for tight bell-bottom pants worn with midriff-baring shirts.

"Cover up your belly boot-ton!" Mr. K said every time she walked into his studio.

For months on end that year, Mr. K gave Michele just one assignment: the first violin part for *Academic Festival Overture*. Every week he rehearsed that piece with her during her lessons. He drilled her on it as if it were a concerto for a solo competition. He did the same with me and his other private students. Before long, we all knew the piece almost by heart.

Michele played piano, too, and for fun would make up songs of her own, sometimes writing out duets that she could perform with Ronni on the flute. One day at school, after she packed up her violin at rehearsal, Michele handed Mr. K a piece of music she had composed herself. For the first time, she had tried orchestrating it for string instruments.

Mr. K walked her into his office as he looked it over. You could see he was singing it to himself in his head. "Not bad," he said, glancing back up at her.

He sat down at his desk with a pencil and called her over. He talked through the piece with her, just as if she were a professional composer, a peer. He praised the harmonies, dissected the structure. Then he offered a suggestion—"Thees part eez awkward for violin"—to improve on a section that needed work. She took his advice, sitting at the piano in our living room and noodling over the harmonies for days. When she handed him the reworked piece, he looked it over and sang it to himself again. Then he nodded in approval.

The piece had no name, so he gave it one: *Petite Fugue*. "Let's haf orchestra geeve eet a try," he said, and if Michele were to pick a moment when she decided to become a music teacher herself, that would be it.

Our gala spring concert that year included the premiere of *Petite Fugue*, with Mr. K introducing Michele to the audience for a round of applause. Then we launched into the finale: Brahms's *Academic Festival Overture*.

In the audience, the first emotion that registered was surprise. The seats were filled with parents who had been driving back and forth to endless rehearsals and listening to their kids sawing away alone on their parts in their bedrooms. In truth, most of those kids had sounded pretty awful. The parents didn't expect much. On their own, there wasn't one kid in the bunch who would make you sit up and take notice. But that night, mothers and fathers turned to each other with looks of astonishment. Could this really be our kid up there on the stage?

It was uncanny. While Mr. K was sweating and spitting and stomping on the podium, I felt myself happily disappearing into the music. The violists in front of me were swaying with the beat. Around me, the other kids were doing the same. Mr. K had achieved the impossible: he made us better than we had any right to be. It's an extraordinary feeling, when you realize you've exceeded your own limits. Maybe Mr. K knew that all along. We had just figured it out.

We couldn't quite believe what we were doing and how much fun we were having. Apparently the audience couldn't believe it, either. It was spectacular. It was impossible.

It *was* insane.

When it was over, the audience members leaped to their feet in a standing ovation.

7

The Mendelssohn

MELANIE

"Dammit, we are going to be late. You girls spend too much time vacuuming you hair!"

I stifle a laugh. "*Blow-drying*, Dad. You mean blow-drying, not vacuuming."

We are in the car, lurching our way toward Maplewood, New Jersey, where my dad's mentor, the famed violin pedagogue Samuel Applebaum, lives. My dad can't understand why, no matter how late we are running, Steph and I will still take the time to fix our hair. We are old enough to appreciate the irony of his complaint, coming from a guy who uses about half a bottle of hairspray every day trying to coax his one overgrown lock of hair to cover his entire balding head.

·"Quiet back there! Stop that asinine laughter!"

Steph and I started weekly violin lessons with Mr. Applebaum about a year ago, when I was in sixth grade. Lots of teachers jealously guard their best students, insisting that they not study elsewhere. My dad is the opposite. When his students reach a certain degree of proficiency, he pushes them from the nest, introducing them to colleagues who teach at more advanced levels. As we take our weekly drives up the Garden State Parkway to Mr. Applebaum's house, my dad alternates between railing at us for being late and issuing instructions.

"As soon as I stop the car, you *run* inside, unpack as fast as you can, and *apologize* to Mr. Applebaum for keeping heem waiting."

"Steph, deed you remember your lesson assignment card?"

"Mel, I hope you really learned your étude thees time. Last week eet sounded like you were sight-reading. *Sheet!* Look at thees traffic! Thees eez why I wanted to leave on time!"

Of all Daddy's colleagues, Samuel Applebaum is perhaps the most well known. He is one of the most influential string teachers in the world, the author of dozens of instruction books. Daddy follows the Applebaum method for all of his students, and uses Applebaum arrangements of songs like "Twinkle, Twinkle, Little Star" and "Au Claire de la Lune" for his beginner orchestra. In music circles, Mr. Applebaum is famous for his fourteen-volume series on teaching, *The Way They Play*, featuring interviews and photographs of him with the great musicians of the day, from cellist Pablo Casals to violinist Yehudi Menuhin to his son, violist Michael Tree. In book two there's one of him teaching me, at age eight.

My father first met Sam Applebaum as a Rutgers student. Since I started playing violin, Daddy has taken me to see him regularly, so he can check on my progress. I am frequently used as a guinea pig to demonstrate various teaching techniques in workshops he leads for string teachers and in master classes he teaches for students. He taught me vibrato, onstage, when I was six.

Mr. Applebaum's house is modest, no bigger than ours, but every room is stuffed with books, manuscripts, and memorabilia. The studio is crowded, with overflowing shelves full of crumbling brown music and stacks of crisp, colorful method books all over the floor. There's barely enough space for me to stand beside his big reclining chair that is placed strategically between the piano and his pupil. The ceiling is so low that even though I'm not yet five feet tall, I sometimes smack it with my bow when I do the dramatic flourishes he asks, and I wonder how his adult-size students manage. Photos covering every surface are inscribed by the world's great musicians, most of whom at one point or another have made a pilgrimage to his home for meals cooked by his poet wife and for impromptu chamber music sessions in the living room.

Mr. Applebaum's first assignment for me is real, grown-up music: the Mendelssohn Violin Concerto in E Minor, my mom's all-time favorite. I have long dreamed of playing it and making it my own. It's one thing to listen to recordings of great artists performing, but that is nothing compared with the magic of being able to create the sounds myself.

Guided by Mr. Applebaum, I practice furiously, learn the concerto relatively quickly, and it soon becomes my "go-to" piece. My father leaps at the opportunity to show me off and, with the aid of the mother of one of his students, who accompanies me on the piano, I take that Mendelssohn concerto on the road, from Pennsylvania to Maine. For me, it's fun to perform a challenging piece that has everything, including beautiful melodies and enough fast, brilliant, showy passages to impress anyone. At eleven, it still hasn't really sunk in that performing is supposed to be a nerve-racking experience.

But that's about to change.

When school lets out, my father and Mr. Applebaum put together a workshop for the summer ASTA conference that will include a performance of the Mendelssohn. I am used to doing these workshops. But my father, who already has his hands full running the growing conference, seems unusually stressed about it.

His stature is growing—he is president of the state chapter of ASTA—and so is his visibility. As he gets more acclaim, rivals are taking notice and sometimes taking aim. The audience will be made up almost entirely of musicians, including the colleagues he admires most. His reputation is on the line.

Before the performance, Mr. Applebaum speaks while I demonstrate. We're comfortable together, and he never fails to charm and entertain his audience. When the time comes to play the piece through, I feel calm as I move into place beside the piano on the stage of Hickman Hall, not feeling the air-conditioned chill even in

Samuel Applebaum gives a lecture about musical interpretation while Melanie, age eleven, demonstrates passages from the Mendelssohn Violin Concerto.

my blue-flowered minidress as my adrenaline begins to flow. Soon I am deeply engrossed in my performance, playing the piece from memory, as usual.

But then something happens, something that has never happened to me before. My mind wanders, just for a split second—maybe it's the flashbulbs popping from the audience, or perhaps I've just absorbed some of my dad's nervousness—but all of a sudden I'm lost. I have no idea where I am, what to play next. Behind me I can hear Mr. Applebaum frantically flipping the pages of my music, in an effort to find my place and rescue me.

I never use the music in performance, never need to use the music; I know this piece *cold*. I could perform it in my sleep. Except here I am floundering away, dying onstage right in front of all my friends, my teachers, my father and all his respected colleagues. Time stands still, and the moment feels like it lasts forever. I don't remember how it finally ends; I get back on track somehow, miraculously get to the end of the piece alive, but all I want is to get off that stage as fast as I can and never, ever, ever, ever get back on it again.

Mr. Applebaum gives my arm an affectionate squeeze as I hurry toward the wings. He has seen this happen countless times and will later regale us with stories of famous artists' worst memory slips.

My dad isn't so sanguine. Afterward, in the hallway outside the auditorium, with the applause inexplicably still lingering in the air, he scowls: "If you had practiced harder, that would never have happened."

JOANNE

Melanie was already a seasoned soloist by the time she performed the Mendelssohn that day. In a demure minidress, her long red bangs swept back dramatically with a barrette, she would always stride with quiet confidence onto the stage, commanding the room even before she started to play. I lost track of the number of times I sat in an audience, watching her perform. The Mendelssohn was my favorite.

You would have thought you were listening to a recording if you were in Hickman Hall that summer afternoon. It seemed like every music teacher and conductor I had ever met, and plenty I had only heard about from afar, was in attendance, crammed into the recital hall's three-hundred-plus seats. The audience was absolutely still, holding its collective breath, not wanting to miss a note. The only movement in the hall was Melanie, onstage swaying with the music as she played. The piece is a virtuoso masterpiece with breathtakingly fast passages and haunting melodies. The cadenza—a showy section played without accompaniment—is one of the most famous in music history and one of the most dazzling, with hyperfast arpeggios that require the violinist to ricochet the bow back and forth across the strings.

Melanie later told me she made some sort of mistake that day, and I caught a puzzling glimpse of her dad glaring in the wings. But if she did goof, the audience didn't catch it. As she finished off the last triumphant chord, the audience was already on its feet, with a thunderous standing ovation that lingered after she left the stage. Of course that was nothing new; she got a standing ovation every time I saw her perform it.

Melanie nodded and bowed graciously at the end of that performance, as she always did. But who knew what she was really thinking? For all the time we spent together, laughing at Steph's antics or rehearsing together, she almost never talked about her own playing. She didn't talk much, period. She was reserved, inscrutable, pouring out emotion and swaying soulfully to the music while on the stage, but an enigmatic cipher off of it. She seemed completely oblivious to the effect of her playing, which alternately inspired awe, envy, and ferocious competitiveness in everyone we knew.

I always figured if I played as she did, I'd be shouting it from the rooftops and dancing a jig on the stage. I couldn't quite understand how she could be so nonchalant about it all. Mr. K, too. He never did more than nod if he approved, scowl slightly if he didn't. My own parents smothered me with kisses for far less. Didn't her parents realize she was really *good*?

The next morning, I stumbled into orchestra rehearsal with an M&M hangover, my throat raspy from whispering way too long after lights out. Still, this was my favorite time of day at ASTA. I loved playing with an orchestra. Whenever the conductor raised the baton and the musicians raised their instruments, whatever little misery might be bugging me disappeared into the music. The sound we made together was so much better than anything I could produce on my own. There was an intimacy about it, a camaraderie, a shared rush of emotion as we played.

I knew most of the other musicians my age by now: Jonathan, the smartest boy in our grade, with the big glasses and a vocabulary to match. Michael, a lanky, gentle violinist who stared at Melanie when he thought nobody was looking. John, a cellist whose mother was a music teacher and a friend of Mr. K. Then there was Paul; after his father left his family, his grandmother sent money each month so he and his brother could continue their lessons with Mr. K.

Jonathan said we were like soldiers in the line of fire. "There's nothing like crawling under the barbed wire together, with machine guns firing over your head," as he put it. He had a point. In Mr. K's orchestra, nobody was literally shooting at us, but we were figuratively diving, rolling, and throwing ourselves in front of his incoming barbs to protect each other anyway.

After dinner each night at ASTA, we had to dress up and attend a concert. I would walk over to Hickman Hall with Melanie, Miriam, and Stephanie, all of us tripping slightly, unaccustomed to our high-heeled sandals, as we navigated the pathway while the sun dipped and glinted between the trees. Sometimes Steph and I would lag behind, dropping on our hands and knees to peer at cicadas and earthworms on the mossy ground, before drifting into the auditorium.

But one rainy Thursday night the summer I turned thirteen, Mr. K was already onstage, pacing anxiously back and forth, as we filed in. He held a white handkerchief hastily folded into a square in one hand and blotted at his forehead while telling us to hurry up and take our seats. He was dressed in his summer best—a tan suit with wide lapels and a fat red, white, and blue tie—and his mustache was fastidiously trimmed. He didn't mention the one topic that was on everyone's mind. But you could tell that for once, he was struggling to focus on the music.

Mr. K had been planning for this day, August 8, 1974, all year. He had commissioned a new orchestral work specifically to be performed at the adult orchestra concert. He had worked tirelessly to bring in exactly the right celebrity guest. He had called the newspapers to alert them. Mr. K had, in fact, planned every detail perfectly.

It was the day he had chosen to introduce a new work: *Declaration of Independence*, written by composer Philip Gordon.

The piece was typical Mr. K. For a Ukrainian guy, he sure had a sentimental streak for American patriotic music. He programmed his favorites into every concert we played. There was *American Patrol*, a montage of American folks songs built around "When Johnny Comes Marching Home." There was *Grand Canyon Suite* by Ferde Grofé, and "Hoe-Down" from Aaron Copland's *Rodeo*, celebrating the American cowboy.

The same was true of the European classics: if a symphonic work celebrated armed rebellion against oppressors, or freedom, or old-fashioned pioneering, it found a way onto our music stands. There was *Finlandia*, which Jean Sibelius composed to inspire Finns to rise up against Imperialist Russia. There were Ukrainian folk songs, which Mr. K arranged himself. There was *New World Symphony*, the Czech composer Dvořák's ode to spirituals and Native American songs.

But that night's piece was particularly significant. It honored American independence and was written at Mr. K's request. It would be narrated by New Jersey governor Brendan Byrne, who was standing off in the wings in a funereally black suit and tie, shifting from one foot to another, looking distracted.

For Mr. K, August 8, 1974, was supposed to be *his* day, to call attention to his music program. He hadn't counted on the resignation of President Richard Nixon, which was expected to be announced later that night.

"Geeves me great pleasure to introduce . . . ," Mr. K announced, "our president."

For a moment he looked stricken. Nervous laughter rippled through the auditorium.

"Uh . . . governor."

Governor Byrne strode onto the stage. The orchestra broke into its opening chords. I couldn't help but notice the irony of the words the governor was reciting. With patriotic strains swelling in the background, he began: "When, in the course of human events, it becomes necessary for one people to dissolve the political bands which have connected them with another . . ."

As he went on, the audience cringed, then tittered uneasily, as he recited those familiar phrases: "when a long train of abuses and usurpations . . ." and "it is their right, it is their duty, to throw off such government . . ."

After the concert, we ran back to the dormitory, gathering around a scratchy portable radio in the common room to listen to

President Nixon deliver his resignation speech. When it was over, nobody could sleep. I darted down the dormitory corridor from room to room, rehashing the Watergate scandal with one group of girls, soliciting opinions about incoming President Ford from the next. I wished I still carried around the *Harriet the Spy* composition notebooks I used to bring everywhere, to record history in the making. I waited in a long line to call home from the pay phone in the hall, so I could ask my parents to save the next day's newspaper.

Truth be told, even when there wasn't a president resigning, nobody got much sleep during ASTA week. We would try to stay up as late as possible, past our eleven P.M. lights-out curfew, without getting caught. Every year, the boys tried to sneak onto the girls' floor; once, Mr. K caught our friends Michael and John shimmying up the outside of the building, attempting to climb up a pipe to the girls' second-floor dorm.

Mr. K trolled both boys' and girls' floors every night, announcing *"Bed check!"* and then poking his head into rooms unannounced. He occasionally reassured the adolescent girls in their baby-doll pajamas, "Eez okay, I am father of two daughters," but no one back then thought twice about the propriety of a grown man patrolling the girls' floor anyway. He warned everybody about "bed check" during his speech the first night of ASTA every summer, getting a laugh when he once garbled his English and announced, "At bedtime, I vant to see two bodies een every bed!"

Most nights after Mr. K made his rounds, we slipped out from under our covers anyway, sharing candy and confessions by flashlight. We got away with staying up late because the adults were off drinking and playing dumb jokes on each other and indulging in Mr. K's Black Russians.

Rumor had it that Mr. K never went anywhere without his portable Black Russian bar, which he set up in his room every year. From the stories that drifted back to us in the dorms, the grown-ups he invited to his nightcaps were unimaginably wild as they drained his favorite concoction of "vodka, Kahlua, and secret Ukrainian incantations." Once, the older campers told us, some drunken counselors Saran-wrapped his toilet when he was out checking beds in the dorm. Another time, they booby-trapped his room with empty cans that went crashing down when he opened his door. He laughed and retaliated with raunchy jokes that made some of the counselors—especially the ones who had grown up with him as their teacher—blush.

But that night, the night President Nixon resigned, there were none of the usual high jinks. The excitement in the air got our adrenaline pumping, but for him it seemed only to unearth some deep, mysterious sadness. We couldn't help noticing it at the concert, how he was somber, more distracted than we had seen him before. Usually, we waited until we heard him stomping down the dormitory hallway before we turned off our flashlights and hid our bags of candy. But that night, his footsteps never came.

PART III

Young people can learn from my example that something can come from nothing. What I have become is the result of my hard efforts.

—FRANZ JOSEPH HAYDN

8

Baba

MELANIE

Everybody I know is afraid of my father. What they don't know is that he has a few fears of his own. There are the Communists, who he remains convinced will try to reclaim him at any moment. Then there's the telephone, which he avoids using because he always bollixes up his English. Driving to new places puts him into a panic, too. My dad has no sense of direction. To compensate, he maps out routes in advance, carefully highlighting directions with a yellow marker.

His greatest fear of all, though, is of his own mother. Up until now, Baba has been mostly a mythical creature in my life, spoken of in hushed tones and in the past tense. You wouldn't have known she was alive, much less that she lived just a few towns away. She stopped speaking to my dad when I was an infant. She never forgave him for marrying my mother, who is neither Ukrainian nor Catholic—and who, in Baba's view, made things worse by going out and becoming an invalid, such a shameful burden to my dad.

Baba is a survivor. My father says she saved his life when he was a boy during the war. But whatever strength got her through those ordeals has metastasized into cruelty and hostility toward those closest to her. My step-grandfather is worse. He used to beat my father and, when they arrived in the United States, made him sleep in the spider-infested dirt cellar—then sued him for rent. The last time my mother saw Baba was when I was still in a crib; she showed up at our house while my dad was at work, threatening to tell the press of the lawsuit and ruin my father's career.

My father has never given up hope of reconciliation. The year I turn ten, my great-uncle dies, and at the funeral, my dad begs Baba for another chance.

The reconciliation has immediate repercussions for Steph and me. Suddenly, we are thrust into Ukrainian boot camp: my dad is determined to show Baba that he can make up for lost time in teaching us our culture.

Our first test comes on Easter, which we are to celebrate at my grandparents' house, in a tumbledown North Plainfield neighborhood that had been elegant once, a long time ago. "Lock the doors," my father says as he turns off the highway. I watch out the car window as we roll past old wooden houses, lined up so close that no sky peeks through. As we get closer, the homes get shabbier, with weeds sprouting from the sidewalks and sofas with the springs poking out sitting on peeling porches.

Finally we pull up to my grandparents' house, a sprawling Victorian with a steep, narrow driveway set far back from the street. Steph and I help set up my mother's wheelchair and follow my dad as he rolls her up to the crumbling doorstep.

"Now remember, girls, you shake hands and look them straight een the eyes. No slouching, stand up straight. Do you remember what I taught you to say?"

My father has been drilling us on the phrase "Pleased to meet you" in Ukrainian, but Steph is having trouble remembering it.

"*Duzhe priemno piznaty*," I pronounce slowly. "Is that right, Daddy?"

"That's eet."

Steph is looking pretty green. "I think I'm going to be sick."

I feel the same way as soon as the front door opens. My grandmother, sour-faced and squeezed into a floral dress edged in bright red rickrack, takes one look at me and pronounces me "homely, but *eenteresting*." My step-grandfather, whom we call Doodie, pulls himself up from his chair in front of the TV set, leaving behind a pile of toenail shavings on the floor. The house is three stories tall, but my grandfather has nailed up wallboard to block off the upper floors for what Baba called her "roomers." My grandparents' living quarters on the ground floor are dimly lit and violently colored, with Ukrainian embroidery everywhere—pillows, table runners, wall hangings—and religious icons and plates full of garishly colored Ukrainian Easter eggs.

I escape to the bathroom, but the long, skinny space, converted from an old butler's pantry, isn't much of a refuge; it has wild red-and-purple carpeting and two swinging doors that don't lock at either end. The bathtub is filled with cloudy used bath water that my grandmother saves for later to wash the kitchen floor.

I search for my dad and find him in the kitchen, where the radiators are covered with paper towels, left to dry so they can be used again. Baba is bent over a steaming pot, making *pyrohy*, traditional Ukrainian dumplings filled with potatoes. I try to help with the dishes, but Baba yells at me for using too much water to wash the plates and then for using too much soap. "Vee don't vaste-it the vater!" she cries, showing me the proper way to wash dishes, with barely any soap and a hasty rinse under a tepid trickle. Later, when my dad is away on business and sends Steph and me to stay with Baba, she will refuse to let us take showers. "Eef you wash hair too much," she warns darkly, "leetle onions on your head weel dry up and you hair eet weel fall out."

If I don't think too much about hygiene, Baba's cooking is delicious. After a few rounds of vodka for Doodie and my dad, she sets out heaping plates of ham, kielbasa, and an Easter bread she makes called *paska* on the kitchen table, which is covered with sticky rings left by glasses of Doodie's favorite homemade cherry brandy. The grown-ups chatter away in Ukrainian that Steph and I can't follow, until Baba notices that Steph isn't eating.

"You no like-it thees kielbasa?"

Steph turns pale. "No, it's not that. It's just . . . I'm just . . . um . . . I'm . . . full." She is a terrible liar.

"Stephka doesn't eat much," my dad cuts in. "She has sensitive stomach. But we are working on that. Right, Stephka?" He shoots Steph a warning glare.

Baba looks at Steph appraisingly. "Your *tato*"—Ukrainian for "daddy"—"ven he was leetle boy, he was beeg trah-ble. He had pepper een hees *dupa*. Stubborn, too." Then she launches into a rant about how our father was a dreadful, colicky baby. She used to rub vinegar on his stomach to make him stop crying, she says. But it didn't work.

"*Ay-yi-yi*," she moans at the memory.

"He have-it gazzzz," she explains. Five decades after the fact she still sounds annoyed. "He was beeg trah-ble."

After that, we see my grandparents regularly. Every Saturday morning, Doodie shows up at our house to give Ukrainian lessons to

Stephanie and me. We gather at our dining room table, the one my mother regrets buying because it's so poorly constructed that the cheap chairs have collapsed one by one, leaving my father with yet another job on his to-do list. Steph and I exchange a nervous glance as Doodie takes his rickety seat.

"Start veeth—how you call-its?—alphabet," Doodie commands.

"Ah, beh, veh," we begin obediently in unison, Steph delaying saying each letter just a fraction of a second so she can hear me say it first.

Mostly, we can't understand anything Doodie says, his accent is so thick and his syntax so garbled. My American-born uncle, John, once printed up a T-shirt with Doodie's constant refrain: HOW YOU CALL-ITS? We manage to stumble through the Cyrillic alphabet and a few vocabulary lists. But when he moves on to the language's complicated grammar, we're lost.

"Thees means these one and that means those one" is one of his first lessons, which serves only to send us diving under the table pretending we've dropped our pencils in order to hide our laughter. Frustrated when we can't seem to catch on, Doodie shakes his head and mutters "*Ayi yi yi!*" under his breath, adding a few choice expletives that are not on our vocabulary lists.

It doesn't seem to matter how hard we work. Under Doodie's tutelage our progress is glacial, and my grandparents let us know they are terribly disappointed. After a while, our sessions dwindle and eventually stop altogether. Doodie gives up on us.

My dad keeps trying. That summer, he packs Steph and me off to language immersion camp at Soyuzivka, a Ukrainian resort in the Catskill Mountains. Set amid thick woods, Soyuzivka was once a sanitarium for Social Register swells looking for a "nature rest cure"—a nice way of saying it was where rich alcoholics went to dry out or depressed ones went to get away. The doctor who originally built the place was the son of the *New York Times* editor in chief who broke the Tammany Hall scandal, and his patients supposedly included *New Yorker* editor Harold Ross and the writers O. Henry, James Thurber, and E. B. White, author of *Charlotte's Web*. During the 1920s, so many literary types swarmed the sanitarium that it was nicknamed "the *New Yorker* Retreat."

But by the time the Ukrainians moved in, its society roots were long forgotten. The sanitarium had closed during World War II and had languished until it was converted into a modest resort that catered mostly to shell-shocked Ukrainian immigrants. The newly christened Soyuzivka was modeled on retreats back home in the Carpathian Mountains, right down to the Slavic-village-style buildings with names like "Odessa" and "Kyiv."

When my dad drops me off at camp and pulls away, all I want is to run after the car and go home with him. I try to hold back my tears. Some of the other girls gather around, attempting to comfort me, but they're speaking in Ukrainian, and I don't know what they're saying. I cry myself to sleep that first night.

Dawn has barely broken when I'm jolted awake by a shrill whistle. "*Mo...Lyt...Va!*"

My eyes fly open. I look around the bunk, noticing the sun's first rays glinting through a window, trying to remember where I am.

"*Mo...Lyt...Va!*"

The whistle blows again. It's the *pani komandantka*, the female commander who runs the camp, shouting, "*Stavanya!*" Wake up! Time for prayers.

I stumble outside, following the other campers, watching to see what I'm supposed to do. We line up like soldiers. A couple of campers step forward to raise American and Ukrainian flags. The girls start singing "Bozhe Velyki," a Ukrainian anthem I have never heard before. I mouth nonsense words along with them.

The flag ceremony complete, the *pani komandantka* turns

toward us to lead us in prayer. In Ukrainian. Then makes announcements. Also in Ukrainian. Then, apparently, she dismisses us, because suddenly I'm standing by myself, everyone scattering in different directions and me looking around, still in front of the flagpole, trying to figure out where I belong.

Over the next few days, I scramble after the other girls, trying to figure out how to keep up with the babble of Ukrainian all around. My one reprieve is when the whistle blows and we rush to line up, by height, to march like soldiers to the next activity. *At last,* I think the first time. *Something I'm good at!* I can keep a beat with the best of them. But then the chanting starts.

"*Ras! Ya ne chuyu. Dva! Holosnishe,*" everyone shouts as they march. I move my lips soundlessly, trying hard to memorize the words that are meaningless to me. This is how I'm going to survive the next two weeks.

Almost all of our seventy or so campmates already speak Ukrainian and chatter on fluently during meals and while swimming, marching, and sitting around the campfire. I am lost, finding it impossible to make friends. Somehow Steph, who knows even less Ukrainian than I do, is unfazed by the language barrier. She doesn't care if she can't understand directions, perhaps because she doesn't pay much attention in English, either. Her easy warmth fills in where words can't as she throws herself into Ukrainian songs, dances, and traditional crafts like embroidery. Soon even the harshest *pani komandantka* is won over.

"Daddy, let me come home! Please!" I beg when my dad arrives for visiting day. I am sobbing, miserable, as we sit in his parked car with the windows rolled down.

He looks at me, his face betraying equal parts pity and shame.

"You must discipline yourself," he says finally, ending the conversation. Ignoring my tears, he turns to Steph. "So, Stephka, which of the girls do you like most? Do you haf a best friend?"

"No, Daddy."

His face falls for just a moment. But by then she has already thrown her arms open wide.

"I love them *all*!"

The following summer, I get a break. I am to start Ukrainian camp one week late, because I'm preparing for my first full solo recital, which I'll perform at Soyuzivka. My father takes great pains planning my program. He digs up some Ukrainian music and teaches me his own favorite piece, Massenet's heartrending "Méditation" from *Thaïs*, a piece whose emotional depths I am not yet old enough to understand. Afterward, Steph comes onstage to offer me a bouquet—the first time I've gotten one for a performance—and the audience laughs and applauds as she trips over the hem of her long dress to give me a hug.

Soon invitations follow to perform at Ukrainian concerts in Trenton, Philadelphia, and New York City. Usually, the occasion is a tribute to a poet, a politician, or a religious figure—often a long-dead priest, pictured on the front of the program in a big black hat and wearing about a thousand crosses and rosaries. The audiences are filled with elderly men whose eyes tear up when I play Ukrainian folk songs and women whose good suits still bear the faint scent of mothballs.

The format is always the same. There are long speeches in Ukrainian, often lasting more than an hour. Sometimes a lot more. Then come the performers: singers, dancers, bandura choirs that perform Ukrainian folk songs on their zitherlike instruments, poetry readings, and me on the violin. Occasionally, my dad includes our quartet on the program and brings Steph, Miriam, and Joanne along, too.

Whenever I give a Ukrainian concert, my dad invites my grandparents to go with us. Predictably, my dad gets lost every time.

Doodie ridicules him and shouts out directions in Ukrainian, but that only makes things worse. Which is how, one weekday afternoon, my father ends up turning the wrong way onto Madison Avenue in New York City, directly into oncoming rush-hour traffic.

"*Oy, Bozhe!*"—Oh, God!—my father shouts as he realizes his mistake.

"*Psia crow!*"—Dog's blood!—Doodie screams back as irate drivers career around us, honking madly.

Baba makes the sign of the cross and starts praying aloud.

Cars whiz by in a blur. Taxi drivers shout at us in languages I don't understand, shaking their fists and giving us the finger. My dad clutches the steering wheel, white-knuckled, cursing and sweating, while my grandfather waves his arms ineffectually and shouts in Ukrainian. Terrified, I lay down on the backseat and close my eyes so I don't have to watch us all get killed, until my dad finds his way down a side street.

The next time we venture to New York, my dad sits down the night before with a map and yellow highlighter and painstakingly lays out our route, like a general plotting an invasion. But the following morning, as we head toward the Ukrainian Institute of America on the Upper East Side, something does not look quite right. There are police cars everywhere. Blue wooden barriers line the streets. When we attempt to make one of our carefully planned turns onto Fifth Avenue, we find the road blocked by a policeman on horseback.

"You can't go this way," he shouts, as my dad opens the window to ask what's going on. "Street's closed for the parade."

Sure enough, cars are turning down side streets. My father looks longingly at Fifth Avenue, spread out right in front of us, and reluctantly turns into unknown territory while fumbling for the map with one hand. The program will start in just moments, and still we remain mired in traffic, separated from the hall by a wide thoroughfare right now occupied by a marching band. Uniformed trumpet and clarinet players march in unison, clowns juggle, floats slowly roll by, and the sidewalks all around are clogged with on-lookers.

Suddenly, I feel a powerful tug: my grandmother, in her floral-print babushka, pulling me from the car with remarkable force. With her hand grasped around my arm like a hawk's talon, she propels me into the middle of the crowd. As I clutch my violin and try to keep my gown from dragging in the street, Baba shoves past the barricades and a startled policeman, right into the path of the oncoming parade. We weave our way through a marching band, which barely breaks its stride, Baba ignoring the shouting police-men as we run toward the concert hall on the other side. No pa-rade, much less the New York City Police Department, is going to stop Baba.

After the performance, Baba is puffed up with pride. "That's *mine* granddaughter, *mey vnoochka*!" she announces to anyone who will listen, while I shake hands with the old ladies and gentle-men who offer congratulations.

"You played beautifully!" the well-wishers say in Ukrainian, as-suming that I speak the language, too.

"*Diakoyu*," I am able to reply. *Thank you*. It's pretty much the only thing I know how to say, and most of the time it's enough.

That day, as concertgoers greet me after the performance, I mur-mur my "*Diakoyu*" to one after the other, nodding and smiling. An older woman in suit and pearls approaches me, burbling prettily in Ukrainian, and I smile back at her. "*Diakoyu!*" I say brightly.

The woman looks at me, confused. Apparently she has just asked me "How old are you?"

Mortified, Baba stalks away, shaking her head in disgust, while the kind stranger switches gears and starts speaking to me in English.

Afterward, Baba berates me for humiliating her in front of her countrymen.

"Vhy you no learn-it to speak good? This eez shame. Shame to me!" she wails. "Shame!"

My Ukrainian never does improve enough for me to converse properly, but my frequent solo appearances are great musical training, and my dad never tires of hearing the music that reminds him of his roots. Maybe, I think, it will help him in his endless attempts to win approval from Baba, too.

Unfortunately, that effort proves to be futile. Many years later, she will inform me that she was never as pleased by the performances as she was ashamed of my inability to speak Ukrainian.

9

The Audition

JOANNE

The first time Mr. K booked our quartet to perform at a Ukrainian festival, I was mystified. I didn't understand a word of the entire evening, which apparently was a tribute to some dead nineteenth-century Ukrainian poet.

But that wasn't nearly as mortifying as the day he sent our quartet to a street fair in the historic district dressed up in Colonial-era villager costumes. I spent the entire afternoon trying to melt into the pavement, hoping I wouldn't see anyone I knew. I tugged at my pink floral-print gown and flattened myself against the brick wall of old Crandall Elementary School, glancing right and left to make sure there were no familiar faces. My hair was giving me trouble, which happened often these days. Long and frizzy, it refused to be tamed. I alternated between the two-hour struggle with a blow dryer required to straighten it, and my clumsy curling-iron attempt at Farrah Fawcett wings.

My mother told me I was going through what she called an "awkward phase," which so far as I could tell had lasted, oh, about thirteen years. The boys at school told me I looked like a scarecrow and called me "four-eyes." What they lacked in originality they made up for in accuracy.

Being in the orchestra was suddenly social suicide. I had just started Hammarskjold Junior High School—named for a Swedish diplomat most kids never heard of whose name many would never learn how to spell—where the pecking order was clear and an instrument case instantly advertised your position at the bottom. After the first few days, I refused to bring my viola to school—I made up some excuse about how it wouldn't fit on the bus—and used a school instrument for orchestra rehearsals instead. I began to avoid the music kids in the hallways, even my friends, even Melanie. I don't think I ate in the cafeteria with her once in three years, even though we spent hours together after school and at ASTA during the summers. If the gods of popularity deemed orchestra kids to be pariahs, I wasn't in any position to argue.

The tension between us was unspoken, but the effect was unmistakable. When we got our yearbooks that first spring, even kids I barely knew wrote knowingly intimate inscriptions. But Melanie's note to me sounded as if it were penned by a distant acquaintance: "Good luck in the future."

Middle school everywhere is the killing field of musical ambition. There's actually a technical term for it—for real, researchers have studied the phenomenon. It's called the "I want to quit" phase. That's the span between twelve and fourteen years old, when, as researcher Theresa Chen put it, kids drop out "because of their desire to seek peer attention and approval."

Lots of teachers ease up on their students when the calamity that is adolescence strikes, hoping to coddle and cajole them through the worst of it. Mr. K did the opposite. He got meaner.

He was especially tough on one of my classmates. Ted Kesler was small for his age, with shaggy bangs he was forever shaking out of his eyes and a sweet, slightly foggy expression on his face. Once, when Mr. K was trying to teach him how to play in fifth position—in which the left hand climbs all the way up the violin neck in order to play high notes—he pressed on Ted's thumb so hard that the knuckle cracked. You could hear it popping, and it hurt like hell afterward.

"That's so you don't forget where fifth position is," Mr. K barked.

"I never did," Ted would say decades later.

As socially humiliating as viola was, I didn't consider quitting. Neither did most of the other musicians in school, not even Ted. "Taking lessons with Mr. K felt like playing for the Yankees," he said. "You put up with the shit because it got you to the championships."

Mr. K, it was true, was on a roll. His students were dominating every orchestra competition, and I was one of them. Junior Regional Orchestra at twelve years old, Senior Regional at thirteen, All-State Orchestra at fourteen, the first year I was eligible. Melanie, naturally, was named concertmaster of all three.

At one audition for a youth orchestra the year I turned thirteen, the primary judge had a particularly intense rivalry with Mr. K. She sneered at me as I carefully closed the door behind me. The door had a glass window, but she had covered it with paper so no one could see inside. She looked me up and down and shook her head in disgust even before I began to play.

"B-flat scale," she said in lieu of a greeting.

On a viola, B flat is the highest three-octave scale there is. It's the scale that requires you to crawl your fingers all the way up the instrument's neck, where it's harder to play in tune and your fingers have to be thisclose together and the bow can scrape and scratch like a screeching cat if you aren't careful. Mr. K had drilled me on it probably a million times by now. I handled it without a problem.

She scowled.

"Faster." She gave me a hard look.

I played it again, concentrating fiercely. I stared at my fingers, willing them to hit their marks on the neck of the instrument as I played all three octaves on a single bow: BflatCDEflatFGAB-flatCDEflatFGABflatCDEflatFGABflat. Then down again: BflatAG-FEflatDCBflatAGFEflatDCBflatAGFEflatDCBflat, also on a single bow. I hit each note. The endless drilling during my lessons had clearly paid off.

Thank you, Mr. K.

The judge gave me a look of loathing.

"Faster!"

I took a deep breath. I had never played it any faster. I had never heard *anybody* play it faster. I had never heard a judge make that kind of demand, either. The cruel expression contorting her features unnerved me. *What did I ever do to her?* I could feel the muscles in my arm tensing up. My palms were sweating. Both hands were visibly shaking. I steeled myself, closed my eyes, and dug in.

BflatCDEflatFGABflatCDEflatFGABflatCDEflatFGABflat, on a single bow. Then down again: BflatAGFEflatDCBflatAGFEflatD-CBflatAGFEflatDCBflat, also on a single bow. The scale went by in a flash. Notes that were too sharp and too flat and off in a variety of ways hung in the air. At least I got through it.

"*Faster! Do it faster!*" Sadistic glee was playing across her lips.

I looked helplessly toward the judging desk. A second teacher sat next to her, but he looked just as cowed as I did. He turned away from me and didn't say a word. By this time my breath was coming in short, shallow bursts. It was clear this woman was out to get me. You could see in the expression on her face that she wanted me to fail, that she was putting all of her energy into *willing* me to fail.

"*I said faster.*"

My hands were visibly trembling as I dug into the scale once more. My brain was telling my fingers to go faster, faster, but like a jockey that whips his horse until the beast collapses and dies mid-race, my fingers didn't have the wherewithal to cooperate. BflatCDEflatFGABflatCDEflatFGABflatCDEflatF—

And *smack*. My left hand spun out of control, falling right off the neck of the instrument.

"Ha!" she said. With a theatrical flair, she lifted her pencil and brought it down with a swoop to mark my presumably failing score.

The rest of the audition was a disaster. Muscles I didn't even know existed tensed into knots I had no idea were possible. Between the flop sweat, the shakes, and the sneering from the sidelines, I barely got through my solo piece and sight-reading. When I finally was dispatched out the door with its square of window strategically taped over, I ran to the closest unoccupied corner of the corridor, sank down against the cinder-block wall, and cried.

MELANIE

"Ewww! It's Melanie!"

I don't remember the first time I was concertmaster of an orchestra, but by junior high, I am earning the title regularly. The year I turn fourteen, I am named concertmaster of six different orchestras. One of them is Senior Regional Orchestra, made up of high school students. It's a qualifier for All-State Orchestra, where all three regions of New Jersey are represented.

When I show up for the All-State auditions, in a big suburban high school a good hour away from home, some of my new acquaintances are already there. In the warm-up room, I'm unpacking my instrument when behind me I hear the girl's voice. "Ewww!" she says again.

Turning around, I see a violist with long, beautiful hair whose name I don't know but whose face is familiar. She's surrounded by a group of her friends. I smile tentatively and continue rosining my bow. The girl approaches me from across the room. She's dressed in tight hip-hugger jeans and smells faintly of cigarettes.

"Hey, Melanie," she sneers. "See that guy over there?" She points to a short boy with glasses who is vigorously practicing the Tchaikovsky Violin Concerto in D Major, one of the most difficult pieces in the classical violin repertoire. "He's really good, and he's your competition. Let's see if you can beat him!" She stalks off, leaving me with my smile frozen on my face.

How could this girl hate me? Why is she so hostile? *She doesn't even know me.*

Confused, I hide behind my instrument and begin to warm up with some scales. This is a new and awful feeling, being singled out for derision. I had first noticed it this past summer at ASTA, when the camp photographer posted candid photos on the wall for parents to buy. It's a coup to get your picture taken, and every year, kids walk up and down trying to spot themselves. But my dad always insists that the photographer take multiple portraits of him with Steph and me so he can get one where Steph isn't laughing or his bald spot isn't showing. "Why are there so many pictures of Mr. K's daughters?" I heard one of the kids complain as I walked past the photo wall.

That did it. When Daddy waylaid us for our next portrait session, his suit buttoned up neatly and his tie smoothed, Steph and I told him we didn't want to pose. Daddy was furious. He exploded, then stormed off and refused to talk to us for days afterward. I felt terrible, writing him a long letter begging forgiveness, saying, "I'm sorry! I didn't get a chance to explain my feelings of embarrassment about the dumb way I look in a picture and the way I feel when people complain . . ."

Now, warming up for my first All-State audition, the feeling comes flooding back. The boy is playing the Tchaikovsky loudly, and his friends, I'm sure, are snickering at me. I try not to notice them, and my heart gradually stops pounding. After a few minutes I'm engrossed in my piece, Max Bruch's Violin Concerto no. 1 in G Minor.

That night, when Daddy gets home from the auditions, he's wearing a huge grin. "Well, sis, congratulations! You made concert-mistress of the All-State Orchestra."

"Concertmaster!" my mother yells from the living room, correcting him. "You can't call her concert*mistress*. A mistress is something between a mister and a mattress."

My dad ignores her. "There eez a boy, a high school junior, and you outscored him by only a couple of points. Really, eet could haf gone either way. This eez his last year in All-State . . ."

I know instantly whom he's talking about. The boy whose friend taunted me.

"I think eet would be the right thing to do to offer to split the concertmastership with him."

I consider what my father is saying. My dad has a firm philosophy about seniority. When he holds auditions in his own orchestra, he gives extra points to upperclassmen, five points for each year of seniority. He always says there has to be some reward for loyalty, some benefit to sticking it out through the years.

He is waiting for my answer. I think about the girl with the beautiful hair, sneering, "Eeew, Melanie!" I don't like to be singled out. Anyway, what's the big deal about being concertmaster? Being awarded first chair seems to come easily. I couldn't care less about it. At least, I don't think I care.

I nod.

"Good," he says. "You weel have other chances."

As far as my social life is concerned, I've hit bottom.

My tiny neighborhood elementary school was located in a corner of East Brunswick that some kids consider "the other side of the tracks." At my new school, Hammarskjold, there are wealthier kids, too. It isn't cool to be smart, or musical, or especially talented at anything except athletics. I figure out the rules pretty quickly but have no hope of mastering them:

A) Appearance and confidence override everything else.

B) It's crucial to have an insulating group of friends.

C) It's helpful to have parents who can assist with A and B by providing a dermatologist, an orthodontist, a ride, and a credit card.

I don't have any of those things. It's hard to blend in when you're a lime-green-plaid-stretch-pants-wearing music nerd. I can't do much about my parents, but I do persuade my dad to give me an old clunker violin that I can stash in the music room semipermanently so I don't have to parade around with my telltale instrument case on orchestra days.

I learn how to hide my grades, too, concealing the A's on assignments by covering them up with my palm as the teacher hands back papers, then quickly stuffing them into my notebook. In class, I never raise my hand or volunteer to answer a question. I adopt a hairstyle that hides part of my face from view, with my bangs swept dramatically over one eye. My mother calls it my "Veronica Lake look." My dad calls it ridiculous.

I haven't given up hopes of reinventing myself. I won't be able to imitate the pretty, wealthy, fashionable girls who saunter by confidently in cute jeans with their shirttails knotted around their midriffs. I'm just hoping I can break free of polyester clothes in colors not found in nature that come from the Sears catalog, arriving wrapped around cardboard and sheathed in plastic bags. Finally, my dad gives me money and allows Steph and me to shop for ourselves at the mall.

Getting real jeans is a dream come true, even though they have to be loose enough to satisfy my dad's sense of decency. I also get a pair of white painter's pants, complete with the hammer loop and the long, skinny brush pocket where I keep a comb for hair emergencies. Tan corduroy gaucho pants and vest come next; all I need is a hat and a rope slung over my shoulder to look like I've just stepped off a cattle ranch in Argentina. A mint-green jumpsuit that makes me look like a gas station attendant becomes one of my favorite outfits. And when I am finally allowed to get a pair of "buffalo sandals"—tan suede two-inch platforms with beige leather straps—I sleep with them beside my bed for a week so I can see them as soon as I open my eyes in the morning.

Baba is disgusted by my new clothes. "Vhy you not take-it nice *dress*? Vhy you wear-it always the *pants*?" she asks.

She takes one look at my new sandals and laughs bitterly. "How you can walk like thees, een these crazy shoes? You looks like you have-it two bricks strapped on you feet!"

I don't care. I love my platform shoes, and I'm not going to take fashion advice from a woman whose wardrobe consists largely of floral-print babushkas. But Baba doesn't let up. A few years later she has a similar reaction to my shoulder pads, snorting "You looks like you have-it two *hard rolls* under you blouse!"

Hammarskjold is a lonely place for me. I have Miriam, of course, and some friends in the orchestra, but if Miriam is absent that day, then I have no one to sit with at lunch. Joanne goes to Hammarsk-jold, too. We laugh and joke at orchestra and outside of school. But inside school, we don't connect much. Joanne excels in advanced classes that I'm not allowed to take. She seems to have lots of friends, most of whom aren't in the orchestra. She's confident, even around teachers and boys, which makes me feel more shy. Joanne is the type of girl who would surely laugh at me for acting uncool. Once, in seventh grade, she does invite me to a Girl Scout party, but the invitation is halfhearted.

"Uh, we're having this party?" She isn't even looking at me. "With my Girl Scout troop? I guess I'm supposed to invite you?"

I'm embarrassed to say how eagerly I accept.

In my scrapbook, I paste an article about one of our orchestra concerts in Atlantic City. On the margin, I compile a list of my friends' names. There's Miriam, whom I've nicknamed Murray. And Michael Grossman, the cute boy our age who plays violin, and our family friend, John Stine, who plays the cello, and his big sister, LouAnn, a violist. Last of all, I write down Joanne's name. Next to it, I pencil in a question mark.

Not long after the All-State audition, at the end of eighth grade, my mother goes into the hospital again.

This is becoming a familiar routine. Her health rallies, then de-teriorates, in an almost predictable cycle. Whenever her illness gets out of hand, she checks herself in to the hospital, usually for a few weeks, which seems to stave off decline for a little while. Lately, she's having more trouble transferring in and out of her wheelchair without help. I have been lending her a hand when she needs it, but that is no longer enough, and I don't have the strength to lift her on my own.

The morning my mother heads off to the hospital, I kiss her

good-bye with my violin in one hand and turn back to the concerto I'm working on. "I'll be back in a few weeks," my mom promises as she leaves.

Dad takes Steph and me to visit a few days later. My mother seems to be in good shape compared with most of the others. At forty-four, she still has the lustrous hair and piercing blue eyes that first caught my father's attention back in college. She is a few decades younger than most of the other patients, the majority of whom have suffered strokes or accidents that leave them with debilitated speech and urine bags tucked beneath their wheelchairs. I hand my mom a box of chocolates to share with her roommates and gather up a laundry bag full of her clothes.

For the next few weeks, that's our routine. My mother calls every day. Once or twice a week, Daddy loads Stephanie and me into the car to visit. Each time we bring her magazines or chocolates or her favorite McDonald's milkshake, and I take home her laundry, which I'll wash and return to her on our next visit. Sometimes we bring our violins and play for her, and Daddy lets us count it as practicing, since she corrects our intonation. She introduces us to Millie and Mary, stroke victims who have lost the ability to speak. She's giving them choral breathing lessons that are so effective that a local newspaper takes note, writing about the music therapy she introduces to patients.

Between treatments, Mom organizes a patients' choir that she conducts. She positions her wheelchair in front of them, looking out at a line of a dozen old stroke and accident victims, most in wheelchairs, their hobbled knees covered by afghans knit by wives or grandchildren. On our visits, she starts asking us to bring her sheet music instead of magazines. Just before the holidays, she leads her patients' choir in a performance, all of them outfitted in Santa hats.

*   *   *

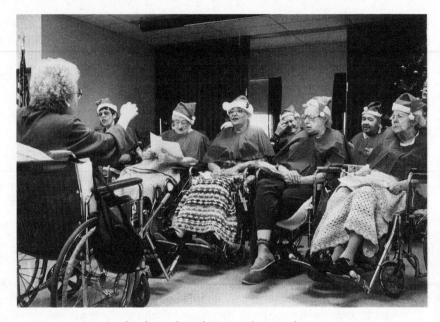

Jean Kupchynsky conducts the Roosevelt Hospital Nursing Home patient choir in a holiday concert, circa 1977.

It's Christmas morning. I'm just getting out of the shower when Steph calls down the stairs, "The ambulance is here! Mommy's home!"

A big white emergency vehicle with flashing lights, its siren mercifully silent, has just pulled into our driveway. It has arrived half an hour early.

I run up the staircase in a towel, my hair dripping on the carpeted stairway. Daddy is already pulling the living room couch out of the way to make room for the medics who will be carrying her inside. Steph, still in her pajamas, is jumping up and down in the open doorway.

Just outside, I can see the neighborhood kids streaming out of their front doors to see what the commotion is about. A group of them gather on the sidewalk directly in front of our house, staring and pointing, as my mother is loaded onto a stretcher, strapped down, and carried across our lawn to the front steps. I feel the familiar blush of embarrassment rising in my cheeks.

"Merry Christmas," my mom sings, as if there is nothing unusual about her entrance. "It's good to be home."

We couldn't have gotten a better present. After a celebratory breakfast and a frenzy of gift unwrapping, Steph and I set to making my mother's annual Christmas meal—roast beef with mashed potatoes and gravy—while she happily calls out instructions. My mother's gift to me, appropriately enough, is my own copy of one of her favorite Fannie Farmer cookbooks, inscribed in a hospital volunteer's unfamiliar handwriting: "To Melanie, as a supplement to Betty Crocker. Love, Mother." My dad plays records of Christmas carols.

Still, even though she is in high spirits, I can see that my mother is struggling. She's trying mightily not to betray how weak she is. Despite being in the hospital for several months and daily physical therapy, she is frailer than when she had checked in. Her hands aren't strong enough to play carols on the piano, as she used to do when I was little.

We have barely finished dinner when, at six P.M., the ambulance rolls up our driveway again.

My mom is going back to the hospital. "Just a few more weeks," she promises as she leaves.

10

Stage Fright

JOANNE

In my old photo album, there is a yellowing snapshot of me at age fourteen, all knobby elbows and frizzy hair and glasses, painfully skinny in a purple gown, the very picture of excruciating adolescence. I am standing awkwardly in my family's front hallway, my cough-syrup-colored dress clashing with the brown-striped wallpaper behind me. Yet in the photo, I have a huge grin on my face.

I remember the moment exactly. After my disastrous youth orchestra audition, I had developed a horrendous case of stage fright. I froze up every time I had to play for anyone, even for my sisters or my parents. If my mother so much as spoke on the phone while I was practicing, my hands would start to tremble and my bow arm would seize up with fear that the caller might overhear me, the notes croaking and the music sounding like a dying frog.

Alone, I practiced for hours, advancing steadily through the standard repertoire: Telemann Concerto, Reger Sonata, Bach Cello Suites transcribed for viola. But when anyone was listening, even Mr. K at my lessons, the dread that started in the pit of my stomach ballooned like some sort of monstrous tumor, taking over my muscles, my nerves, my organs, until it squeezed out every iota of music in my body. I was paralyzed.

The first audition after my tryout trauma was for Senior Regional Orchestra, a qualifier for All-State Orchestra. I was supposed to be a shoo-in for principal violist. But when I woke to the insistent ringing of my alarm clock that morning, my head felt like it was being pinched between pliers while simultaneously being suspended upside down on a broken Ferris wheel—the kind my mother had warned me about years ago. My eyes refused to focus. When I sat up, my body lurched forward while my brain sloshed backward. I pulled off my lime-green covers and stumbled toward the bathroom, but before I could get a look at myself in the mirror, I fell to the floor in a dead faint.

My parents found me there, crumpled on the linoleum tile next to the washing machine. After much whispered discussion and desperate entreaties from me after I revived—"I feel fine! I can't miss the audition!"—they allowed me to go. But they both came along, insisting that I lie down and rest in the leather backseat of my dad's brown Oldsmobile 88 on the way. They kept watch over me while I warmed up and then sat outside the audition classroom when it was my turn, as if they were holding vigil for an accident victim in an emergency room corridor. Afterward, they took me to the doctor. Diagnosis: nerves.

I was too embarrassed to admit my fear to anyone, especially my intimidating teacher. Mr. K never acknowledged that he knew my secret. If he noticed my cramped gait and sweaty palms, he didn't let on. But one day not long afterward at my lesson he announced, "You weel play solo at next orchestra concert. Eet eez all arranged."

He pulled out one of my favorite pieces, *Tema con Variazioni*, a pretty Renaissance-era work composed by Marin Marais, a court musician at Versailles. The piece wasn't originally written for viola—not much is—but it had been transcribed by Paul Doktor, the violist I idolized and followed around like a groupie. His autograph was one of my prized possessions.

The day of my solo performance, I woke up with creepy silent fireworks exploding in front of my eyes, splashing garish splotches of color anywhere that I tried to focus my gaze. I took deep breaths to calm myself before gingerly stepping out of bed. I forced myself to choke down an English muffin. After showering, I spent two hours trying to tame my hair into submission. My arms were shaking while I maneuvered the lime-green blow-dryer and stared back at the fearful reflection in the mirror in my bedroom.

When we pulled into the high school parking lot, I smoothed my purple dress, pulled back my shoulders, and pretended to feel a confidence I didn't remotely possess. I pushed through the rehearsal room door, viola case swinging behind me. Mr. K greeted me with a hug.

The concert featured the orchestra playing typical Mr. K music, heroic and patriotic and celebrating the triumph of right over might. After Richard Rodgers's World War II–inspired "Victory at Sea," I quietly stood up and headed to the wings to prepare for my piece.

Backstage, I felt my bravado crumbling. I paced back and forth in the wings, unable to concentrate on the Mozart echoing through the auditorium now. The increasingly familiar feeling of panic set in. I could taste bile in the back of my throat.

That was when I felt an arm slip around my shoulder.

"Shh," Mr. K said. "You worked hard. You are well prepared."

His left arm firmly encircling me, his right hand holding my own, he fell in beside me, matching the rhythm of my pacing, whispering in singsong in my ear.

"You weel have fun. You weel go out and have a good time."

Back and forth we paced in the wings. In the distance, a string quartet was playing onstage. Beyond the footlights, hundreds of pairs of eyes were watching, paper programs were rustling, a few muffled coughs were echoing faintly from the back rows. But backstage, it was just the two of us. It was just Mr. K and me now. My own face felt rigid with fear, but when I looked at his, I saw serenity. Certainty.

"Shh," Mr. K said again.

Onstage, the group before me was finishing up, and applause filled the hall.

With a gentle nudge, Mr. K propelled me from the wings.

"I'm proud of you" was the last thing he said, looking into my eyes as I drifted away.

From the front of the stage, I looked out at the full auditorium. I had that feeling of approaching the very top of a roller coaster—when you hear that ominous *click click click click* sound on the tracks before you plunge into a free fall. The taste of bile was making a return appearance in my mouth. Whenever I was at an amusement park and heard that *click click click click* of the roller coaster, I always looked frantically around for an escape route, reeling at the dizzying sight of trees and people on the ground and concession stands all receding into tiny primary-colored plastic toy figures. *Can I get off?*

I couldn't. There was no turning back now, only going forward.

I plunged in.

For the first few notes, I was excruciatingly aware of every twitch of my muscles and every throat being cleared in the audience. But very quickly, Mr. K's words came back to me, pushing away the fears and helping slow my panicked heartbeat. He believed I could do this. He was sure of it. He had confidence in me. I was ready.

This was the good kind of roller coaster, not the kind that spits unsuspecting kids into the ocean. It was hard work, but it was . . . fun.

When the piece was over, a wave of relief washed over me, rushing like white-water rapids in my ears so loudly that it drowned out even the applause. As I bowed to the audience, the way Mr. K taught me, I caught sight of him offstage. He was handing a bouquet of flowers to Ronni, who ran onto the stage to present them to me. I threw my arms around her. As I hugged her tight in joy and relief, I could see Mr. K over the top of her shoulder. He had stepped out from the wings to lead the applause.

At home just after the concert, my dad snapped the photo of the awkward, skinny girl in the purple dress with the huge smile on her face. She has frizzy hair and glasses, and the color of her dress clashes with the striped brown wall behind her. She is holding a huge bouquet. It is the first time anyone has ever given her flowers.

The picture is of a girl who has just gotten her confidence back.

Somehow, despite fainting just before the audition for regional orchestra, I had scored well enough to be named principal violist. Not long after, though, I landed in another youth orchestra, this one conducted—in a cruel twist of fate—by the audition judge who had so effectively tortured me.

Like the church, student orchestras hone to certain traditions from which they never deviate. They rise in unison at the conductor's command. They show appreciation not by clapping but by tapping bows on music stands or stomping feet. And at the end of the final concert, the concertmaster presents a gift to the conductor and makes a short speech of thanks. Usually, that last task fell to Melanie. But Mr. K took me aside after rehearsal one day.

"At the performance, you weel geeve conductor flowers and make speech," he said.

"But that's Melanie's job."

"She won't mind."

"But the conductor hates me!"

"Exactly." He nodded.

On the way home, when I explained the plan to my dad, he broke into a grin.

"Mr. K is right, Jo. Take the high road," he said, glancing back at me from behind the wheel of the Olds 88.

Mr. K's plan clearly appealed to my father. As a kid, my dad had stayed in the Boy Scouts all the way through high school. He reminded us regularly that he would have made Eagle Scout if only his parents had sprung for the swimming lessons he needed to complete that last badge. Barely a day went by when he didn't cite the Boy Scout motto "Be prepared." He believed in hard work and dedication. But he also was a skilled negotiator in business, who understood that graciousness, properly applied, was the ultimate expression of power.

A few weeks later, when I took my place onstage for the final concert, I was prepared, all right. I quietly slipped off into the wings before the last number, noticing the look of consternation mixed with suspicion on the conductor's face. When I reemerged, I was cradling a bouquet of long-stemmed roses in one arm. I faced the audience, threw a smile in her direction, and launched into my prepared speech.

"There is no one else quite like our conductor . . ." I began.

I went on to thank her, on behalf of the whole orchestra, for the "unique" experience she had given us. "Personally, she has taught me so much," I added, looking away from the audience to gaze directly into her eyes. My eyes locked on hers, and I spoke my next words slowly. "She has set an example that I know I will never forget."

She shifted uncomfortably on the stage.

I turned back to the audience. "Ladies and gentlemen, please join me in acknowledging our conductor. She is really something."

I presented the roses to the conductor and gave her a hug. When I stepped back, she was smiling graciously for the audience, but her eyes were wary, like a German shepherd that's been cornered by a kitten.

After the concert, my parents came to find me, embarrassing me with big affectionate kisses planted on both cheeks.

"Good for you for taking the high road," my mother said.

Backstage, as I was packing up, Mr. K had a big old mischievous grin on his face. He used a different expression to describe my performance, one that I had never heard before. So later, at the ice-cream parlor for a post-performance celebration, I asked my parents between spoonfuls of a hot fudge sundae with no nuts and extra whipped cream: "What does it mean to be 'a wolf in sheep's clothing'?"

That year, it seemed like the quartet was performing every week. There were few opportunities Mr. K wouldn't consider. In my room at night, I carefully cut out and pasted into my photo album scores of newspaper articles, with such notable entries as this one from November 1975: "An ecumenical group of four young girls provided the patients of Villa Maria with a string concert on the eve of All Saints' Day."

I played at funerals, weddings, and every school in town. Once,

Mr. K bused the orchestra to downtown Newark, where a hostile audience of inner-city school kids drowned out the music with shouts and jeers. Another time, I played at a New Jersey polka festival where a sleazy promoter tried to pass off recordings of our group as an "internationally famous polka orchestra." My illicit favorite as a nice Jewish girl was performing the *Hallelujah* chorus each year at midnight mass at Our Lady of Lourdes Roman Catholic Church.

"You just can't teach children an instrument and then hide them in a hole," Mr. K explained.

Most of all, Mr. K made us perform in nursing homes and hospitals. These were well-meaning sorts of places, and they attempted to be cheery, with cardboard cutouts of candy canes and Santa Clauses around Christmastime and jack-o'-lanterns near Halloween. But the decorations couldn't mask the air of futility that wafted through the halls, an aroma equal parts disinfectant and despair. We had to perform loathsome old-people musical standards that would make my stomach churn—"Begin the Beguine," "Moon River"—in fluorescent-lit rooms filled with ancient women with thinning wisps of hair and decrepit old men in wheelchairs or leaning on walkers.

"Slush museek," Mr. K called it. It made me a little bit nauseous.

The first time I performed at a nursing home, with the school orchestra, Mr. K stood up from his seat at the front of the yellow school bus as we rolled into the parking lot. He planted his feet shoulder-width apart, blocking the aisle, cutting us off from the door. We were trapped.

"Seet down," Mr. K yelled. "You keeds don't move yet."

Whatever we had done, we were in trouble now.

Then he launched into a speech I would hear him give probably a dozen more times.

"Don't be afraid," he said.

We looked back up at him, puzzled.

"They going to want to talk to you, and touch you or hug you or kiss"—it sounded like *kees*—"you."

Really?

"Let them. They don't see a lot of young people."

Mr. K told us some of the patients inside were old and others were sick, near death. Some of them were senile. We might be repulsed by what we saw inside. Too bad.

"After concert, you weel stay and circulate. And you weel like it."

Then he turned and trotted off the bus.

Resolutely, we filed off, clutching our instruments and taking a deep breath of fresh air before plunging into the sour-smelling, linoleum-tiled all-purpose room.

As promised, the crowd was needy. No sooner had Mr. K lowered his baton on the final notes of "The Girl from Ipanema" than gnarled hands began grabbing at us like something out of the graveyard scene from the movie *Carrie*. I shrank away from an old woman clutching at me from a wheelchair. Out of the corner of my eye, I saw Mr. K. He was staring at me, his expression hard.

With a glance back at him, I forced a smile and approached the old woman. She told me I reminded her of her granddaughter and stroked my cheek. I could see Melanie and Miriam and Stephanie, too, circulating slowly among the old and the ill, Mr. K's words seared into our brains even as they patted us on the head or cooed at us. The prospect of Mr. K's wrath was without a doubt much scarier than the old people were.

We only stayed a few minutes before Mr. K called for us to get back on the bus. But the next time we went to play there, and with each time after that, I could have sworn we stayed progressively longer. The trips would continue regularly for years. Mr. K was always packing us off to some old folks' home or hospital or rehab center. I wouldn't admit it out loud, but I began to look forward to the conversations afterward with war veterans and old ladies who reminisced about their lost youths.

Each time, Mr. K gave us the same lecture, refusing to let any of us off the bus before he said his piece. "They're going to want to hug you...Let them."

On one of those visits, I noticed a new resident among the crippled bodies and gnarled hands. She was younger than the others. Her metal wheelchair was secured with a brake, and her body leaned at an awkward angle against its right armrest. She was Mr. K's wife.

MELANIE

The weeks turn into months; the months turn into a year; and still my mother is in the hospital. I only realize how long it's been when All-State auditions roll around again.

When the results are posted, I have to check twice to make sure I'm not misreading the list. There it is, in black and white: I am named *assistant* concertmaster.

Second place.

My dad holds me on his lap in the big brown easy chair in our living room while I cry so hard that my tears soak his shirt and tie.

I never realized I would care so much about losing an audition. The thought of disappointing him is devastating. Disappointing myself, though, comes as an even bigger shock. I didn't practice enough, I silently berate myself. I didn't measure up. I didn't do what I was supposed to do. I was too sloppy. I didn't work hard enough. I had no discipline. *How could I have been so lazy? I've let everybody down.* The familiar old cocktail of self-recriminations and guilt overpowers me.

He holds me for a long time, stroking my hair and saying little. "I know you tried your hardest. Shhh. It's okay, Lastivko."

He hasn't called me that in years.

I look up at him, sniffling. "You're not m-m-mad at me?"

"Mad at you? Of course not!"

"But I made it last year, and I gave it up."

"That was the right thing to do. You ween some, you lose some. You weel audition again next year."

He straightens his tie and pats his wet shirt with the handkerchief from his pocket.

"Now, no more crying. Discipline yourself."

My dad surprises me again when he allows me to go to the ninth grade dance with a boy. Michael Grossman is the cutest boy in the orchestra. I'm not his first choice, but I don't care.

Michael and I will go on to date all through high school. My dad allows it only reluctantly. "Do not trust heem," he often says of teenage boys, "but do not let heem know you do not trust heem." Of course, my dad has a point. Michael and I sneak into the empty auditorium to be alone at lunchtime. Once, I steal the key to my dad's office while he's away so we can use it for a make-out session. We steam up the windows of Michael's parked car, getting caught by the police in both of our neighborhoods.

Our boldest plan comes when my dad is out of town, Stephanie is away, and I decide to make a romantic dinner at home. We plan the evening carefully. Nothing too momentous—we are not ready for *that* yet, or at least I'm not—but we'll have the whole house to ourselves for a few hours, until Michael's curfew.

After I make the chicken and potatoes and put brownies into the oven, I decide it would be quite grown-up to have a drink before dinner, like I've seen my dad do countless times. So I pour myself a glass of vodka, straight. Michael will be arriving soon, so I figure if I have a big drink it will take effect faster. It tastes awful, but I quickly gulp down about a half cup of my dad's Smirnoff. *Wow! How can people drink this stuff?* After just a few minutes, when I don't feel anything, I repeat the process.

The next thing I remember, I am lying on the blue linoleum bathroom floor. I open my eyes. *Where am I? What happened?* Michael is there, and for some reason our music teacher Sandy Dackow, who works for my dad, is there, too. My nose is assaulted by the smell of vomit and burned brownies.

"It's okay, it's okay, you did the right thing to tell me," Sandy is saying to him. "If she threw up, then she'll be okay. Do you know how much she drank?"

Reassuringly, Sandy is her usual self, in charge and quick thinking. I close my eyes as wave after wave of nausea passes through me. I am lucky I didn't die of alcohol poisoning, though I almost wish I had. *Can you die of embarrassment?*

I try to focus on Sandy's face. She has become not just a teacher but also a close family friend. But she works for my dad; isn't it her duty to report back to him?

"Please don't tell," I murmur, before succumbing to another surge of nausea and guilt. I don't think she will. She'll be just as afraid of his reaction as I am.

My dad keeps lining up solo performances for me, but the older I get, the more I dread them. I wish I could conjure up the childish fearlessness I used to have, before I was old enough to understand stress and anxiety.

Orchestral playing, on the other hand, has exactly the opposite effect. It's exhilarating. I can plug into the energy surging around me and lose myself in the music. It offers an escape from the loneliness of my practice room and the solitary pursuit of solo playing. It's a way to connect with my fellow musicians, to become part of something greater than me. I'm fourteen years old the first time I realize it. At an All-State Orchestra rehearsal of Wagner's triumphant Overture to *Die Meistersinger von Nürnberg*, just before the climactic cymbal crash near the end, I glance down to see goose bumps rising on my arms. My scalp is tingling, as if my hair is sticking straight up. When the music stops, it takes a moment before I am earthbound again. I am surprised to find myself in a folding chair in a school rehearsal room in New Jersey. *I just want to keep doing this, over and over again, for the rest of my life.*

Teaching music is almost as good. I've been helping my dad since I was twelve years old. He always enlists the aid of more advanced students to help less advanced ones. At first my job is to help the beginners, putting marker tapes on fingerboards and bows and patrolling through the violin section, pushing down left wrists and helping the kids arrange themselves with their violin scrolls pointing inward so they won't whack each other with their bows.

By the time I reach high school, my job also includes demonstrating difficult passages. Sometimes my dad makes every violinist in the orchestra play alone, in turn, and when someone has trouble, he makes me play along.

"Who eez deaf een first violins?" he yells one day, as he often does. It's a rhetorical question, but this time a hand is sheepishly raised from the back of the section.

"I don't need to know! I just want you to fix eet!"

My dad beckons me to stand behind Ted Kesler, in the back of the first violin section. Together, we play the passage again and again, while the rest of the kids in the orchestra wait patiently. Ted grimaces, but he is used to this by now. My dad spends extra time on the kids like Ted who he thinks need the most help. He may not show it, but I've learned over the years that the underdogs are the ones whose progress fills him with the greatest pride.

Sometimes I feel as if my dad is testing me, too, to see how much I can take. Once, when the violins are fumbling a passage from Aaron Copland's "Hoe-Down"—an orchestra favorite—he threatens to pull the piece from the program unless I stand and play it perfectly. The room goes dead quiet. I can see a cellist crossing her fingers, eyes closed. When I do manage to play the passage to my dad's satisfaction, I feel as if I've scored the winning goal just as the buzzer is about to ring.

Another time, after a particularly trying rehearsal, my dad tells my mom, "You know, I was pretty tough on Melanie today een front

"Who eez DEAF in first violins?" Mr. K solves the problem by having Melanie play along with students, including Ted Kesler (seated at left), while he keeps the beat. In front of Ted sits Stephanie Kupchynsky. At far right, watching Melanie, is Michael Grossman.

of the whole orchestra. I gave her a really hard time. Probably a leetle too hard. And she never reacted, never got upset. Just smiled and deed what I told her."

"Daddy," I say, looking him straight in the eye, "that was not a real smile. That was controlled hostility!"

My dad laughs and looks at me with new appreciation. Behind the amusement I can see a hint of pride—and respect.

You wouldn't think a mother's absence, her lingering stay in a hospital, should ever feel normal. But over time, to Steph and me, it does. It's just the way things are. I've already been doing the cooking and cleaning for some time. I tend to my dad's Qiana shirts the way he likes, hanging them up still warm from the dryer and buttoning the top button to make sure the collar lays properly. I wash and fold my mom's laundry from the hospital, then return it to her when we visit. I learn to make cheese sauce to cover the taste of the vegetables Stephanie hates. I clean the house each week, then bake brownies as a reward, then yell at Daddy and Steph for tracking crumbs all over my spotless kitchen floor.

Stephanie, now in middle school, just smirks. She is preoccupied with a new group of friends who sometimes come by the house when my dad isn't there. They smell like smoke and look at you with narrowed eyes. They wear dark clothes and thick black eye makeup. Steph's best friend scares me the most. She is long and lanky and has an evil look about her. I'm sure Steph is telling her friends things about me that aren't true.

After my dad leaves the house in the morning, Steph changes into pants he thinks are too tight and lines her eyes with kohl. When I collect her laundry, sorting through her piles of black clothes, I find unsettling clues about the life she is no longer sharing with me. I uncrumple the scraps of notebook paper that I find balled up in her pockets and read the scrawled notes that she and her friends have been passing back and forth to each other in class.

"I hate everything."

"My life sucks."

"Homework is a joke."

"I'm SO bored."

"My parents are assholes."

"I have to get out of here."

It's confusing; I don't know what to do. When my mother was in the house, Steph and I were aligned, a unit, each other's greatest defender. But since my mom has been in the hospital, I've had to act as Steph's caretaker instead. I can't be her ally anymore. She's my responsibility now. The strain between us is unbearable, and we fight more than ever. Most of what Steph is up to is uncharted territory for me anyway; I don't have the benefit of having "been there, done that." I have no idea what I'm supposed to be doing to help her.

If I tell my dad, he'll just get mad. I don't want to worry my mom, whose condition is aggravated by stress. Nor do I want to make Steph mad at me.

But I can't just let it go.

One night after dinner, I bring up the subject after my dad goes downstairs to his studio.

"Uh, Steph? I was thinking. What ever happened to Chrissie and Arlene? And Liz? They were so nice, nicer than your friends are now ..." I trail off.

"What's wrong with my friends?"

"I don't know. They're a little scary. Tough. Smoky."

"They're my friends. They care about me!"

I back off. "Sure, I know. I just wondered, you know, about the other girls?"

"They're dorks!" she announces, leaving the room.

Steph's grades start to slide as she falls in with the girls who smoke cigarettes in the field behind the school and cut class. At first it's easy for her to keep my dad from seeing the warning notes that come in the mail. She simply throws them out before he gets home. It's trickier to keep her report cards a secret, but she's able to fool my dad by painstakingly changing the D's to B's, or F's to A's.

One day I see her report card lying on the table. As I pick it up she grabs it from my hands.

"What are you doing? That's mine."

"I know, I just wanted to see. What did you get?"

"Well, if you must know, I got a bunch of B's, and one C. And one D."

I inhale sharply. A D! "What did Daddy say? Did you tell him yet?"

"No, and I'm not going to. I can bring it up next quarter."

"But he has to sign your report card! He'll see it!"

"No, he won't. Look." She has neatly forged his name in the space provided. It doesn't really look like his writing, but I have to admit I'm a little impressed by how bold Steph is. I say nothing to my dad and hope for the best.

Of course Stephanie and I are both kidding ourselves. My father is a teacher, and one who knows every other teacher in the entire school system. He practically explodes when he finds out what is going on.

"Stephanie! You are failing math! How eez this *possible*? *What the hell eez going on?*" He is yelling so hard his face turns purple, and I'm afraid he'll give himself a stroke.

My dad can't figure out why any daughter of his would squander the chance to get an education. To him, nothing is more important. He's saved every one of his own report cards, even the ones from when he was a boy in Ukraine during the war. His framed diplomas hang on the walls of his studio.

Steph is grounded.

"It's not fair!" she cries when I sit down with her that night to go over her homework.

Dad stomps angrily down the steps after dinner to teach, leaving me with my sullen sister, her teary face smeared with eyeliner that she isn't supposed to be wearing in the first place. I'm the enforcer now.

Though Steph doesn't confide in me anymore, I can hear her thoughts when she practices the violin. Longing, sadness, anger, melancholy, all of them come through in the strains of her playing. Our vicious old great-aunt Titka, who scares me almost as much as her sister, Baba, is right when she remarks: "You, Malanka, play with energy. But Stephka—she plays with heart."

Sometimes I see glimpses of the sweet, funny little girl behind the eyeliner. But those flashes appear less and less frequently. In eighth grade, Steph develops a cough and hoarseness that will not go away. My dad is worried. "Thees eez what comes from not eating your vegetables!" he says, insisting she eat more greens. Every time she leaves the house, he calls after her: "Bundle up!"

Only after he discovers a hole in the window screen of the downstairs bathroom and a little pile of cigarette butts underneath does he realize the reason for her cough. His feet come pounding up the stairs and down the hallway to her room, and another round of screaming, ranting, and threatening ensues. He's running out of weapons, of things to take away. She is already grounded and forbidden to use the phone. At his wit's end, Daddy extends her sentence. She's now grounded indefinitely. But none of the punishments seem to make any difference to Stephanie.

11

"Mr. Jerry"

JOANNE

"E-flat scale."

Without so much as a hello, Mr. K began my lesson. He sat at his piano, arms folded, a pencil protruding from one balled-up fist, staring at me as I dug into the strings. Upstairs, the after-dinner dishes were clattering as Melanie cleared the table. In the waiting room, my mother was flipping through a magazine. Mr. K didn't seem to be aware of any outside disturbances. He didn't believe in small talk during lessons. He never asked how my day was, or if I liked school, or what was my favorite subject. He never asked me anything at all. He just gave orders.

"Flat!"

He sprang forward in his chair to bang the offending note on his piano.

I adjusted my fingers and tried again.

"Smooth wrist! Again!"

The formality of lessons always made me uncomfortable. I would walk in and hand Mr. K the seven dollars my parents had counted out carefully beforehand. He would stuff it into his pocket without looking at it, as if it were something vaguely distasteful. Then without another word he would begin.

First, he would drill me on scales. He almost always picked the hardest ones, where your fingers had to climb awkwardly all the way up the neck of the viola. When I hit a sour note, he banged the right one on the piano with a single finger, with such force the whole room seemed to shake. Sometimes he would make me just bow on open strings, back and forth and back and forth, teaching me to fluidly move my wrist so there was none of that painful crunching or croaking at the beginning or end of each note.

"More! Again."

We were interrupted by a knock on the door.

Stephanie peeked into the room and tentatively walked in, handing her father her math homework. I tried to catch her eye. In our quartet, Steph was my kindred spirit: she loved to write stories like I did, and had a wild imagination, and always made me laugh. While Melanie was serious and obedient, Stephanie did a wickedly funny imitation of her dad and cracked herself up with her own jokes. We shared a tomboyish streak and a love of rock and roll. At orchestra parties, we compared our favorite musicians—I knew she was currently swooning over Peter Frampton—and she got headphones so her dad wouldn't know she was listening to Bruce Springsteen instead of Bach.

She could always make her father laugh, and she would smother him with kisses without embarrassment. When she was a little girl and got too rambunctious, he would gently swat her away. But lately, the dynamic had changed. He seemed to start yelling at her before she had a chance to do anything wrong. She was sullen more often than not, and she cried more easily than ever.

Now, I waited in awkward silence while he looked over the division and multiplication problems she had worked out in pencil on a mimeographed homework sheet. Her brown hair was askew, as if she had been pulling on it while working through the calculations. She watched him concentrate on her homework, absolutely still, not meeting my eyes.

Feeling like I was intruding on a private moment, I shifted from foot to foot and averted my gaze. I busied myself by studying one of the framed photographs on a bookshelf.

There were lots of photos in the studio. Most of them were in black and white and offered a glimpse of Mr. K in younger days. One on top of the piano showed a young man in an army uniform playing the cello. A while back when I played out of tune, Mr. K banged out the proper note on the piano so furiously that the whole instrument shook and the picture fell to the floor with a crash. Mr. K picked it up and, as he was brushing it off, told me it was taken when he played with a U.S. Army string quartet in Korea.

In another of his photos he is also wearing a uniform. This one is white and double-breasted, with shiny buttons and a sharp black stripe along the collar and cuffs. In this photo, though, he is laughing. He is surrounded by a group of children, who are also wearing uniforms. On his head is a paper crown.

The picture is a glimpse of a young man who didn't yet know his future held a sick wife and crushing medical bills and rebellious teenage girls. It was taken in rural Shawneetown, Illinois, hard by the Kentucky border. I learned later that Mr. K got his first job there as a marching band director in 1954—right out of college and the Korean War—and that he helped desegregate its schools.

There wasn't much to Shawneetown back when he arrived. Families had lived there for generations. The foreigner who barely spoke English must have been an odd sight, wandering through a town whose roots dated back to 1800, almost two decades before Illinois even became a state. The area was so rural that neighboring hamlets got by with one-room schoolhouses. But Shawneetown had two schools for white kids, and "Mr. Jerry," as he was known there, was hired as band director for both.

Almost immediately, though, he started teaching students in the "Negro school" in town, too. The same impulse that always drew him toward the underdog, that stirred his passion for music celebrating freedom and rebellion against oppression, animated him there as well. "Naturally there were more objections," he would remember later, "but I remained adamant, explaining that they were necessary for the band."

He strong-armed almost every family in town to get their kids to start playing instruments; he needed all the recruits he could get. Within a couple of years, he had assembled a marching band sixty-one members strong, piling them into yellow school buses to perform and compete all over the county. He rehearsed them endlessly and trotted them out shamelessly. Broadway's *The Music Man* wouldn't open for a couple more years, but he was already a real-life Harold Hill, coaxing tunes out of his ragged crew through raw willpower, his own particular "think system." Soon they were winning competitions all over the state.

After one particularly sweet victory, in the nearby town of Metropolis, band members poured into the center of town, buying up streamers and crepe paper to decorate their two buses. They were greeted at the Shawneetown border by a fire truck and police escort, sirens wailing, kicking off a town-wide celebration.

"The students obviously love and admire him very much and their respect and admiration is mutual," reported the *Metropolis Sun-Sentinel*. The *Paducah Sun-Democrat* celebrated the win with the headline: "Shawneetown Director Is Hero of Metropolis Fest."

Mr. K found a friend in a farmer named Cedric Drone, who taught him to hunt raccoons and squirrels that they skinned and ate. When the nearby Ohio River flooded, they clambered onto Cedric's boat to hunt ducks with shotguns. Mr. K never missed one of the Drones' coon barbecue suppers, where they grilled raccoons they had hunted themselves.

The two men even owned a coon dog together, keeping K-D (its name a combination of their surname initials) at Cedric's farm. When they took the dog hunting in the woods, they'd outfit themselves in old mining hard hats with gas-powered lights on them, borrowed from an elderly coal miner and moonshine runner who lived nearby. When someone stole the dog, they went to court to lay their claim; the case made the local front page, with a photo of the hound in front of the jury box. " 'Every Dog Has His Day,' it has been said; but not every dog has his day in court as did the above pictured hunting dog," the paper reported.

Cedric would invite him to his farmhouse for dinner, and Mr. K would join him for a smoke, puffing on a pipe that he filled with cherry-flavored tobacco so pungent it would make your eyes water. "You could be a mile away and know he was at our house, it just reeked," Cedric's son, Walter, told me years later. Mr. K would stay to watch wrestling matches on the black-and-white TV, "getting so excited he'd start jumping up and down and throwing punches. He finally broke the springs in the chair. He was totally entertaining. We just used to laugh our tails off."

*   *   *

I was caught up in the photo, looking at the crisp military band uniforms and shiny snare drums, when a loud bang jolted me out of my reverie.

It was Steph, who had run out of the room after grabbing the homework sheet back from her father, slamming the door behind her. The sound reverberated in the silence of the studio. I stared at the back of the door, its paint faded and scuffed, still shuddering in its frame.

"I hate you!" I could hear her crying.

I had grown accustomed to Steph's sobbing, but this was new.

Paducah Sun-Democrat, April 14, 1957   —16-A

KING IS CROWNED—Jerry Kubchinyski, Shawneetown band director is crowned by students at Metropolis after band won first superior rating award ever given to a Shawneetown band. Band was preparing to leave Metropolis for home town and a big celebration in their honor.

"Mr. Jerry" with his marching band at his first job in Shawneetown, Illinois. "King is Crowned," says the caption, in the *Paducah Sun-Democrat*, April 14, 1957, reporting on a band competition victory.

Mr. K was the one who was supposed to be angry, and Stephanie was the one who was supposed to take it. I waited for him to tear out of his chair. I figured he'd be out the door in a split second, running after her and screaming for her to get her *keester* back here. This instant.

Instead, Mr. K turned back to me. His face was immobile. He said nothing. Then, with one finger, he began banging out a note on the piano. "E flat E flat E flat E flat," he sang to the pitch.

"Again," he said.

As I started my scale one more time, I could hear him sigh.

The end of junior high couldn't come soon enough. I was a triple threat of thick glasses, bad hair, and good grades. Compounding the indignity, I had just gotten braces on when everybody else was getting theirs off, at a time when the other girls at school were already starting to get their Sweet Sixteen nose jobs.

Salvation came from an unexpected quarter.

"Good news," Mr. K said when I showed up for my lesson one Tuesday evening. As usual, he was sitting at the piano in his cramped studio, a ratty wool cardigan sweater pulled over that day's dress shirt and suit pants, a cup of tea in its china saucer in one hand.

"I haf spoken to Paul Doktor, and he weel take you as a private student."

Paul Doktor, world-famous violist, whose penciled autograph was carefully preserved between plastic sheets in the green photo album in my bedroom?

"Really? He really said so?!" I didn't even bother to cover my huge metallic grin with my hand.

"I haf taught you as much as I can," Mr. K said solemnly, setting down his teacup and turning from his piano to face me. "Eet eez time for you to move on."

I was too excited to notice the hint of melancholy in his voice.

I suppose I should have felt a twinge of regret about leaving my teacher. I had spent almost half my life being tutored by him. Listening to him, being pushed and prodded by him, coming weekly to his studio. Could I even imagine what it would be like to suddenly stop? Could I imagine what it would be like not to spend each Tuesday night at a private lesson before quartet rehearsal? Looking back, I feel a pang of guilt for taking and taking all he had to offer, and then running off to the fancier teacher the moment I had the opportunity.

I'd like to think all those thoughts flooded through my brain right then. But that wouldn't be honest. I was too excited about Paul Doktor to think about Mr. K at all.

Nor did I appreciate the novelty of the situation: the best teachers usually don't send their best students elsewhere. And Paul Doktor wasn't just any teacher. He was one of the great violists of the century. Like Mr. K, he had come to the United States after the war, but unlike Mr. K, he was born into music royalty. The son of a renowned Viennese violinist, Mr. Doktor was courtly and impeccably mannered, with an elegant Austrian accent and a gracious air that evoked the salons of Vienna and the opera houses of Europe. When he wasn't gracing a stage somewhere, he was teaching at Juilliard and the Mannes College of Music in Manhattan. Mr. K had met him through musician friends and convinced him to spend a week each August giving master classes to the sweaty adolescents at his ASTA conference.

"Thank you thank you thank you!" I spun around, giddy. I couldn't believe my good fortune, and I was unexpectedly flooded with gratitude for the man who made it happen. Forgetting for a moment how much Mr. K intimidated me, I threw my arms around him.

For the first time, I realized with surprise that my larger-than-life teacher was shorter than me.

*   *   *

My viola lessons with Paul Doktor brought an unexpected benefit. Every other Saturday, my parents drove up the New Jersey Turnpike and through the Lincoln Tunnel to take me to his apartment on the Upper West Side of Manhattan. We would emerge from the tunnel promptly at eleven A.M., and I would see the same over-the-hill prostitute on the corner of West Forty-Second Street, in hot pants and high heels, with long bottle-blond hair that you could just tell was covering up her natural gray. For some reason, the senior citizen hooker always made me teary, as did the stooped old ladies in black making their way slowly along the sidewalk, gripping a cane in one hand and a half-empty plastic bag of cereal and cat food in the other. The shuffling old women reminded me of the patients I visited in the hospital with Mr. K. I wished I could hop out of the car to talk with them.

Mr. Doktor gave me two-hour-long lessons in his living room overlooking Broadway, where the streets were alive with *abuelas* yelling at children in Spanish. While he taught, my parents sat doing crossword puzzles on his couch. At each lesson, I popped a fresh cassette into my portable tape recorder, so I would be able to listen to his instructions again later when I practiced.

When we were finished, my dad would say, "Let's have an adventure!" and off we would go, usually to a fancy restaurant, where the lunch specials were affordable. I loved those afternoons, taste-testing the cheesecake at Maxwell's Plum with its glamorous mirrored walls and ferns, or twisting pasta on my fork at Patsy's Italian Restaurant with its signed photos of Frank Sinatra. Sometimes we stopped at the Frick Collection before we went home, or splurged on twofers for a Broadway show or on a backstage tour at Lincoln Center.

Soon after I started lessons with Mr. Doktor, I was named

principal violist of All-State Orchestra. First in the state! Melanie was concertmaster of the orchestra again, of course. It was a record year for Mr. K, with ten East Brunswick kids in All-State Orchestra and two of us leading the string sections. Half of us scored well enough to be chosen for All-Eastern Orchestra, which pulled together the top high school musicians in a dozen states up and down the coast.

It was around then that my braces came off. Then I figured out how to stick contact lenses in my eyes. In a happy confluence of events, big '80s hair was making its first appearance, a fortunate development for my out-of-control frizz. I was still an honors-class music nerd, but my social life improved.

That summer, I picked up a job as a camp counselor at the local swim club. The club was dominated by a large, L-shaped pool, which was surrounded on both sides by grass that was crushed into unappealingly scratchy turf. Nearby, the alarmingly warm kiddie pool was hidden behind a brown wood fence. A few tired paddleball and tennis courts sprouted from the crab grass out back.

Nate, the middle-aged guy who ran the snack bar and should have known better, threw a party at his house for the counselors one night. I lost count of the Seven-and-Sevens I downed during the barbecue. I don't remember much after that. I'm told that the other teenage counselors threw me into the pool, fully clothed, to sober me up, then had to dive in to save me when I sank to the bottom. The water-sports counselor drove me home, and I puked all over her father's brand-new car on the way there.

"You've learned your lesson," my mother said when I stumbled through the door, caked in vomit. She undressed me and threw me into the shower. Ronni took out my contact lenses. I fell into bed. My mother woke me up a few hours later to go back to work.

"Rise and shine," she said cheerfully as I struggled to sit up, my face as green as my shag carpet and my head about to explode. She ticked off brisk instructions: Get to work early. Stay at work late. Be cheerful no matter what. I got her point: Suck it up.

"I don't need to punish you," she said, taking an appraising look at the dehydrated, nauseated, Kermit-colored creature before her. "You're doing it to yourself."

My mother was right. I never again got falling-down drunk. I joined the school newspaper and the literary magazine. I did all my schoolwork as soon as I got home, the better to carve out a couple of hours to practice before rehearsals. But I did stay out past curfew on occasion. Once, my mother spent a couple of frantic hours on the phone in the middle of the night, prying an unlisted phone number out of a telephone operator as she tried to track me down at an unchaperoned house party.

I thought my parents were way too strict, but I did find one loophole. I was allowed to push the rules—stay out extra late, or take the bus into New York City—as long as I was with a Responsible Boy. A Responsible Boy was defined as one they trusted, which was further defined as somebody with good grades who played the violin. My orchestra friends Michael and Paul became my constant companions. With Michael I went to see Queen and Yes in Madison Square Garden. With Paul I got to go to a midnight showing of *The Rocky Horror Picture Show*, where the marijuana smoke was so thick that I almost blacked out after that first scene with the giant singing lips.

The orchestra boys were just friends; my crush was on a Camaro-driving upperclassman who dreamed of becoming a diesel mechanic and had no idea of my existence. Still, I was annoyed when Michael started dating Melanie and had less time to spend with me. "I don't like that girl," I wrote in my diary.

In a creative writing class at school that fall, our assignment was to write new lyrics to a familiar tune. I chose "Hava Nagila"—the song you dance the hora to at weddings and bar mitzvahs—and renamed it "The Jewish Mother's Song." Here's how it went:

Straight A's, They told me, Straight A's,
They told me, Straight A's, They told me
That's what you should get!
Good grades, my child
No run-ning wild
Stay sweet and mild
You're not eighteen yet!
Show up the Goldberg's son
You can be number one!
Don't shlump, now eat your food
Chicken soup is good for you!
Shmatas will never do
I only want nice clothes for you
Find yourself a Jewish boy
Who plans to be a doctor.
Go! Find!
GO AND FIND A
Jewish boy with lots of money
Faithful, sweet, and calls you honey
He won't beat you
or act funny
And who will be—absolutely!—
The perfect son-in-law!

Melanie and Miriam weren't impressed with my expanding social life. One day, I showed up for our weekly quartet practice, now held during school hours, to find I'd been replaced by another violist.

Miriam and Melanie "told Mr. K that I smoked cigarettes and pot!!" I wrote in my diary with great indignation.

But there was one person at school who took my side, who believed I was being unfairly maligned and had faith that my inner common sense would prevail. I never would have expected it. One person had my back, no matter what.

"Mr. K wouldn't believe them," I wrote.

After a few weeks of exile, I was back in the quartet.

MELANIE

Quartet without Joanne just isn't the same. For a few weeks, we get other players to fill in for her. They're talented, but something is missing.

It's true that Joanne is different from the rest of us. My life revolves around the orchestra. All my friends are musicians. Even though there are almost eight hundred students in our grade, to me there may as well be just a few dozen. Joanne, on the other hand, has friends beyond the music room. At lunch, she sits with kids I don't know in the cafeteria, some of whom head out afterward to the smokers' patio. She goes to parties that I'm not invited to. I did go to a keg party once, but only because my dad, with his limited command of English, thought it was a "cake" party.

I can't help but feel funny when Joanne goes to rock concerts in New York City with my boyfriend, Michael; concerts given by bands I've never heard of that I wouldn't even dream of asking for permission to attend because I know what the answer would be. They both say they're just friends, and I'm pretty sure she's not interested in stealing him. Not that she couldn't if she wanted to—she's way cuter and cooler and smarter than I am. But I get the feeling that Joanne is looking for something more than he, or any other mere high school boy, has to offer.

It doesn't take long to realize, though, that none of that really matters: the issues dividing us are trivial compared with the ties that unite us. They go beyond our inside jokes, and surviving my dad's yelling, and the sheer amount of time we've spent sweating over tricky passages. Creating music is one of the most intimate experiences that people can share, and because we started so young, at such a formative time in our development, we couldn't help but bond as we grew. Our quartet's chemistry is what makes it all work, like the transformation that occurs when oxygen and hydrogen combine to make water, and we've come too far to let petty differences break us apart. I'm relieved when Joanne comes back to where she belongs.

The day I get my SAT scores back, a tiny doubt that has been flickering unnoticed in the back of my brain flares up suddenly like a struck match.

I am excused from school that afternoon, missing gym class so that I can get in extra practice time. Standing in the living room, holding my test scores in one hand and my violin in the other, I consider my future. There has never been any question in my house that I will major in music education at a music college and become a music teacher, just like my parents. I have never thought that I could, or would want to, do anything else. I've been training to be a music teacher almost my entire life.

But looking from the SAT scores to my violin and back again, it occurs to me that my future doesn't have to be preordained. The test scores have come back well enough to qualify me as a National Merit Scholarship semifinalist. I could, if I really want to, think about some other kind of path.

What would I be, if I could be anything in the world? What do I really want to do for the rest of my life?

I look out the big window of our living room, focusing on some faraway horizon, not noticing the cracked driveway that always needs repair or my father's garden, which he tends so aggressively that it threatens to take over the whole front lawn. Around me is the silence of a suburban weekday afternoon. Steph and my dad are still at school, my mom in the hospital.

Certainly, I love the violin. But I love reading and writing, too. I've devoured everything on my mother's old bookshelf, from *Valley of the Dolls* to *Great Expectations*, and lately I'm immersed in the red leather-bound copy of *The Lord of the Rings* that Michael gave me for my birthday. My favorite class is biology. The best part of the school day is while I'm in biology lab, wearing safety glasses, dissecting a frog or examining an amoeba pinned between two glass slides under a microscope.

How do I know that music is for me when I have never been allowed to try anything else? Did I ever even choose music, or did my parents choose music for me?

That is one question I know the answer to. My parents chose, not me.

I was so young when their decision was made. I just walked the path as it spread out before me. Now, it seems too late to turn back.

If I go to music school, I think, swinging my bow absentmindedly from my pinky, I know I will never again use a microscope or see the inside of a lab. It will cut me off from that. Forever.

My father no doubt will be furious if I bring up the subject. Nothing arouses his contempt more than the expression "He eez steel finding himself," which he delivers with a mocking sneer and an eye roll. Back where he came from, the Communists decided who would be allowed to pursue what careers. There was no such thing as "finding yourself." I know how grateful he is to have come to America, where he can follow his passions and make his own dreams come true.

But what about people who aren't as sure of their dreams? He has little respect for those who don't have the "guts" to be certain, the way he was. He doesn't have patience for kids who are confused by the variety of choices, who resist the deep, difficult work of becoming excellent in favor of "flitting from thing to thing, a jack-of-all-trades and a master of none!" My dad never mentions the aspirations of his own that he may have abandoned in pursuit of his career, though he used to write poetry as a young man and perhaps would have been a writer himself. I only know that he is driven, focused, and single-minded. His goal: to be the best music teacher it is possible to be.

Later, I muster my courage, expecting a confrontation.

"Daddy? How come I can only apply to music schools?" I take a breath. His face is impossible to read, so I rush on.

"Is there any way I can still take some other classes, like science, even if I major in music ed? It just doesn't feel right, that I never picked this for myself. You started me on violin when I was too little to know what other choices there were. I feel like I'm always going to wonder if music was the best thing for me to do. I like other things, too, maybe even better than I like music . . ."

I trail off, afraid of my dad's reaction. I have already said too much. I wait for him to fly off into one of his rages where he yells about what an "ungrate!" I am.

Instead, he regards me sympathetically.

"Look, sis. You were talented from the start, extremely talented. I've seen enough kids over the years to know what I'm talking about. Maybe you would haf been good at something else, but to become excellent on the violin you had to haf discipline, you had to put een the time, you needed to be focused. You weel never truly know what other things you might haf been good at. But we do know that you are good at violin."

He pauses. I may be having a moment of doubt. But he speaks with absolute certainty.

"You weel thank me one day."

12

Yesterday

JOANNE

In high school, I started to suspect there was a method to Mr. K's concertizing madness. One year, he hauled the high school orchestra all the way to West Virginia University, a twelve-hour bus ride, to perform for an audience that included prominent music professors.

On the way there, Stephanie took out her violin on the bus and entertained us with TV theme songs—*The Love Boat*, *The Brady Bunch*, whatever we called out to her, she nailed it. At a rest stop somewhere in rural Pennsylvania, I slid into a faux-leather booth at Bob's Big Boy next to Melanie and Miriam. Through the big plate-glass window, we could see Jonathan, the class brain, picking at the ground with a tool he pulled from his pocket, searching for fossils.

"Where do you think you'll go to college?" Melanie asked me.

"Don't rush me!" I laughed.

Ever since our quartet had gotten back together again, I couldn't help noticing a difference in our playing. We blended better than we had before, the music flowing a little more easily. Maybe it was because we were progressing as musicians, but more likely, we were growing up. College was getting closer, our shared childhood a little further away. The differences that had grown between Melanie and Miriam and me seemed suddenly childish and long ago.

In West Virginia, our quartet would be performing a piece that composer Philip Gordon had written especially for us, with each one of our personalities and abilities in mind. We knew we wouldn't be playing together much longer. I gazed out the window at Jonathan in the parking lot, then looked from Melanie to Miriam across the table littered with hamburger scraps and a congealing side order of greasy fries.

"Time to go," Mr. K ordered from the front of the room.

I took a last sip of my Coca-Cola and then, with a wink toward Miriam, poured the rest into her glass of milk. She upended a bottle of ketchup and conked it on the bottom until it spurted into the mix. Melanie picked up the salt and pepper shakers to add the finishing touch. Then we sat back to admire our masterpiece: a perfectly gross concoction, just like we used to make as little girls.

The West Virginia performance went well, so well that four orchestra members were awarded music scholarships there. Miriam was one of them, and so was our cellist friend, John Stine.

Mr. K, it turned out, had quietly been helping to arrange college music scholarships for his students for years. He also gave lessons to some of his students for free. Miriam told me about what she laughingly called the every-other-Simon rule—she and all six of her siblings studied privately with Mr. K, but he only charged for half of them.

Now Mr. K was focusing his attention on recruiting the next generation of students. He had lots of help, including from a new student teacher: Miss Lipman. Michele was following in his footsteps, studying music education while playing violin as concertmaster of the Rutgers Symphony Orchestra. Another of our teachers was Darlene Morrow Brandt; the violinist whom Mr. K had yelled at twenty years earlier for crying onstage was now one of his most trusted colleagues.

Mr. K looked for every angle, and every gimmick, to fill the pipeline with prospective new recruits. That's why one day he handed Donald Meyers a red costume. We're playing *Orpheus in the Underworld,* he said. We need a devil.

Don, a few years behind me, was one of the most impossible students Mr. K had ever had. His left thumb was always creeping up in an ungainly way alongside the neck of his violin. It drove Mr. K nuts. "I weel cut thumb off and feed eet to cheekens!" Mr. K would warn him. Don loved the violin madly anyway.

Don's role was perfect for him. Jacques Offenbach's *Orpheus in the Underworld*—an operetta best known for giving the world the cancan—was a crowd favorite, especially for little kids. The piece starts slowly before picking up steam. Just as it winds up to the big cancan moment, Don as the devil ran onto the stage, pushing Mr. K off the podium. With theatrical melodrama worthy of an old vaudeville act, the two of them went at it in front of the audience, pushing and shoving, while the orchestra threw itself into an increasingly maniacal rendition of the dance, until Mr. K finally triumphed as the piece rushed to its climax.

Don Meyers never did make it beyond the back of the second violin section as a musician. But at the end of our orchestra concert that day, Mr. K ushered him to the front of the stage to take his solo bow.

* * *

The truth is, there weren't too many stunts Mr. K wouldn't try, if it would win him just one more young student. He was especially eager to recruit boys. When he took the high school orchestra to elementary schools, he always called on the two tallest, most handsome violinists to perform a duet. "Now eef any of you boys in the audience steel think violin eez for sissies," he would say when they finished, "these two young men weel be happy to discuss weeth you afterward on the playground. Eef you dare."

The high school boys, the braver ones, were the ones who pulled pranks on Mr. K. Before each concert, they would hide a *Playboy* magazine centerfold in his music. When he was in a good mood, he would chuckle and give the boys an appreciative wink. But once, when his mood was sour, the boys mistakenly slipped the centerfold into the middle of the most difficult piece. As Mr. K turned the page mid-symphony, his eyes widened, his face contorted with rage, and he furiously tore the centerfold out of his music with a grand sweep of his arm. As the orchestra played on, Playmate of the Year Miss 1978 fluttered slowly over the front rows of the startled audience.

Senior year, when auditions for regional orchestra rolled around, Mr. K won the trifecta. Melanie made concertmaster of the orchestra for the fourth year in a row. Miriam was named principal cellist. I was principal violist. Stephanie, in her first year of eligibility, was a first violinist. In all, twenty-three East Brunswick students made the cut. Perhaps it wasn't surprising when the Music Teachers' Association announced its choice to conduct the orchestra: Mr. K.

For our final concert, the high school orchestra chipped in to buy

Mr. K a present: a new podium. It was fresh and clean and sturdy, with not a scuff on it. It had a brass plaque with his name engraved on the side. Best of all, it had carpeting on top to muffle the stomping we'd been listening to for the past ten years. He thanked us politely but stopped using it as soon as he could. He preferred the worn, old, hollow wooden box—the one on which I had first seen him as a kindergartener—where his footfalls echoed out as loud as gunshots.

As we barreled toward graduation, Mr. K offered to help me make an audition tape for college applications. Walking into his studio for the recording session, I was struck by how small and dark it was. I hadn't played for him in this room for a long time now. It seemed a lifetime ago that I had moved on to lessons with Paul Doktor at his apartment in Manhattan, with its airy high-ceilinged living room and two walls of windows looking out over Broadway.

Perhaps noticing my unease, Mr. K asked me about my thoughts on college.

I told him about my visits to campuses, about the schools I liked most. I told him I wanted to be a journalist. Then I confessed that I narrowed down my college list based not on journalism courses but on music programs. I had talked it over with my parents. We figured that any of the places we visited would offer a fine education—but only a few would also offer the chance to play with a great student orchestra.

"I love music. That's why I could never do it for a living," I said. "It would ruin it for me."

Mr. K nodded. He understood. Then he turned to the tape machine, his finger hovering over the "record" button, signaling the conversation was over.

"Again," he said.

He spent hours with me making that tape. I think I thanked him when he was done, but I don't remember. When it came time to get a recommendation letter for college, I didn't ask him. I figured colleges would rather hear from somebody important. I asked Paul Doktor instead.

One of the last times the quartet performed together was during our senior year of high school. There was a terrible car crash that weekend, just around the corner from my house. Two classmates died in the wreck.

Mr. K called us together afterward to tell us we would be performing at the funeral of one of the boys, a popular athlete. We gathered in the small high school classroom Mr. K used for chamber music rehearsals. He handed us the music selection: the Beatles' song "Yesterday." The boy's little sister was a beginner violinist, Mr. K explained. "He loved to listen to her play." Our quartet would symbolize that devotion.

The funeral was during a school day. Melanie, Miriam, and I drove to the church in silence, with our teacher Darlene Brandt at the wheel of her car. She was going to fill in for Stephanie on second violin, since Steph was still in junior high school on the other side of town.

Inside the church, we set up in the balcony and waited for our cue. From our perch, we looked down on an unimaginable sight: a casket being carried by teenage pallbearers wearing their varsity jackets buttoned up to the neck. In the front of the church sat the boy's sister, a beautiful little blond girl. At one point she turned around. She glanced up at us in the balcony. I could see she was looking straight into Melanie's eyes.

None of us spoke. When it was time to play, we gently eased into the bittersweet strains of the song, trading melody and harmony, one to the other. There's a bond created by musicians who play together. It was clear to us then that the bond wasn't something that comes and goes or depends on your mood. It stays with you and gets stronger with time; the more you test it and try it and push it, the more you punish it even, the more powerful it becomes. We played the song, and, without exchanging a word, we mourned together.

PART IV

Neither a lofty degree of intelligence nor imagination nor both together go to the making of genius. Love, love, love, that is the soul of genius.

—WOLFGANG AMADEUS MOZART

13

The Conservatory

MELANIE

My dad narrows down my college choices for me. I am only allowed to apply to music schools and only those with a music education program, so that I can become a teacher. That eliminates Juilliard and the Curtis Institute of Music. Indiana University, with its superb music department, is too far away. The Manhattan School of Music is in New York City, according to my father a "wolfish" place where I might not survive.

After much thought, my dad settles on the Eastman School of Music in Rochester, New York, where he knows a violin teacher, and the New England Conservatory in Boston. When I am accepted into both, we choose New England because it offers a larger scholarship.

My first day, Dad and Steph help me move into the eight-story dorm. We wait for the ancient elevator with a line of other families stretching almost out the door to Gainsborough Street. Milk crates overflow with sheet music, and garbage bags are crammed almost to bursting with bedding and clothes, all stacked high around tuba and cello cases, with barely enough room for the people squeezed in between. The elevators groan in protest as the doors laboriously slide shut. After we finally make it up to the top floor and unpack, I hug my dad and Steph good-bye near the stairs.

As they head down on foot, the stairwell is deserted and silent. Then Steph's voice pierces the air.

"Daddy? Are you crying?"

If you listen hard, you can hear the faintest sound of sobbing.

"Just a little. Okay?" comes my father's reply.

My dad may be the one crying, but I am the one who is worried. I have been running our house for four years. Before I leave for school, I go over the checklist with Steph: cooking, cleaning, laundry. I show her how to bake chicken with lots of garlic, the way my dad likes it. His roast beef must be so well done that it's almost burned. No pink! Mashed potatoes have to come from a box: my dad, having discovered American convenience foods, thinks potato buds are like a small miracle from God.

I am afraid that with those two tempers on the loose in the house, their battles will get out of control. I can imagine Steph after a screaming match, flying out the door and slamming it so hard behind her that the windowpanes rattle. I can see my dad, alone in his studio late at night, after his last student has left, eating tuna fish from the can. Without me there to mediate, who knows what will happen?

My mom, still in the hospital, isn't able to help. After I head off to college, she moves into a single room. It has the heavy air of permanence, rather than the transience of the room she shared with two rotating patients. She converts the shower stall into a closet for the dresses she continues to buy; a seamstress splits each one straight down the back so she can slip them on while in her wheelchair. The new room is a tangible manifestation of the realization we all share but that none of us speak aloud: My mother isn't coming home. She will never live in her own house again.

At school, worried about my dad and Steph, I call home as frequently as I can. On Saturdays, I commandeer the lobby pay phone next to the cafeteria, watching the swarms of waist-high conservatory prep students carrying tiny violins, parents in tow. The little kids, some of them barely out of preschool, remind me of Steph and me, in what seems like a lifetime ago.

"How's it going at home?" I ask anxiously, when Steph answers the phone.

Surprisingly, things aren't as bad as I feared. In my absence, it seems, a truce of sorts is forming.

"Not bad," she answers.

"Are you guys eating cereal for dinner every night?" I ask.

"Nope." In fact, Steph tells me proudly, she tried a new recipe for egg-drop soup for dinner just the other night.

"How was it?"

"Awful."

Steph giggles as she tells me how my dad choked it down anyway and tried his hardest to be diplomatic about it. "He ate most of it," Steph tells me. "Then he said, 'Eeet's good . . . buuut let's not haf eet again for a looooong time.'"

From a distance, I can see more clearly that the two of them—my father and sister—are far more like each other than either one is like me: short, dark, with fierce tempers. Passionate. Emotional. "Steph's eyes were soulful from the moment she was born," my dad's old student Darlene Brandt always says.

For my dad's birthday, Steph writes him a poem:

> *The father looked at his daughter*
> *But he saw only rebellion in her gaze*
> *Not recognizing it as the same fire which brimmed in his eyes*
> *But insolence, which masked their light...*
> *So alike—so unyielding*
> *Emotional mirrors staring at each other*
> *Yet not recognizing the images reflecting back*

More than twenty-five years later, looking through my dad's papers, I will find that poem carefully packed in a shoebox and tied with a frayed brown string. Beneath the poem lies a stack of all the cards and pictures, in bright crayon with bits of yarn and felt attached, that Steph had made for him since she was a little girl.

"Don't play like a music *educator*!" My chamber music coach, Benjamin Zander, spits out the words as we rehearse Schumann's Piano Quintet. "Play like a violinist!"

At the New England Conservatory, I quickly learn that life is all about performance, not academics. My double major in music education along with violin performance mostly earns me grief. Some of the students don't know the school even *has* a music education department. My violin teacher, Eric Rosenblith, thinks there must be some mistake.

"My dear, my paperwork has you down as an education major? You'll have to go see the registrar and correct this..." Shuffling through a sheaf of forms, Mr. Rosenblith peers at me over his glasses.

I'm unpacking my violin in his big, sparsely furnished studio for our first lesson.

"No, that's right. A double major, actually, education and performance." Nervously, I wipe my sweaty palms on my pale pink skirt. I'm eager to get started and determined to make a good first impression. I am also clueless about the implications of what I have just said.

As head of the string department, Mr. Rosenblith can have his pick of any student at the school, and places in his violin studio are highly coveted. Why should he squander one of them on someone who might end up conducting a high school band someday?

In my naïveté, I don't realize then what a disregard for his stature I have just betrayed.

"But, my dear, may I ask why?"

I answer honestly. "My father wants me to. I mean, I want to, too."

He regards me with curiosity.

Nervously, I plow ahead.

"He's a teacher, the head of a music department actually. I'm going to be like him, I hope, do what he does someday. Also, he thinks it's important to have a degree that will help me get a job when I graduate."

My dad's words still resonate in my head. He has ranted countless times, how "keeds grahduate from conservatory weeth useless degree, like piece of toilet paper, that qualifies them to do ahbsolutely nothing!" But I don't think Mr. Rosenblith would want to hear that part.

He is silent, so I go on. "But I also love playing, I want to see if I can get really good . . ." I trail off.

Mr. Rosenblith nods and changes the subject.

We talk for a long while. He asks about my family, former teachers, pieces I know and would like to know, practice routines. When he finds out that I usually practice about two hours a day, Mr. Rosenblith is taken aback.

"I am surprised that you got this good on so little practicing. Things are different here, and that's what concerns me about your schedule. How are you going to find the time to practice your thirty-five to forty hours per week?"

Forty hours a week? Is he serious?

"You will have to take so many classes..." He draws out that last word with obvious distaste. "I would hate to have to drop you as a student..."

I hastily wipe away the tears brimming in my eyes. "I'll practice, I'll work hard, I promise! I can do it, please just give me a chance." I'm confused. I have spent my entire life surrounded by music, and in my world, music teachers are admired, even revered. It never occurred to me that there could be a stigma attached to pursuing a music education degree.

Mr. Rosenblith isn't the only one who is puzzled. I notice conductors, coaches, and teachers looking at me quizzically. Sometimes they pull me aside, asking, "Why would you want to be an *education* major?" I explain that I want to be a teacher, and they walk away baffled, shaking their heads.

I don't get it. They're teachers, aren't they? Don't they value teaching? At my sophomore violin performance evaluation, one of the faculty members writes a comment: "Excellent talent. Don't waste it!"

Juggling both majors leaves no time for anything other than rehearsals, lessons, coaching sessions, and classes. I get good grades, though I know better than to advertise this to Mr. Rosenblith. "If you are getting good grades it means you are working too hard in your classes and not hard enough on your violin. Can't you get away with a gentleman's C?" he queries one of my fellow students in our weekly master class after "too much studying" is given as an excuse for a poor performance. To me it is unthinkable not to do whatever classwork is required. Besides, I can't imagine trying to explain a C to my father.

Somewhat to my surprise, it turns out that I love the extra practice time. The hours melt away as I find myself utterly absorbed in the regimen Mr. Rosenblith assigns. My dad is right: hard work really does lead to happiness. Actually, for me right now, hard work *is* happiness. And even though he is no longer there every day to tell me to practice or to say "discipline yourself," I realize that somewhere along the way my father's words have become a part of me. In return for my efforts, Mr. Rosenblith showers me with praise, affection, and extra lessons, all of which I eagerly accept.

Gradually, teachers begin to overlook my odd penchant for flute classes and choral conducting seminars, and to consider me a "real" violinist, though I never make it into the group that I mentally dub "the elite string players." They are the principals in the orchestras, the concerto competition winners, the most sought-after chamber music partners. During their breaks they congregate in the cafeteria, smoking cigarettes and sipping black coffee while comparing opinions about Beethoven's metronome markings. They ignore me as I trudge by with a stack of textbooks, a clarinet under my arm, and a violin strapped to my back, and I can't help feeling envious. They are the confident ones, the ones who never doubt that they'll make it in the performance world, the ones who don't worry about having a teaching degree so they can be sure to have a job someday.

The workload is crushing, but I don't consider abandoning the music education degree. I never think about being anything other than a music teacher, just like my father. That's what I'm meant to do . . . isn't it?

With one semester to go, I finally reach the home stretch. Almost there. The final requirement for my education degree is student teaching in a classroom. Just before I start, I drop by the apartment of a friend, another music ed major who is already deep into his student-teaching gig.

He's at the kitchen table, poring over his lesson plan. That is the moment it strikes me, the realization that for an entire semester I will be working at a school all day and planning at night. How will I find forty extra hours a week to practice the violin? So far, I've managed through a combination of long hours, skipped meals, caffeine, and no sleep, but I'm about to run up against the finite number of hours in a day. It will be mathematically impossible.

Can I get by for the next five months without enough time to practice? Can I imagine not playing the violin?

Maybe I can do it, I think.

No, I can't *do it! I can't give up playing my violin for a whole semester!*

My decision is made. Just one step away from getting my music education degree, I drop out of the program. I will graduate with a single major: performance.

Who knows if I can really make it as a performer? The vast majority of conservatory graduates don't ever land jobs with major symphony orchestras, and many don't make a living in music at all. But I am determined to give it my all to find out.

The next step is telling my dad.

I brace myself for recriminations. I rehearse in my head how I will explain.

"I love kids...I love music...I love teaching..." I tell him over Thanksgiving break. "But it turns out that I love playing most of all." I have already been accepted into New England Conservatory's graduate school performance program.

"I wish you'd get your teaching degree," he says regretfully. But then he smiles. "I understand about the playing. I guess all those years of forcing you to practice paid off."

Together, we start to believe, or at least to hope, that my violin will take me where I want to go.

14

The Gig

JOANNE

When I landed on campus freshman year of college, I knew where I wanted to go. I knew I wanted to become a journalist. Unfortunately, I knew very little else.

My first day of class at Yale, I watched classmates reciting—by heart, in the original Middle English—the prologue to Geoffrey Chaucer's *The Canterbury Tales*, a book I hadn't heard of. Everybody in beginner French already spoke fluently. The psychology professor yelled at me for nodding off, as it turned out from a raging case of mononucleosis, during his lecture on B. F. Skinner.

The only subject for which I felt well prepared was viola. I qualified for graduate-level lessons at the Yale School of Music with another one of my viola heroes, Raphael Hillyer. Mr. Hillyer was a formidable presence, the founding violist of the renowned Juilliard String Quartet. His demeanor was intense and his pedigree daunting: Curtis Institute, Dartmouth, graduate studies at Harvard, where he gave recitals with his friend and classmate Leonard Bernstein. When I showed up with a sky-high fever from the mononucleosis and dragged through my lesson, Mr. Hillyer had no sympathy.

"I suggest you warm up before you arrive," he said drily, not inviting further comment. I suspect he wasn't interested in hearing about my fever convulsions the night before.

Between practicing and symphony rehearsals, I spent more time on music than on the school newspaper. Still, there was an addictive pleasure to sitting in the musty *Yale Daily News* offices, in a paneled room hung with formal portraits of the all-male editorial boards of decades past, tapping out stories late at night on a typewriter. I would stay until dawn, gorging on other people's leftover cold pizza and then heading in to the composing room. There, the pages were laid out on easels, and the editors literally cut out pieces of articles that needed to be fixed using razor blades, then pasted the new, corrected versions on top.

After my *Yale Daily* articles were put to bed—as my mother insisted, I always asked a Responsible Boy to walk me back safely to the dorm, in this case a Responsible Boy being anyone still standing at five A.M.—I would grab a few hours of sleep before class. Then in the afternoon, I would carve out time to practice, turning down the Crosby, Stills, Nash & Young that my roommate Carol and I usually played on the stereo while we studied.

My goal in college was to get a summer internship at the *Wall Street Journal*. My father had read that paper every day since before I was born. It landed on our driveway at home while it was still dark out each morning. He loved the excitement of the business world; he always said that it was "an adventure." As a kid, I never looked at it. But the summer after freshman year, I won a magazine internship in New York City and commuted on the bus every day with my dad. Out of boredom and desperation one morning, I picked up his newspaper. I was transfixed: the front page had the best writing I had ever read.

That first magazine internship had been humbling. At my job interview, when I closed up my slit-front skirt over my knees, the interviewer barked, "If you want the job, you'll leave that open." My boss, the editor in chief, gave me assignments like buying presents for his wife. Still, I managed to report and write several pieces. That was enough to get me a job the following summer as a "copy girl" at my hometown newspaper, the *Home News,* where I would run to the printing press when it started rumbling and deliver the first copies to editors in the newsroom.

An internship at the storied *Wall Street Journal* would be a long shot. But junior year, I sent my article clippings anyway. Weeks later, I was surprised and a bit terrified to learn I was a finalist, invited with other aspirants to a lunch with editors in New York. This would be my most important audition yet.

At the *Journal* office, in a conference room set up with sandwiches and cans of soda, I met the judges—a small group of editors and reporters—and was introduced to the competition: about a dozen other students, one more intimidating than the next. They had interned at fancy places like *Time* and *BusinessWeek*. They casually dropped business buzzwords into their conversations and nodded knowingly at the jargon the *Journal* reporters in the room tossed around with ease.

But looking around, I realized something. Unlike at an orchestra audition, I wouldn't be called into a closed room and asked to play scales by people with pencils and judgmental expressions. I didn't have to worry about shaky arms or cramping fingers. I didn't have to fret that my muscles might betray me. The overwhelming pressure of viola auditions, and Mr. K's years of putting me through hell, made everything else seem easier by comparison. Once that realization struck, my fear receded.

As the bureau chief gave us a tour of the newsroom, I peppered him with questions. How did the news ticker work? Why was he so interested in the story that broke during our tour, about AT&T breaking up? I worried that I was asking too much, betraying how little I knew. But a few days later, a letter arrived: I had made the cut.

That summer, I threw myself into learning how to write earnings reports, cover shareholder meetings, and pitch story ideas. One of my pieces even made the front page. I didn't have a spare moment to practice my viola.

Back at school in the fall, my *Journal* boss called to offer me a job as a bona fide reporter, starting after graduation. I was so excited that I didn't ask what the salary was.

"*Yes!*" I shouted into the phone.

"Don't you want to know how much we're paying you?" he asked.

No! I wanted to scream, before I got hold of myself and answered with what I thought was studied nonchalance: "Sure." I was too elated to pay attention to his answer.

At the *Journal*, my first front-page story as a full-time reporter wasn't about high finance: it was a first-person account of being a street musician. To report it, I paired up with my childhood orchestra friend Michael to play Bach duets all over Manhattan. We earned the most in Times Square, from tourists on matinee day. We earned the least in front of the New York Stock Exchange, where the biggest contribution was five dollars from a bewildered investment banker I had once interviewed ("Joanne Lipman! What happened?!" he asked in alarm as he rushed by).

We averaged twenty-one dollars an hour in spare change from onlookers. The piece was headlined: "Our Violist Finds the Income Better than a Reporter's."

I sent a copy of my street-musician article to Raphael Hillyer at Yale, with a note thanking him. Our relationship had been strained ever since my bout of mono, which marked me as an insufficiently serious student. But he replied with a long, beautiful letter, saying that in writing the piece, "you became a professional musician." I heard from Federal Reserve chairman Alan Greenspan, too, who later wrote wryly, "[Y]ou magically combined three subjects dear to me: the warmth of classical music performance, the kaleidoscope of humanity traveling the streets of the city, as well as the sheer joy of engaging firsthand in comparative wage analysis." My parents had seen the article, of course, and cut it out to show their friends.

But somehow in my excitement, something slipped my mind. Perhaps I was careless, or perhaps I thought it wouldn't matter to

During a summer break from college, Joanne works the July 4 shift at her first newspaper job, as a copy girl/reporter for the New Brunswick, New Jersey, *Home News*.

him. Whatever the case, it didn't occur to me to send the article or a note of thanks to Mr. K.

MELANIE

While I'm home on a school break, my dad helps me record audition tapes on the big reel-to-reel recorder in his studio. I send them out to every major symphony in the country. The first response comes quickly. I can't wait to share the news with my boyfriend, Ed, a fellow conservatory student.

"Ed! They liked my tape! Chicago liked my tape!" I am thrilled. My first try, and I've already gotten a positive response, and from the legendary Chicago Symphony Orchestra, no less. This is going to be easier than I thought.

Chicago is one of the few major symphony orchestras that doesn't require a preliminary tape. Anyone can show up to audition. But it's expensive, flying all over the country. So if you can get a thumbs-up on a tape, it means you at least stand a chance in the live audition, where 250 players often show up for a single opening.

"Really? That's great! Really? Wow! Really? When is the audition?" Ed is stunned. He knows lots of people who have taken auditions already. Often it takes years to land a job, or even to start making the finals.

"It's in a month. And they sent out a new list of excerpts. I have to get one more piece to learn." Symphonies generally require at least fifteen orchestral excerpts, most of which I have already been practicing.

"What piece?"

"A Strauss piece, *Also Sprach Zarathustra*. Is that hard? I've never heard it before."

"Sure you have. Remember *2001: A Space Odyssey*? 'Open. The.

Pod. Bay. Doors. Hal," Ed intones in a mechanical voice. "That's the theme they used in the movie, it's from that piece. I think it's pretty hard."

By the time I get hold of the music, I have run out of time. I brazenly fly to Chicago anyway, hoping the audition committee won't ask to hear it. After all, they only allocate a few minutes to each person. I've learned everything else on the list. Maybe I will get lucky.

No names and no gender-specific pronouns are used when the proctor makes his announcement as I make my way onto the stage. I'm shielded by a tall white screen, so that the audition committee— nine members of the orchestra—can't see me and I can't see them.

"Candidate number sixty-three will play the Brahms concerto."

For me, the concerto is the easy part, and I feel calm and focused. I play Brahms for about two minutes, then we move on to the excerpts. So far so good. The audition is going well. I can tell they like me because they keep asking to hear more.

"Strauss, please," comes the disembodied voice from behind the white wooden screen.

My heart sinks. *Damn! Now what do I do?* There is no way to communicate directly with the committee. To ensure fairness and anonymity, this is how it's done in the first round: no talking allowed, a carpet laid on the stage to mask the click of high-heeled shoes, a designated entrance for candidates so they will not accidentally run into the orchestra members.

The proctor places the music on the stand. I shake my head and lean toward him.

"I didn't learn that one. It wasn't on the first list!" I whisper urgently.

He looks at me, perplexed. I feel about three inches tall.

"Uh, the applicant did not learn this excerpt!" he announces loudly into the void.

Whispers, then, "Have the applicant play it anyway."

Are they kidding? There's no way I can sight-read this!

The proctor flips to the hardest section, a passage in a crazy key, so full of fast notes and markings that the page is more black than white.

I have no choice. It's fight or flight. *Okay, here goes.* I go for it. I doubt I play one correct note. It sounds so bad it would be funny, if I hadn't just blown my savings on an airline ticket.

"Try it again."

Unbelievably, the committee is giving me another chance. Maybe they really like my playing? Maybe they can't reconcile my painstakingly practiced and executed pieces with this god-awful mess? Maybe they're having a laugh at my expense?

I play the passage again. It's even worse than before.

"Thank you."

There is a painful finality to their dismissal.

My first audition is over and so is my chance to play with the Chicago Symphony. I mentally kick myself. I recall the first time I blew an audition, years ago, when I sat crying on my dad's lap. *Don't worry, Lastivko*, he told me then. *Pick yourself up and work harder next time.* He's right: I have learned my lesson. I will never be unprepared again.

I have a few hours to kill before my flight home. I go to a bar and get drunk by myself, then go shopping at Lord & Taylor, then stop to buy a Chicago pizza to bring back to Ed. When my plane lands, he's waiting at the airport with a single red rose.

Steph and my dad still clash at times, one digging in more stubbornly than the other, but Steph's passion for the violin is equally fierce. She wins a scholarship to West Virginia University, where my dad has already sent about half a dozen of his other students on music scholarships.

My dad and I drive her to school. In the dormitory, as we say good-bye, we linger. We know that this could be a final step, that Steph might drift away from us. But Steph surprises us both. Once she's on her own, almost imperceptibly at first, the ground shifts. At West Virginia, my dad isn't there for her to rebel against. Steph is finally free to be herself. She can "find herself," in the words my father so loathes.

And the person she finds is ... a lot like him.

Steph, like my dad, has a ferocious work ethic. She earns her music education degree while winning the university concerto competition. During the summers, she joins our dad to teach at his ASTA conference, coaching young string players and soaking up teaching tips. When she graduates, she is awarded a place in the same graduate performance program at the New England Conservatory that I have completed, studying with the same gifted teacher, Eric Rosenblith.

In Boston, we move into an apartment together. It is a tiny, roach-infested place on Westland Avenue, with a kitchen so small that my shirt once catches fire from the stove at my back while I stand at the sink washing dishes. I'm waiting for an audition break, hoping to get into a major symphony, while teaching and playing freelance gigs in Boston.

Steph's love for music, like my dad's, is full throttle. She has a lusty appreciation for it that is constantly reminding me of him. Writing to a friend about an advanced chamber music camp she gets into that summer, she describes her excitement:

They assigned me the Elgar Piano Quintet, 1st violin, and I had never heard of it ... [I] found a recording of it & was shitting because it's hard but so beautiful! I only have 1 week to learn this bitch part, plus 2nd fiddle Beethoven op18 #1 (the infamous "How do you like my feet?" quartet). That's not too hard. But of course my recital stuff needs to be kicking ass also ...

Meanwhile, I practice like crazy to try to win an orchestra job. I've read somewhere that playing an audition feels similar to running up six flights of stairs and standing on one leg on a rickety chair while trying to execute perfectly the most difficult passages in the violin literature. So while I practice, Steph makes noise, claps her hands, knocks into the furniture, flicks the lights, and whacks me with her purse, to see if I can keep playing no matter what. Anyone who passed by and looked in the window would have thought we were nuts.

After my first year of graduate school at the conservatory, I'm named a fellow with the Tanglewood Festival, an intensive orchestral training program in the Berkshire Mountains, where the Boston Symphony Orchestra is also in summer residence. There, early every morning, I run two miles and practice scales for an hour before the first orchestra rehearsal of the day begins at ten A.M., pausing only long enough to chug a glass of orange juice and pop a multivitamin.

All the students at Tanglewood—most of us conservatory upperclassmen or graduate students—want to get real jobs. We are all highly aware that during orchestra rehearsals, the Boston Symphony's personnel director stands just offstage and watches us, ostentatiously taking notes on a clipboard. Harry Shapiro has the ultimate power to hire subs for the orchestra and for the Boston Pops Orchestra. Everybody wants to impress Harry. As we rehearse, the students all watch him watching us, adding another dimension to the already supercharged, competitive atmosphere. The students whisper that sometimes in the spring he holds first-come, first-served unofficial auditions, if you know the right day on which to call him.

My second summer as a Tanglewood fellow, I am named one of the concertmasters of the student orchestra. Coached by Boston

Symphony and Juilliard String Quartet members, I get over some of my timidity. At a joint concert with the Boston Symphony, I sit in the front, between the symphony's concertmaster and principal second violinist. Composer Aaron Copland, in one of his last public appearances, comes to hear us perform his Symphony No. 3; during the fourth movement, which starts with the "Fanfare for the Common Man," I find myself weeping at its power and beauty and innocence. At an after-concert party at Miss Hall's School, the swanky girls' boarding school where students are housed, I muster all my courage and dance with Leonard Bernstein.

"Mr. Bernstein, playing with you has been the most amazing experience of my whole life," I shout over the stereo thumping out the music of the Pointer Sisters.

The legendary composer of *West Side Story* twists his arms to the music, his head thrown back to the beat. "Your whole life is just beginning, my dear," he shouts. "It's all still ahead of you."

Back in Boston, I get an unexpected phone call.

"Melanie. It's Harry Shapiro."

My brain freezes. I seem to have forgotten how to speak.

"Hello?"

"Um, yes. Sorry. Hi, Mr. Shapiro."

"Melanie, we have some work for you."

Mr. Shapiro needs an extra violinist, he says, to fill out the Boston Pops Esplanade Orchestra. The orchestra will spend several weeks in Boston, then tour the United States and Japan, conducted by composer John Williams.

"Let me give you the dates so you can check your schedule," he is saying.

John Williams? Star Wars' *John Williams? Check my schedule? What, is he kidding?*

The Boston Symphony Orchestra combines with the Tanglewood student orchestra for a concert. Conductor John Williams, the composer of film scores, including those for *Star Wars* and *Schindler's List*, congratulates Melanie. Also pictured, from left to right, BSO concertmaster Malcolm Lowe, principal second violinist Marylou Speaker Churchill, and violinist Rachel Goldstein, far right.

"Yes!" I say.

"The season starts in early June and runs through August."

Damn. Early June?

"Um, is it possible to miss just one weekend? I have something planned for June twentieth."

"No, it's not. I'm sorry. It's the whole summer, all or nothing."

I only hesitate for an instant.

"Yes! I'll do it!"

Now I just need to tell Ed that we'll have to reschedule our wedding.

* * *

The life of a musician is a series of auditions. After touring with the Boston Pops and exhausting my savings flying around the country to audition for other big-city orchestras, I land a one-year contract with the Pittsburgh Symphony Orchestra. Ed and I, newly married after our hastily rescheduled wedding, pack up the battered Toyota Tercel that looks like a toaster oven on wheels and move to Pittsburgh.

Our wedding had been a cheerfully no-frills gathering at a local restaurant that we paid for ourselves. My ever-practical father had offered me a choice: he would buy me a violin or pay for the wedding. I didn't have to think twice. My mother came, and Steph pulled out her violin to serenade us with Bach's Air from Orchestral Suite No. 3. Baba scowled through the ceremony and boycotted the reception, furious that I didn't get married in her Ukrainian church. My great-aunt Titka mocked my dress and makeup, then announced that her wedding gift was to buy a new dishwasher for my *father*. It didn't matter. Ed just laughed and said that anything nice anyone did for my father meant more to him than any gift to us ever could.

That spring, the Pittsburgh Symphony, under conductor Lorin Maazel, is to perform in New York City at Lincoln Center's Avery Fisher Hall, one of the great concert halls in America. It's a thrill to be playing there on tour with a major orchestra for the very first time. Before the concert, we file onstage to warm up.

"What's that?" my stand partner says, squinting into the crowd.

He's pointing to the balcony. I look up from the music for Strauss's *Don Quixote*, which we will be performing in a few minutes. Leaning over the edge of the balcony railing, a man is frantically waving a large white handkerchief.

"Look at that guy!" my stand partner laughs.

Stephanie plays Bach's Air from Orchestral Suite No. 3 at Melanie and Ed's wedding in 1987. The piece, one of Stephanie's favorites, would be played at a much more somber occasion more than a decade later.

The handkerchief waver is flapping so energetically and leaning so far forward he looks like he might fall right off and plunge into the expensive seats below.

I take a closer look.

It's my dad.

There he stands, pressed up against the balcony railing, his handkerchief unfurled. He is waving that thing like crazy, putting his whole body into the effort. He looks like a *mahnyiak*, as he might say. I'm overcome with the urge to either jump up and wave back to him or dive under my chair in embarrassment.

Instead, I wave my bow surreptitiously a bit in acknowledgment, trying to suppress a smile. My dad sits back in his seat, content that I know he is there. Across the darkened space of Avery Fisher Hall, I can see his face, lighting up his spot on the balcony just as sure as if he were plugged into an electric socket. He's pointing me out to everyone in the seats around him.

"Mel, it's unbelievable! People are leaving notes under my windshield wipers in the grocery store parking lot: 'Do you have room for one more student?'"

After Steph earned her graduate degree, she took a position teaching violin on Martha's Vineyard, the Massachusetts vacation haven seven miles out at sea. During our frequent phone calls, Steph gives me vivid updates about her new life. "I had to order more violins from the mainland, it's been crazy!" she says. "*Everyone* wants to play. I'm not sure how I'm going to handle them all by myself."

Steph has developed into an accomplished violinist. But like my dad, she has discovered her true passion is for teaching. Years earlier, he had told a newspaper reporter, "I believe teaching is a profession all its own. It's no place for a frustrated maestro." Teaching, for him, isn't a fallback position. It's a calling. And Steph has heard the call, too.

As a teacher, Steph is as gentle and soft-spoken as my father is loud and intimidating. But her approach to the fundamentals is the same. Like him, she assigns her students "Twinkle, Twinkle, Little Star" and "Lightly Row," but then she mixes in her own transcriptions of Madonna and Bruce Springsteen songs. She rewards her students with stickers, stars, fuzzy-bear pencil toppers, and cookies and milk. Sometimes she allows them to play with one of her pet birds perched on their shoulders.

As well suited as she is to teaching, though, Steph is ill suited to the isolation of island living. After the seasonal crowds leave, she

Stephanie teaches multitudes; here, with her Suzuki class on Martha's Vineyard in 1990.

finds herself alone, living in a house at the end of a long dirt road. Life outside of work is dreary.

During the long winter evenings, Steph turns to her violin for company, preparing a full-length recital program that she schedules for the end of the school year that June. My dad, Ed, and I all come for the occasion. For old time's sake, Steph and I perform our childhood favorite, Bach's Concerto for Two Violins. Ed, succumbing to Steph's entreaties, drags a vibraphone all the way out to the island on the ferry so he can perform a few jazz tunes for the crowd. My dad beams in the audience. He has presided over more concerts than he can count, but he is never more proud than of this one.

It is a fitting finale to her time on the island, since Steph has decided it's time to move on. The next year she takes a new job, to teach violin in a burgeoning suburb—a town named in one survey as among the ten safest in the country—outside of Rochester, New York, called Greece.

That December, between Pittsburgh Symphony rehearsals, I fly to yet another orchestra audition. I am the last person to play that day, number 23 out of more than 250 applicants, and the committee is tired. Luckily, I don't know that at the time. Downstairs in the fluorescent-lit basement hallway, after the votes are counted, the personnel manager gives me the good news. I am a finalist for the Chicago Symphony Orchestra.

Coincidentally, my father is also in Chicago for a music convention. I run down Michigan Avenue from Orchestra Hall as fast as I can in high heels, with a violin strapped to my back. The hotel elevator ride takes forever, and when my father opens his door, I fall into his arms, laughing and then dancing around the room.

"I did it! I did it! I made the finals!"

"Really? *Wow*," my father says, unable to find the words. "*WOW.*"

"You're my good luck charm. You should be in town for all my auditions!"

"So now what? What's next? When are the finals?"

"In April. I have to come back then."

"April? That weel give you four more months to practice. Lots of time—you can really prepare."

"Don't you worry, I am going to be prepared."

For the next four months back in Pittsburgh I do nothing but sleep, eat, work, and practice. No fun allowed. I set a goal of practicing eight hours on a free day. If I have one rehearsal I can do six hours, and if I have a rehearsal and a concert I can do four. No days off, of course, but that's nothing new; my dad has prepared me for this since I was little. My fingers bleed, and my neighbors call the police, but nothing is going to get in my way.

I am playing the best I ever have, but there is more to it than that. In my brain, something has clicked. In the old days, when I used to go to auditions, I would walk into the group warm-up room, looking around in awe at the great players surrounding me. I would find a corner and practice frantically until the last possible second before my number was called, fighting the irrational fear that I might somehow forget how to play the violin during the time it took to walk from the warm-up room to the stage.

Along the way, though, I realized something. There is a missing piece to the puzzle, and it doesn't involve more practicing. My dad once told a newspaper reporter about student auditions: "Even though they might be strenuous, it's part of growing up. And we work to prepare the kids, both musically and psychologically." Now, finally, the psychological piece clicks into place. Before an audition, instead of exhausting myself in the warm-up room, I begin playing just a little to loosen up. Then I take out my knitting. While everyone around me is practicing the hardest parts over and over again, just like I used to do, I instead sit calmly knitting, centering my thoughts, focusing, relaxing.

The first few times it is difficult to break the pattern, to believe that it is more than just the sheer quantity of hours, the number of miles logged on the bow, that is going to win me a job. But I realize there is something else, something far more elusive. It's not in my fingers, it's in my head.

When I figure that out, everything else falls into place. And in April, Sir Georg Solti offers me a position as a violinist with the famed Chicago Symphony Orchestra.

15

Duets

JOANNE

In the decade after I graduated from high school, I only saw Mr. K once. Melanie gave a recital on the East Brunswick High School auditorium stage, presenting the program she had prepared for her New England Conservatory master's degree in performance.

I brought along Tom, the boy I was dating, and introduced him to Mr. K at the punch-and-cookies reception in the old orchestra rehearsal room afterward. Mr. K gave Tom an only slightly suspicious "What are your intentions?" once-over before extending his hand. As Mr. K moved along to speak to other well-wishers, I made a quick exit. I had to get back to work.

There wasn't much room for the viola in my new life as a *Wall Street Journal* reporter. I wrote about the insurance business, then about the real estate business. I was in awe of the other reporters in the newsroom. They were smart and funny; sometimes I just sat back in my cubicle and listened to them working their sources on the phone, then tried to mimic their technique for cajoling and coaxing information out of reluctant executives.

I worked on a manual typewriter, on carbon paper in triplicate— the *Journal* was among the last technological holdouts and still hadn't warmed up to computers in the newsroom. My boss, Larry, marked up my copy with vast swaths of red pen, peppering me with fifty questions on stories that ran only fifteen sentences.

Where is this company based? What does it do? How old is the executive? Is he AN executive vice president or THE executive vice president? Is that earnings or revenue? Is she a "Miss" or a "Mrs."? Do you realize you used twenty-seven semicolons in three paragraphs?

I had a lot to learn as a reporter and even more to learn as a business reporter. I didn't know how to read a balance sheet and had taken only one semester of economics. The most useful skill I had acquired so far was a legacy from years with Mr. K: a thick skin. I didn't get easily intimidated. Executives could bluff or badger or patronize me, or yell at me after a story ran, but whatever they dished out, I could take. I had already been toughened up. I had Mr. K to thank for that.

My musical activity steadily dwindled and soon consisted primarily of listening to my Walkman on the subway. I practiced my viola every once in a while and briefly played in a community orchestra, but it was dispiriting to realize that my technique was getting rusty and there weren't enough after-work hours to fix it.

I did make time to volunteer with a local senior citizens group.

Every Sunday, I spent the afternoon sitting in the musty living room of a housebound widow who was nearing one hundred years old. She couldn't remember what she did yesterday or this morning, and she frequently forgot who I was. But every week she recounted vibrantly detailed stories about her childhood. She told me about her father, a Confederate soldier in the Civil War who lied about his age to enlist at fifteen; the southern plantation on which she grew up; her twelve older brothers. Her mother just kept on having babies until she finally got a girl.

The widow's apartment, a study in faded elegance, was a small, dark two-bedroom on the second floor of a fancy building off Park Avenue. The living room faced an airshaft. When you looked out, you couldn't tell what the weather was, or whether it was morning or night. She spoke in wistful detail about the eleven-room Park Avenue apartment she and her Harvard-educated lawyer husband shared until they lost everything and downsized during the Depression. Each week, before I left, she offered up her papery cheek for a kiss.

I couldn't have told you why, but I enjoyed our visits at least as much as she did. They reminded me of something. It was only later that I realized I was re-creating those trips to nursing homes and hospitals with Mr. K. *They going to want to touch you, to hug and kiss you*, I could still hear him saying. *Let them.*

Most of my hours, though, were spent at work. My boss wisely paired me up with one of the most experienced reporters in the newsroom, a ferociously competitive fireball named Dan Hertzberg. I would trot after him, tripping over my scuffed black pumps, as he sped along the pockmarked sidewalks and through Wall Street canyons. One day, after we cowrote a short and not terribly momentous news story, I came running into the newsroom, waving a copy of the *New York Times*.

"Dan, Dan, our story is better than the *Times*'s story!"

Dan just looked at me in stony silence. Then he shot back: "Not better enough."

I had to smile. *Not better enough.* That could have been Mr. K's motto. Dan was articulating something that had been drilled into me for my entire life: *Next time work harder. Again!*

In the newsroom, my colleagues and I laughingly called that kind of thinking a "healthy neurosis," but we meant it as a compliment: it was that quality of having just enough anxiety to triple-check a fact or make one more phone call. The Danish philosopher Søren Kierkegaard famously said, "Whoever has learned to be anxious in the right way has learned the ultimate."

Kierkegaard had nothing on Mr. K, who could have taught the course on that one.

I would have mentioned that to Mr. K if I talked to him at all. But I didn't. I was preoccupied with my job and my boyfriend and my friends and the new life I was making in New York City. Most days I worked until late at night. On occasional summer evenings I ran out by seven P.M. to go with Tom to hear the free New York Philharmonic concerts in the park. We listened to Tchaikovsky and Rachmaninoff on a batik blanket while eating the romantic picnics he packed of champagne and cheese and fresh bread from Zabar's delicatessen. When I turned twenty-five, I married him.

I tried to keep up with the viola. For a couple of months I played duets with a violist friend. Sometimes I made it to symphony concerts, but they frustrated me. I would watch the viola players, who usually were performing some orchestral work I had once played myself, and feel guilty: I should be practicing. When I was nine months pregnant, I briefly joined a quartet through the Ninety-Second Street Y, figuring I would get some time to play during maternity leave. Like many mothers-to-be, I was hopelessly naive about how life was about to change.

When Rebecca was born, and then Andrew two years later, it was clear my playing days were over. I shoved my viola in its case, the address of my college dormitory still stuck on front with peeling tape, into the back of my closet and forgot about it.

MELANIE

As the plane touches down in Leningrad, I glance apprehensively at my father next to me. "Are you okay, Daddy?"

He is clutching the armrests of his seat, his chin bobbing ever so slightly up and down. His eyes are fixed on the window. I follow his gaze. Uniformed soldiers are stationed on the tarmac outside, machine guns at their sides.

"Fine, fine," he says with an awkward shake of his head, apparently intended to convey confidence. "It makes me uncomfortable to see all these guns, that's all."

My father has been ill at ease since we embarked on our trip. I've been with the Chicago Symphony Orchestra for more than a year now, and I invited him to join me on the orchestra's tour of the Soviet Union. He hasn't been back to the Old Country since he fled Ukraine forty years earlier. The Communist threat has haunted him ever since. As a little girl, I thought his name was on a list somewhere in the country, and that he could be snatched away from me and banished to the gulags. But now, in 1990, the Soviet Union is in the thrall of glasnost. The Berlin Wall has fallen. Shouldn't he have gotten over his fear by now?

Traveling together this way is new to us, a strange role reversal. We're on my turf now. I give my dad instructions, anxious that he not misbehave somehow and embarrass me in front of my new colleagues. I feel my face flush when, at the airport, he struggles with the buttons on his coat. In line for security, while he fumbles with his carry-on bag—"eet's new, the zippers are treecky"—I snap at him: "Hurry up, Daddy! We don't want to get left behind the group."

I grab the bag away from him and close it myself, glancing around to make sure none of my colleagues have seen. *Oh my God, he's getting old,* I think.

On the long flight over, my dad calms himself with a double vodka before falling into a fitful sleep. I stay awake, watching him covertly from behind my book. He has never had time or money for "gallivanting" all over the place like some people, as he always says. But he's given up his orchestra conducting duties, passing his baton to a new generation, including Gordon Tedeschi: the boy who challenged me at ASTA when I was nine years old now directs the East Brunswick High School orchestra. My dad has cut back on his private teaching schedule, too. As I turn the pages of my book without reading them, I steal a glance at his snoring form. He has always taken energy from his students, as if they fueled him with some sort of hormone-amped adrenaline cocktail. Without them, he seems suddenly older, tired. A little bit lost.

The seat belt sign turns off. Around us, my colleagues are pulling on their shoes, digging in their bags for sweaters, and grabbing flute and violin cases out of the overhead bins. Some are grumbling because our trip is during the Thanksgiving holiday, and they resent being away from home. I understand their irritation, but how can they not be as excited as I am to go to an exotic foreign country, behind the Iron Curtain? In any case, even if I do miss Thanksgiving with my family, it will be worth it if I can make a good impression on the conductor and earn tenure with the orchestra when I become eligible at the end of my second year.

I put away my book and give my father a teasing grin as we edge down the aisle toward the cockpit door.

"And you're *sure* your name isn't on some list somewhere . . . ?"

"God, I hope not!" He smiles weakly.

*   *   *

Leningrad is in the midst of a food shortage. The government is planning emergency food rationing. There are no restaurants to feed us, so the hotel serves dinner each night. As the old joke goes, the food is bad and there isn't enough of it. But the vodka is plentiful. After dinner, my father makes himself at home with my orchestra colleagues at a makeshift bar he sets up in his room. "You must try my famous Black Russians," he announces. "Vodka, Kahlua, and secret Ukrainian incantations."

In Leningrad, the streets are rutted, and the few stores that are open have nothing on the shelves. In our concrete bunker of a hotel, the water in the bathroom faucet spurts out brown. On the streets, soldiers offer to sell us their medals and caps; on the train, the ticket taker tries to sell his uniform. Moscow, where we travel a few days later, isn't much better. On Thanksgiving Day, our hotel gamely attempts to serve us a festive meal, notable mostly for the large rat that scampers across the middle of the dining room floor.

This tour will be one of the last for Chicago Symphony conductor Sir Georg Solti, who is nearing the end of what will be his twenty-two-year run as its maestro. Sir Georg thoroughly intimidates me. A Hungarian-born music legend, he, like my dad, fled his home country and ended up in Germany after the war. He built his conducting career there and at Covent Garden in London, before taking over the Chicago Symphony in 1969.

Like a benevolent monarch, Sir Georg is warm and affectionate but doesn't mingle much with the rest of us. His thick Eastern European accent is different from my dad's but just as difficult to decipher. He floats through our lives trailed by a flurry of attendants. I can't imagine him buttering his own toast.

My dad and I are waiting to go down to the lobby when the elevator opens. There inside is Sir Georg himself. I clear my throat tentatively and introduce my father.

"You have a good girl there!" the maestro says, turning toward my dad.

My dad stares back blankly.

My father, who can so intimidate his students, has turned into a starstruck teenager right before my eyes. He looks mutely at Sir Georg. I worry briefly that he will lose his command of the English language as he moves his lips, trying to form the words he wants to say. His chin sways a bit from side to side.

"Thank you! Thees eez a wonderful opportunity for me, to travel weeth you and hear such great music!" he finally blurts out.

I exhale, relieved, but then my dad tumbles on. "I feel eet has galvanized me professionally!"

What?

Sir Georg smiles politely and steps off into the lobby.

"'*Galvanized professionally*'?" I hiss at my dad. "Why did you have to say that? What were you thinking?"

My dad looks hurt. His head bobbles a bit as he glares at me. I have no idea what he was thinking. But I'm pretty sure I know what Sir Georg was thinking: *Weird girl has weird father . . . no tenure for her!*

On the overnight train ride from Leningrad to Moscow, we cross through snow-covered steppes, illuminated by moonlight. The trees are heavy with fresh snow. The scene from our window is straight out of the film *Doctor Zhivago*, which my dad and I have watched together many times.

Inexplicably, the train comes to a stop in the midst of the frozen landscape. Everyone else is asleep as we sit, transfixed, staring out the window. My dad begins to hum. We often play a game of "Name That Tune," where I hum a few bars of whatever the Chicago Symphony will be performing that week and my dad guesses the name of the piece and the composer. His accuracy is uncanny. This time,

I am the one who recognizes the song: "Lara's Theme" from *Doctor Zhivago*. I join in, harmonizing with him. Predictably, the water supply on the overheated train has run out. Porters come around offering big bottles of vodka instead. My father and I swish the glasses in our hands as we hum. "I feel like Strelnikov could appear at any moment," he says, a reference to the film's evil commissar.

My dad has had so much trepidation about this trip. Although he has told me very little about his childhood, I know that for his entire life, the Soviet Union has meant fear, death, men in uniform with bayonets. Yet coming here, he's struck instead by the similarities with his home. He is enveloped in the warmth of the familiar— the snowy landscape, the white birch trees, the people, the meager food and plentiful vodka, and, especially, the music.

There is something utterly magical about bringing a piece of music home and performing it where it was born. It sounds different—more powerful—in its own home than it does anywhere else in the world. It comes alive, it's almost tangible, a bridge not just to other people but across time and place. I imagine it must be like standing on magnetic north, holding a compass. There the needle spins wildly, as if brought to life. Playing the music of a particular people in its original place has that enchanted quality as well. My dad, in the audience, feels it as powerfully as I do onstage, as the symphony plays Shostakovich in the hall where Tchaikovsky himself was once the conductor.

At one of the concerts, my father sits in the audience next to a Soviet school music teacher. As a boy, he had refused to even speak Russian, though he knew the language better than any other. "The Russians came to our country," he would say. "Let them speak our language." But now in the audience, he falls easily into Russian with the teacher, who like him has a gravely ill family member, in her case a young daughter. The little girl's condition is treatable, but the medication she needs isn't available in the Soviet Union. My father jots down the teacher's address before he leaves.

I can see that my dad, swept up in the music and the landscape, isn't a scared little boy anymore. He's faced his fear. He has finally moved on. It strikes me that he's like that compass needle, coming alive as he comes home to his own true north. He's traveled willingly into the heart of evil that has haunted him since childhood, only to realize that what he feared is just a ghost. The horror is in the past. The music and the landscape and the people that remain are the same as those he had so loved.

We talk quietly for hours, watching as the snow transforms from moonlit blue to sunlit pink. In the reflected glow of the dawn, his is the face of a man who has confronted the demons that have tortured him for his entire life. For the first time, the demons don't win.

A few months later, my dad and Steph come to celebrate Easter with me in Chicago. Easter has always been one of my mom's favorite holidays. When we were little, she dressed my sister and me in frills and made a big dinner of ham with cloves, with a festive Easter cake for dessert. But as my mother's health declined, Baba took over the holiday.

Baba's Ukrainian Easter was another matter entirely: a dark, days-long ritual that began with a mandatory egg-decorating session that entailed painting elaborate designs using beeswax. Ukrainian legend has it that if you don't decorate eggs, an evil serpent will destroy the world. The holiday ended with hours in church, where we knelt before the *Plashchynytsia*, a plastic tablecloth with a portrait of the crucified Jesus. Elderly women in babushkas, for whom kneeling wasn't a sufficient display of devotion, crawled slowly on hands and knees from the back of the church all the way to the altar, then kissed each of the wounds on the portrait while crossing themselves profusely.

On a spring day, in my rented house in Chicago, I do my best to meld both my mom's and Baba's traditions for my family. Like my mom, I make glazed ham and, for dessert, a bunny-shaped cake. For Baba, I agree to take my father to a Ukrainian church across town. I don't bother with the complicated egg-decorating ritual. I have to draw the line somewhere.

"It's in a dicey neighborhood," I tell my dad, as he scours a map to find the church Baba has specified. "Can't you just tell Baba you went? Fib a little?"

My dad gives me a dark look. "She's my mother. I can't lie to her."

It is a beautiful church. It's relatively new, with a colorful mosaic above the entrance that depicts the baptism of the Ukrainians in 988 by Saints Vladimir and Olga. But when we file inside and take our seats for the service, we are surprised to find it almost empty.

"Ah! Damn!" My father has realized something.

"Okay, Daddy, spill," Steph demands.

"Well . . . eet isn't Easter here."

There are only a handful of Ukrainian churches in the entire country. As it turns out, two of them are here on this street—and we're in the wrong one. This one celebrates Easter according to the Orthodox calendar, not the Gregorian calendar used in the West. It was, in fact, built by a group of die-hard parishioners who were outraged when the other church switched calendars back in 1969.

After the service, Ed is incredulous. "Let me get this straight. At the Ukrainian Catholic church across the street it's Easter? But at this one it isn't? They couldn't agree on what day to have Easter so they built a whole new church?"

"Apparently so," my father says sheepishly. So much for celebrating Easter Ukrainian style. We haven't decorated the eggs with beeswax, and now we haven't made it to the right church. Baba would have been outraged at the bad luck of it all. Had she been here, she surely would have warned that evil spirits would now rain down upon us.

Instead, we laugh it off.

234 · JOANNE LIPMAN AND MELANIE KUPCHYNSKY

Over dinner at home, we tease my dad as we heap big helpings of ham and macaroni and cheese onto our plates. Afterward, Steph and I snuggle on the couch while my dad and Ed pick over the leftovers and share a nightcap. Steph lays her head in my lap and lets me stroke her velvety cheeks.

This is what I've been missing. My family.

My whole life, this is all that I've longed for. Finally, I feel like I have a normal, happy family. I sleep soundly that night.

At the airport the next morning, I can hardly let go of Steph, and I unexpectedly find myself sobbing. We talk about how we'll see each other in August, when she, my dad, and I will spend some time together again at his house in New Jersey. I try to console myself that it's only a few months away.

"Sounds like a plan," Steph says, as her flight is called. "I love you, Mel. Say bye to old Ed for me. I'll call you, okay?" She gives me a squeeze.

I wipe my eyes as I watch her walk down the jetway. She's happily hugging a grocery bag of leftover ham and cake to her chest.

That is the last time I will see my sister.

PART V

I shall seize Fate by the throat;
it shall certainly not bend and
crush me completely.

—LUDWIG VAN BEETHOVEN

16

The Disappearance

MELANIE

Ed and I are all packed, our boxes scattered across the bedroom floor, ready for the movers to take us to our first real home, a three-bedroom bungalow we bought on the outskirts of Chicago. It's a pretty little house in a good neighborhood, where we hope to start a family.

We're counting down the last few nights before moving on to our new life, when I wake up with a start from the worst nightmare I've ever had. I shake Ed awake, crying. In my dream, Steph and I are walking up a hill, when she disappears over the rise. I search for her and call her name, but I can't find her. In front of me stretches a dark forest, and I run into it, but no matter how hard I look, I can't see her. I can't hear her. She has simply vanished.

"Ed! Ed!" I sob as I wake him. "I dreamed I lost my sister!"

I try to shake off the awful feeling the next day. The movers are on their way, and I need to focus. No sooner have they deposited all of our belongings in the new place than Ed is heading off to a summer job playing timpani at a music festival in Connecticut. I struggle to unpack while adjusting to the traffic-clogged forty-minute commute from South Oak Park to the Ravinia Festival in Highland Park, twenty-five miles north of the city, where the Chicago Symphony performs in the summer. Complicating matters, our new neighborhood is prone to power outages.

"Damn!" I say aloud, slapping the steering wheel with my palm as I drive over the Eisenhower Expressway into our new neighborhood after a performance a few weeks later. The streetlights, which had been glowing encouragingly all the way down Harlem Avenue despite the recent thunderstorms, suddenly disappear as I cross over the highway and near home. The electricity in our neighborhood is out again.

On my doorstep, fumbling blindly with my house key in the blackness, I hear the phone ring inside. Not relishing the prospect of being home alone in the dark, I rush to answer it. *Don't hang up! Please don't hang up, whoever you are!* Shoving my way through the maze of boxes littering the entryway and tripping toward the kitchen, I manage to grab the phone in time. It's my father. He doesn't even say hello.

"We cannot locate Stephanie!"

What? I'm confused. "Calm down," I say, still catching my breath.

"We cannot locate her!"

"Is she not answering her phone? I just spoke to her a couple of days ago. There must be a logical explanation," I reassure him.

During our latest conversation, Steph sounded good. She loves her new job in Greece, New York. She chattered on happily for an hour, telling me about her violin students; like my dad, she works

The Kupchynsky family
(left to right Mr. K, Stephanie,
Melanie, and Jean)
in 1976. . . .

. . . And the Lipman family the same year.
Left to right: Michele, Ronni, Burton, Diane, and Joanne (with Skippy).

Can you say "awkward stage"? Joanne at age fourteen in her purple dress, after Mr. K featured her in a confidence-boosting solo performance.

Joanne at her first lesson with renowned violist Paul Doktor. Mr. K sent his best students to study with more advanced teachers.

Mr. K was tough on the podium, but always appreciative when he sat in the audience. Here, applauding for his students in the mid-1970s.

Melanie with her high school boyfriend and fellow violinist, Michael. Mr. K allowed her to date only reluctantly. When Michael got his driver's license, Mr. K wouldn't let his daughter into the car until Michael took him on a test drive.

Joanne, age sixteen, at a rehearsal for the New Jersey Senior Regional Orchestra.

Mr. K, conducting the New Jersey Senior Regional Orchestra, poses with the principal players from each section. He has one arm around Melanie and the other around Joanne; Miriam Simon stands next to Joanne.

Joanne and Tom married at the National Arts Club in New York City on June 13, 1987. Tom's brother, pianist and composer Jed Distler, perfomed at the reception as his gift.

Stephanie gets a kiss from her father at Melanie's wedding, September 5, 1987. Stephanie serenaded the newlyweds on her violin at the ceremony as her gift.

THE WALL STREET JOURNAL.

© 1983 Dow Jones & Company, Inc. All Rights Reserved.

★ ★ ★   EASTERN EDITION   FRIDAY, OCTOBER 7, 1983   PRINCETON, NEW JERSEY

What's News—

Business and Finance

MEXICO soon will disclose that its estimated 72 billion barrels of oil and gas reserves were overestimated by at least 17%, say industry sources. Such a step isn't expected to hurt oil exports or talks related to Mexico's $85 billion foreign debt.
(Story on Page 3)

Brazil's bank advisory group agreed to interest-rate concessions on $6.5 billion of new loans. Banks advising the nation also agreed to recommend to Brazil's lenders that only interest payments be made on those credits for five years.
(Story on Page 2)

Argentina's foreign debt, which has been estimated at $40 billion, might be overstated by $10.8 billion, according to an Argentine court-ordered investigation. The discrepancy may reflect secret loan repayments by firms evading exchange controls.
(Story on Page 3)

IBM won a victory in its battle to safeguard its technology as Hitachi settled a suit IBM brought against it.

World-Wide

A CAR BOMB KILLED a pro-Israeli Moslem leader in southern Lebanon. Hussein Wahbe, head of an Israeli-supported militia, was killed in Adloun, 30 miles south of Beirut. Separately, U.S. diplomats think they are near breakthroughs to solidify the cease-fire in Lebanon and start talks on political reconstruction. Talks are under way with Lebanese factions to arrange international observers to police the Sept. 26 cease-fire. (Story on Page 2)

Moscow apparently is preparing to send a surface-to-surface missile to Syria that would represent a new threat to Israel, U.S. intelligence sources said.

The leaders of Nicaragua, El Salvador, Venezuela, Honduras and Costa Rica agreed to principles for peace in the region, Mexico said. They include an end to outside military intervention. Separately, a plane that crashed last month during a bombing raid in Nicaragua reportedly was provided to anti-Sandinista rebels by the CIA.

Reagan's reelection campaign committee is to be created officially Oct. 17, raising speculation that he is nearer to announcing his 1984 plans. White House political director Edward Rollins will become director and GOP Sen. Paul Laxalt of Nevada will be general chairman.

Office Glut

OFFICE SPACE remains in oversupply. The nationwide vacancy rate rose to 11.7% in June from 7.1% a year earlier. Construction slowed to $13.4 billion in the second quarter.

Street Musicians Get A Mixed Reception, But Sizable Rewards

Our Violist Finds the Income Better Than a Reporter's; Scourge of the Boom Box

By JOANNE LIPMAN
Staff Reporter of THE WALL STREET JOURNAL

Washington Wire

A Special Weekly Report From The Wall Street Journal's Capital Bureau

U.S. HOPES for early extrication from Lebanon appear doomed.

The front page of *The Wall Street Journal*, October 7, 1983. To report her article about street musicians, Joanne played her viola in Times Square, in front of the New York Stock Exchange, and in the concourse of the World Trade Center, among other locations.

Members of the Chicago Symphony pose in front of St. Basil's cathedral in Moscow during the orchestra's historic 1990 tour. This was Mr. K's first trip back to Eastern Europe since he fled in 1946. He and Melanie stand in the first row, far right.

The Kupchynsky family on Christmas Day, 1990.
From left to right: Jean, Stephanie, Ed, Jerry, and Melanie with Allegro the cockatiel.

The poster that volunteers distributed throughout upstate New York immediately after Stephanie's disappearance, August 1991.

Mr. K's influence, the next generation:
Joanne's son, Andrew,
plays the French horn. . . .

. . . while her daughter,
Rebecca, dances classical ballet. . . .

. . . and all three of Melanie's children play the violin. Here, a gift of music
for Baba's one hundredth birthday celebration, November 2004. Left to right:
Laura, Melanie, Greg, and Nick.

Joanne performs for the first time in years, at Mr. K's memorial concert, Hammarskjold Middle School, East Brunswick, New Jersey, February 14, 2010.

Melanie leads the orchestra at Mr. K's memorial concert. Her son Nick sits directly behind her. Michael Grossman sits behind Nick.

And the orchestra played on. . . . The podium may be empty, but Mr. K was very much with us all that day. With Dr. Sandra Dackow, conductor.

with them through the summer, even when school lets out. We finalized our plans to meet next month in New Jersey. We talked about my dad's shakiness, which has been worrying us both, and debated over how to get him to a doctor. I told her about the tiny bedroom in our new house that will make a perfect nursery.

"*Ooh!* I can't *wait* to be an aunt!"

Steph told me about her new boyfriend, Ken, a violin maker. She's certain, she said, that he is the one. She assured me that at twenty-seven years old, she's old enough to know.

"Now that you have Ken, do you still love me?" I asked her jokingly in the little-girl voice we used when playing with Keester the parakeet.

Steph answered me softly, not joking at all. "I'll always love you."

My dad fills me in on the details of Steph's disappearance while I hunt around for a flashlight and some candles. He tells me that Steph didn't show up for a date with Ken. Hours later, Ken and his sister, also a friend of Steph's, let themselves in to her apartment. Inside, they found a bag of groceries on the kitchen floor. The light on Steph's answering machine was blinking. They listened to messages from parents of her students who had shown up that day for violin lessons, only to leave in frustration when Steph didn't answer her door.

"Did we come on the wrong day?" they wanted to know.

That's when Ken called my father. Steph wouldn't forget her students. Then they called the police.

They pieced together the sequence of events. Steph went out for ice cream with a friend and her little girl the previous evening, then stopped at the grocery store on the way home. The receipt was still in the bag, along with the cookies she had bought to give to her students.

As my dad recounts the story, he works his way through possible explanations, trying on one after another like he's shopping for a hat that fits, looking for one that will make sense. Maybe she left early for her trip to New Jersey, he ventures.

"I told her to get her car serviced before the drive," he says. My dad is a bit of a fanatic about proper car maintenance. "What eef she broke down, or had an accident?"

"She would have called," I answer. "Or the police would have called."

"Maybe she went off somewhere, to be alone, to think," my dad says. "Maybe something awful happened that made her leave. She might haf been having second thoughts about Ken—"

"No way." I cut him off. "It's not that. Her birds are still there, right? She wouldn't leave them. She wouldn't leave, period. Not without at least telling me!" I want to believe one of my dad's theories, but none of them makes sense.

After hanging up with my father, I first call Ed in Connecticut and then Ken, exchanging awkward pleasantries—"I've heard so much about you," "Nice to meet you, too"—before plunging into intimacy with a near stranger as we work out a plan. By candlelight, the flame flickering across my face, I unearth my phone book and start calling everyone who might know where Stephanie could be. I lose track of time, waking up people all up and down the East Coast, from Martha's Vineyard to West Virginia University. No one has heard from my sister. I move on to calling hospitals and police stations. Somewhere near daybreak, I fall asleep fully clothed across my bed and awake with a start, the early dawn light filtering through the windows and the hot, sticky telephone still grasped in one hand.

I don't want to be alone. Pulling myself out of bed and showering, I head back to Ravinia. Music will be an escape. It's always been a salve before, a way to lose myself when I am upset. At Ravinia, we are performing Beethoven's Seventh Symphony, one of my favorites. Usually when I play the piece, the world falls away. But tonight, the music speaks to me more urgently than it ever has before, especially during the powerful, mournful fugue in the second movement. It soars around me and expresses my feelings in a way words never could. It's a spiritual feeling; what some people feel in church, I feel on that stage. For a moment, my heartbeat slows and my mind is eased. But once the last familiar note fades away, fear comes rushing back, a tsunami crushing everything in its path.

Eight hundred miles away, Ed is performing Beethoven, too. For him, the timpani part to the *Missa Solemnis* is no match for the distraction of worrying about Steph. Minutes after completing one of the worst performances of his career, he jumps into the car and heads for Steph's apartment outside of Rochester, New York, driving through the night.

The next day, I get on a plane—abandoning my job—to join him.

"Stephanie! *Stephanie!*"

A little girl with her nose in a book almost bumps into me as her mother tries to get her attention. For a moment, I think that the voice in my head has become real. It's the first time I have noticed my surroundings in twenty-four hours.

The woman grabs her daughter by the hem of her shirt. "Watch where you're going!" she admonishes the child.

I have somehow gotten myself to the Rochester airport. Before I leave my house, I tape a note to Stephanie on the front door. It's a slim hope, that she might just turn up on my doorstep, but that is all I have right now. As the plane is landing in Rochester, my head is pressed against the window, my eyes scouring the landscape. I wish I could swoop down and fly over every inch of the earth until I find her. Lack of sleep combined with an icy-cold fear deep in my chest gives the world around me a surreal, dreamlike quality.

Ken's brother-in-law meets me at the airport with Ed.

"I found Stephanie's car," he blurts out.

"Where?"

"The airport, long-term parking," he replies. "The police aren't really taking this seriously. They keep saying that she probably had a fight with her boyfriend or something and just ran off."

He drives us to Steph's apartment. Inside, the kitchen countertops overflow with heaping platters of food—casseroles, breads, salads—dropped off by anxious friends and neighbors. Just like at a funeral. I shake off the thought. The food is untouched; no one can think of eating.

The rest of Ken's family is there, too, turning out en masse to help. As the hours ticked by with no word from Stephanie, they had begun their own search of the area. After the car was found, they asked the police to check whether Steph had taken an unscheduled plane trip. The absurdity of the situation crashes over me, and I feel hysterical laughter rising in my throat, while Ken's family looks on, perplexed.

"If she did drive to the airport, it would have been for the first time!"

Steph, like me, inherited our dad's awful sense of direction. My dad wouldn't let her get her driver's license at first, he was so worried about her. After he relented, she routinely got lost going to even the most familiar places in our hometown. "I doubt that she could even find the airport. She always takes a cab!" I say. The idea of her arranging a secret trip and driving her car to the airport is ludicrous.

The police had searched the car, too, of course. "My heart almost exploded when they opened the trunk, I was so afraid she would be inside," Ken's brother-in-law admits.

Thank God she wasn't. But where *is* she?

As the hours wear on, and then days, I bury myself in the details of the search. Horrible, graphic images keep working their way into my mind, threatening to consume me. What if someone is holding her in a cellar somewhere, even as I sit here at her kitchen table? What if she is lying in a ditch, bleeding, on the side of a road? My imagination tortures me, playing one more unspeakable image after the next vividly in front of me. When my eyes are open, the awful images play out like a sick horror-movie reel on an endless loop. When my eyes are closed, they're worse.

Every time those images work themselves into my mind, I try to discipline myself, to push them away. The police have told us that the odds are that Steph ran away. She had been prescribed Prozac for depression during a long, lonely winter on Martha's Vineyard and had stopped the medication once she moved to Greece. Maybe she is depressed again, the police say, or maybe she had a fight with her boyfriend and bolted. That's what happens in most of these missing persons cases. I know that isn't the case with Steph. But I have to be strong; I won't allow myself to ponder the alternatives.

My dad, still in New Jersey, is engaged in the same struggle against his thoughts. The night before she disappeared, at 10:30 P.M., the last call Stephanie made was to him.

My father can't forgive himself for not answering the phone that night. He was just finishing up teaching his last student of the evening, and he let the answering machine pick up. By the time he noticed the message light flashing, he figured that Steph was in bed.

Now I call my father several times a day to update him. He stays in New Jersey, hoping that somehow she might find her way to him. He tries with no success to get the Federal Bureau of Investigation interested. With what little savings he has, he hires a private detective.

My mom, confined in her hospital room, feels even more help-less. She is convinced Steph has been kidnapped and is being held against her will somewhere. She refuses to contemplate any other scenario. One day she receives several hang-up calls in a row and insists that they are "clues" from Stephanie.

At Steph's apartment, Ed and I go through her garbage, laundry, clothes, shoes, and cosmetics. With Ken's family, we search her bills and schedules. We hunt for her purse and checkbook, both of which are missing. I even go through her violin case, looking for evidence.

Ed and I drive around aimlessly, looking for we know not what, and walk through wooded areas calling her name. Thrashing our way through the undergrowth near her apartment complex, desper-ately calling out, "Stephanie! Stephanie!" Ed breaks down and weeps.

In Rochester, we speak to police, detectives, reporters, and psy-chics. We trace every lead. When someone calls to say something pink is lying in the median on the highway, we race over immedi-ately. It turns out to be a shower curtain. Friends and local volun-teers go out searching with dogs and on horseback. We go to church and pray and pray.

We meet with the police and the private detective on a daily basis. We retrace Steph's steps from the last day, and speak to the health club staff and the mechanic who serviced her car. We speak to her neighbors, her students and their parents, her ex-boyfriends and former teachers, and call hospitals and police stations across New York State. We print up flyers to distribute all over town. We go to bars frequented by local lowlifes to eavesdrop. We speak at length with her landlord, who had received a note from Stephanie on the day that she disappeared saying there was a leak in her bathroom.

I've always taken strength from my dad. Now, I try to be strong for him. Everything he has tried to teach me—about discipline and focus and persistence—suddenly becomes useful and urgent in a way that, in my worst nightmare, I could never have imagined.

Since I was a little girl, I've had this feeling that infinity exists, that there is always something more you can do. It's true for practicing the violin. I pray it is true as we search for Stephanie.

When the police ask for Steph's passport, I call my dad. He has been holding on to it for safekeeping after a trip he and Steph had taken the previous month to his native Ukraine. His beloved country has finally gained its independence. Traveling back there for the first time since he was a young boy, and bringing Steph to experience it with him, had been one of the greatest joys of his life. They brought along an extra suitcase full of toddler clothes and medicine donated by a doctor who was one of his former violin students. My dad had never forgotten the Russian music teacher with the ill child whom he had met during the Chicago Symphony's Soviet tour. With the help of that medicine, the child will grow up healthy.

My dad is at work when I call. He is running his summer ASTA program, now held at Glassboro State College, more than an hour from home.

"The police need Steph's passport. Can you get it?"

"I'm een the middle of the conference. Can't eet wait?"

I explode. I can't understand how he can work at a time like this. "Daddy! I cannot believe you're hesitating. How can the *conference* be more important than your own daughter?" I accuse him of not taking this seriously, of not caring enough about Stephanie.

There is a long silence on the other end of the line.

Oh my God! What have I done?

"Daddy? Daddy! I'm sorry, I didn't mean it! I know you love her, too. I'm just so scared . . . What if she's being held prisoner, or lying hurt somewhere . . ." I break down, sobbing into the phone, unable to finish my sentence.

"Melanie. *Stop!* Pull yourself together. Do not allow yourself to imagine the worst," he orders me. "I haf a job to do here. But I weel get the passport."

As I hang up the phone, it occurs to me that my dad is coping with Steph's disappearance in the same way I am. At his music conference, surrounded by his closest friends and colleagues, most of whom have known Steph since she was born, he doesn't have to be alone. Like me, the music is his escape, his deliverance. It helps push the most horrible thoughts out of his head. He can lose himself in the music that has given him strength since he was a little boy.

For him, his salvation is teaching music; for me, it's playing it. It is the only way to keep both of us sane. Teaching music at the ASTA conference for him; playing Beethoven's Seventh Symphony at the Ravinia Festival for me. They are one and the same.

We are in Rochester for a few days before we realize that Steph's bed has no sheets—only pillowcases and a quilt. Steph is just as gloriously sloppy as she had been as a child, and her apartment in the best of times is a mess. Her furniture is borrowed and make-shift: milk crates, baskets, TV trays. Nothing is contained, and piles overflow on every surface. The novel she was reading lies open, facedown on the nightstand. At first we didn't notice the bedsheets stacked next to it.

"Here, she must have been intending to put these on the bed," Ken's sister says. When she holds up one of the sheets and starts to unfold it, the room suddenly falls silent.

"Wait, this is a single bedsheet, and that's a double bed . . . ," she begins in confusion.

The realization washes over me in a rising tide of fear.

"She was *packing*." Those are the sheets she was bringing to my dad's ASTA conference in New Jersey, where the dorms have twin beds. The bed in her apartment is full-size.

I can barely say the words: "Her sheets are missing."

Up until that moment, we all have been hanging on to the hope that Steph would call and tell us she was ready for us to come pick her up. She would tell us she was sorry she left without telling us. She would explain that she needed to get away to think and to have time alone. She would beg us to forgive her—she would smile sheepishly and shower us with hugs and kisses—and of course we would.

But as we look from one to another in Steph's bedroom, the single sheet draped over her bed like a flag draped over a soldier's coffin, the fantasy dims and goes dark. Why would Steph pack up her sheets and leave everything else behind? Why change the sheets but not the pillowcases?

The horrific mental images of my sister and what could have happened with the bedsheets that are now missing cue up again in my head. Eyes shut, eyes open, it doesn't matter. The images are playing out in an endless loop. I do my best to discipline myself, to make the images go away. I can't.

JOANNE

The first thing I noticed about Mr. K, when I got the phone call at my desk while on deadline at the *Wall Street Journal* that August, was how vulnerable and uncertain he sounded. The man whose image was seared into my brain—I pictured him always with a conductor's baton or an unsharpened pencil clamped in one hand—was an intimidating giant. He had a loud, booming voice and a presence that loomed so large in my mind's eye that he blocked the noonday sun streaming full on through a window.

It took me a moment to reconcile the daunting teacher of my youth with the disembodied voice, hesitatingly asking for me on the telephone.

"It's Jerr ..."

"Yes?" Impatiently.

"It's ... your Mr. K."

He sounded small, and scared. And old. As he started telling me about Stephanie, he spoke in halting cadences, stumbling over his words, and you could feel the pain in his voice each time he uttered her name. I twisted the coiled cord around my finger and felt my face redden. I was ashamed. I hadn't spoken to him in years. At that moment, I couldn't have told you where my old viola was. I hadn't thought much about Mr. K at all since I left East Brunswick more than a decade ago.

I had lost track of Melanie and Stephanie, too. My waking hours were consumed by work and the demands of one baby, with another soon on the way. I was writing a daily column now, and each day was a fresh frenzy of searching for a topic, reporting it, then pushing the deadline as late as I could possibly get away with. My schedule was so tight that I slept in earrings and wristwatch to save time in the morning, but still ended up arriving at the office late most days with baby spit-up stains on my shoulders.

My lawyer husband's hours were even longer. We put our one-year-old daughter, Rebecca, on our schedule, so she napped all day long and woke up in time to eat dinner with us, often at midnight. We had moved to a new apartment a year before, when Rebecca was born, but our lives were so hectic that our few pieces of artwork—if that's what you could call our college-era framed posters—were still leaning against the walls, waiting to be hung.

As Mr. K filled me in on Steph's disappearance, I stared across the chaos of my desk at a photo of Rebecca. The picture was encased in one of those dime-store paperweights, and in it she had a ribbon in her dark hair and a smile playing across her little cupid's-bow lips. It was incomprehensible, unimaginable, to think of a child just disappearing.

How could Stephanie vanish? How could he bear not knowing where she was, at this very moment?

"Maybe she hit her head," Mr. K was saying. "Maybe she has amnesia."

He told me about her teaching job outside of Rochester, New York, about how much she loved her young students and how she had found a nice apartment and was dating a violin maker. How she had gone to the store to buy cookies for her violin students, then disappeared. How her groceries were still in the kitchen.

How the sheets were missing from her bed.

I tried to get my bearings. As a reporter, you are taught to be in control of a conversation. That's your job. But hearing Mr. K's voice, I became a kid again. I was twelve years old, with frizzy hair and glasses.

I was tongue-tied. I was of no use to anyone.

I had to pull myself together.

"Maybe she's somewhere that no one knows her. If we could get the word out, maybe someone weel recognize her," he was saying.

I shook myself out of my childhood stupor. I *could* do something, I realized. I pulled out a fresh reporter's notebook, picked up a pen, took a deep breath, and steeled myself.

For the first time in my life, I was about to give my old teacher instructions. "Tell me everything," I said. "Tell me your story."

In between deadlines those next few days, my cubicle-mate Kevin put Mr. K in touch with some true-crime TV producers he knew. I called friends at the *New York Times*. It was late summer, and we didn't know who, if anyone, might be interested in writing about the case of the missing violin teacher.

On Labor Day, my parents came to visit. The last blast of humid summer weather was pushing the temperatures up into the stratosphere. We spent the day swimming in the freezing-cold pool of our upstate New York weekend house, a fixer-upper we'd bought the year before and hadn't yet had the time or the money to fix up. Rebecca splashed happily with her grandparents, sitting on the top step in the shallow end, wearing the Pebbles and Bamm-Bamm bathing suit that was a gift from Tom's dad.

At the end of the day, after we barbecued hot dogs and hamburgers and fresh Jersey corn, my parents walked with me to their car in the driveway. My dad popped open the trunk, and my mother reached inside, retrieving a copy of the local *Home News* newspaper, dated the previous Thursday. "I didn't want to upset you before," she said.

The paper was folded neatly to an article inside. A large photo of Stephanie stared out at me. She was older than the last time I saw her, but not by much. She looked beautiful, with her wide dark eyes, pale skin, dark hair, and, of course, a smile on her face. It was one of those studio pictures, the kind they take in school, where the photographer sits you against a backdrop and tilts your head at all kinds of awkward angles and then tells you to act natural. But even so, you could see in the photo that she wanted to laugh. Stephanie always wanted to laugh. The next frame after this photo she no doubt ruined the picture by collapsing into giggles.

The headline over her photo made my heart sink into my stomach. "Police Perplexed by Disappearance of Ex-Area Woman," it said. The article quoted Mr. K. "I think she was abducted," he said. "But I'm pretty tough. As long as the worst doesn't happen, I feel she will turn up somewhere, somehow."

A few weeks later, a fat manila envelope arrived at my office. Mr. K had sent the police report, some news articles, and the missing persons report. He had enclosed a two-page handwritten letter. It was written on lined paper in small, neat script, unlike the big, sloppy instructions he always used to scrawl across my music—

"AGAIN!" in a dark splat of big block capital letters. This letter had obviously been carefully thought out, perhaps written and rewritten several times.

"Your kind words reassure me that human beings are basically good and that my existence on this planet has not been totally pointless," he wrote. He talked about how the police and the private investigator he hired had run into a dead end. He tried to get the Federal Bureau of Investigation interested, but ran into a wall. Perhaps if there were some news reports, the FBI would be convinced that the case was worthy of its time. "Dearest Joanne," he wrote, "whatever you can do will be very much appreciated. I will be eternally grateful..."

In a postscript to the letter, an oddly well-mannered coda that reminded me of his Old Country background, he asked to "remember me to your husband. I assume he is the same young gentleman I met at Melanie's concert in East Brunswick some years ago." He also sent "a big kiss to your little Rebecca Leigh."

Stephanie by this time had been missing for almost three months, and you could see that he was struggling with how to frame her fate—Is she alive, in the present tense? Dead, in the past?—as he talked about my own young daughter:

"When the time comes, I would love to teach her violin. Or better yet, if we find Stephanie, she would teach Rebecca via 'Suzuki' method. Steph (was) is a brilliant teacher!"

The letter was signed, with quotation marks carefully marked around his name: "Love, 'Mr. K.'"

As it turned out, TV producers and journalists did care about the case of the missing violinist. Several of the true-crime shows featured her story, resulting in hundreds of tips but no solid leads. As summer turned to fall and fall slipped into winter, Stephanie still hadn't surfaced. Mr. K drained his savings, posting a reward of $5,000, then $10,000. Three months passed, then four. Then five.

In early December, the *New York Times* piece appeared. I read the paper religiously early each morning, checking up on the competition. Even so, when I first glanced at the piece, I had no idea it was about Mr. K. The headline is what flummoxed me. I assumed it was referring to some other person, not the music teacher I had known for my whole life. Here's what it said:

"One More Blow to the Heart for Survivor of Nazi Terror."

Up until that moment, when the headline slammed me in the face, I never would have put Mr. K and "Survivor of Nazi Terror" in the same sentence. Sure, I knew he was Ukrainian and had immigrated to America sometime after the war. My music friends and I first trembled, then, as we got older and braver, laughed at his mangled English, his references to "cheeken plocking" and girls "vacuuming you hair."

But in all the years I knew him, Mr. K never talked about the war. I guess if I had thought about it at all, I would have assumed he was a kid at the time, far removed from the action. World War II was something I studied in school and read about in books, but never with a spark of recognition that would link that awful history to him.

Growing up, around the corner from my house was a street called Schindler Court, built by a local developer, a Jewish Holocaust survivor rescued during the war by Oskar Schindler. In eighth grade, every student had to bring in a signed permission slip to watch a gruesome documentary that included footage of Hitler's wartime atrocities. In the cafeteria beforehand, there were anticipatory whispers about the horrors that that film would unveil: firing squads, bodies being bulldozed into ditches, and emaciated prisoners with no shoes and bloodied feet being forced on death marches through the snow.

But I didn't connect that to Mr. K. We students never wondered what had happened to our own music teacher back in the Old Country. Or what stories he would have had to tell, if only we had asked.

If the headline threw me, the lead of the story seemed even more foreign. It talked about how as a young boy Mr. K had been "snatched" from his family and "shipped to Germany" as a laborer. It described how he "walked down a rubble-strewn Munich street past a bombed house. Strangely, one window was not shattered. The boy peered in. Then, he walked on. A scream. The window flew open. There stood his mother, now a refugee herself."

This was the story Mr. K had never told.

It came out in bits and pieces, as if he had great difficulty allowing himself to travel back to that time. At first, in the *Times* interview, he parted only with a few anecdotes, like the one about his mother on that shattered Munich street. But in the months after Stephanie went missing, the memories flowed a bit more, then came back in a flood, in reminiscences and poems that he began writing down in his native Ukrainian. Still, it wouldn't be until later that I was finally able to piece together the whole of our teacher's story, with the help of translators and documents and his childhood friends. That's when I finally understood how he himself learned the lessons he would pass on to his students.

Mr. K acknowledged, to himself at least, how painful it was to confront his past. "Having survived two wars and great tragedies in life, I learned to neutralize my emotions," he wrote in Ukrainian after Stephanie disappeared. "Such strict discipline was indispensable to maintain my physical and intellectual existence. Circumstances have forced me to learn self-mastery!"

Those circumstances were something I couldn't have imagined

when I was sixteen years old. Back then, I was whining about Mr. K and worrying about getting invited to a party on a Saturday night. By the time Mr. K was sixteen, he had different concerns: He had been shot at, stabbed, and starved. He had fled his home twice. His country had been occupied by three different powers, and both his father and his stepfather had been imprisoned. He had joined the Ukrainian underground army. He had almost died violently. It says something about the boy's life that things first started looking up when he landed in a rat-infested former concentration camp outside of Munich.

Jarema, as his mother named him, started out life as a coddled only child. He was born in 1928 in western Ukraine—that is, his family referred to it as Ukraine, though by then the country didn't officially exist. It had been split in half after World War I, with Poland claiming the west where he lived and the Soviet Union controlling the east.

A sensitive boy, Jarema loved poetry and Ukrainian folk songs. He inherited his artistic bent from his father, a teacher and painter who once spent an entire week making a costume for his son for a children's ball. But Jarema could be stubborn, too. He inherited that quality from his mother. Once, he went to the town square with his grandfather, a priest who lived on a nearby farm. As they made their way on the cobblestone streets slick with rain and manure, past horse-drawn carts and merchants hawking live goats, Jarema threw a tantrum in front of a toy-seller's stall, pummeling the old man with his little fists until he bought his grandson a carved wooden horse.

"*Dziadzio* [Grandfather], buy me a horse!" he cried.

"You already have many horses at home."

"I must have one more!"

Grandfather shook his head.

"Then I will park myself here until you buy it for me!"

Jarema thought himself fortunate to have such a happy child-hood. But it was over by the time he turned four years old.

That year, the killing began. In Soviet Ukraine to the east, millions of people were starving to death as Stalin's government collectivized farms, confiscating crops and grain. Entire villages were wiped out; adults dropped dead in the streets, distended-bellied children at their school desks. The Holodomor, it was called in Ukrainian: killing by hunger. Jarema knew of a boy his age who disappeared, supposedly eaten by his own family. Ultimately, twenty-five hundred people in Soviet Ukraine would be convicted of cannibalism. The Soviet regime put up posters warning: TO EAT YOUR OWN CHILDREN IS A BARBARIAN ACT.

Jarema's parents were Ukrainian Nationalists, a group whose leaders tried, unsuccessfully, to expose the mass starvation. They paid the price. Jarema's father was arrested and jailed as a political prisoner. Later, he died under murky circumstances. On occasion, Jarema spoke of seeing him shot by the Russians on the family's doorstep. He was devastated.

His mother told him to pull himself together. *Discipline yourself,* she said. She was a hard woman—and practical. "If the Communists hadn't killed him, the vodka would have" was her assessment. She remarried another activist, a man who had disdain for his gentle stepson and beat him.

Worse was yet to come. When war broke out in 1939, Jarema found himself surrounded by bloodshed, violence, and betrayal, as his country was occupied by Russia, then Germany, then Russia again. Each time another army invaded, the Ukrainians were treated as chits for the victors. They were hanged or shot in the streets, shipped to concentration camps or forced into labor. Neighbors turned on each other; the Jewish population was decimated. Ten million Ukrainians would die during the war, a quarter of the population. By some estimates, more Ukrainians died than any other nationality.

Late one night, Jerema's mother pulled him from bed. She took him to the river, where she paid a smuggler to take them across the border to Poland. But before they could get across, Soviet soldiers gave chase. On the banks of the opposite shore, the smuggler quickly shooed them into a fishing cabin, where Jarema fell, exhausted, into a bunk. A bullet whistled through the window and lodged in the wall inches above his head. He was eleven years old.

Despite the violence at home, Jarema and his mother eventually returned. Like other Ukrainians, they hoped that life would improve under the Germans, who held out the promise of independence. They were wrong. The Nazis considered Ukrainians to be *untermenschen*—literally meaning subhuman, their lives worthless, fit only for labor and servitude.

So at fifteen years old, Jarema joined the Ukrainian guerrilla army, opposing both occupiers. He was put to use as an ammunitions courier. One afternoon, he was transporting a knapsack of grenades when his train was searched by German soldiers. The soldiers moved down the aisles, ripping open valises and inspecting packages. A soldier approached Jarema and kicked at his bag. With relief, Jarema saw the soldier move on to the next passenger.

Jarema's mother, whose ferocious will seemed to be a match for any invading army, managed to keep her son in school at first. On his way home one afternoon, he heard something that stopped him cold: the sound of a violin. He was transfixed. The music wafted through an open window and to the street below where he stood, motionless. Inside, a German soldier—one of the occupying forces—was practicing.

The music transported Jarema. It took him away from the war, away from the death surrounding him, away from the uncertainty that was his future. It opened up, instead, a world suffused with beauty. The music filled him with so much joy that it pushed out the darkness. Jarema yearned to play the instrument, too. It was a revelation, these melodies that lifted him up and chased the demons away. It was an escape. It sparked in him an almost spiritual belief in the power of music to heal.

"I want to learn the violin," he told his mother.

"You will," she said. "We will get you lessons."

She was never able to deliver.

One day, the window was closed. There was no music. There never would be again. The soldier was gone; to another posting or to his death, Jarema would never know for sure.

As fierce as Jarema's mother was, even she couldn't hold their family together. By 1943, the depleted German Reich was shipping off thousands of Ukrainians a day to work in German factories and farms, packing them into locked cattle cars without food or water. Jarema's parents were among them.

Jarema, on his own at fifteen years old, joined thousands of other Ukrainians who were fleeing west, abandoning houses and schools, as the Soviet army advanced again in the spring of 1944. The Ukrainians escaped by train or cart, on horseback or on foot. Every day was a battle to survive—and for Jarema, a fight to finish the school year. He found his way to a hastily set up gymnasium staffed by fleeing teachers, about fifty miles to the west, where he lived with a dozen other boys and managed to complete the equivalent of his sophomore year in high school. Even with chaos reigning around them, his bunkmate Ihor Hayda would recall him as "a romantic. He was a poet. He liked girls."

But the boys weren't safe there, either. German soldiers commandeered the school one day, rounding up Jarema and his classmates and dispatching them to a youth antiaircraft artillery unit as auxiliary "volunteers." Almost immediately, the boys were assigned to be human decoys, ordered to man lights at a fake artillery factory at night to attract Allied bombs. The bombs were supposed to target them instead of the real factory, blacked out several miles away. The boys were being given a death sentence.

"We were sitting ducks, so the bombs [could] fall on us," Ihor recalled. But at least the fake factory was near orchards, which meant the boys could get food: "For us, compared to what happened later, it was a paradise. It's all relative."

The boys survived, only to be transferred to Linz, Austria, where a massive armaments factory was under attack from Allied bombs. They were ordered to clear the rubble. The war was in its final months by then, and food was scarce. The winter was brutally cold. Jarema and Ihor shared a triple-decker bunk in a flimsy wooden barracks, where they talked at night as they tried to distract each other from the freezing winds. Jarema was starving and exhausted, his worn clothing woefully inadequate. He contracted pneumonia.

Remarkably, he was able to escape again—once more with the help of his mother, who managed to track him down. During that vicious winter of 1944–1945, he landed in a military hospital, near death from the pneumonia. One day, his mother marched in with a bribe for the guard and a purse full of clothes. When she left the hospital, she was accompanied by her pale, ill son, dressed as a local schoolboy.

"He had an extremely good mother. She followed him, no matter where he went," Ihor said. "She devoted her life to taking care of him. She risked her life. He was like the only precious thing she had."

Missiles were raining down as Jarema and his mother left the hospital and joined thousands of other refugees trying to flee. Fighting the crowds at the Salzburg train station, his ever-resourceful mother muscled her way to a guard in front and flashed papers to prove their right to transport. The guard had no way of knowing the papers, written in Ukrainian, were actually her son's report card. After the train pulled away, the station was bombed. The crowds still left on the platform perished.

Mother and son were separated again in the chaos. By the time they found each other, on that shattered street in Munich, the war had ended. By then, the city was decimated; it had been bombed sixty-six times during the last two years of fighting. But again, their reunion was short-lived. While his mother tried to find a job, he found his way, alone, to a refugee camp outside of the city.

He was skeletal and infested with lice when he arrived at the Karlsfeld camp. The place was grim. Until just a few months before, it had housed forced laborers who worked at a BMW plant. The wooden barracks were surrounded by barbed wire and teeming with rats. Families were housed together, separated by U.S. Army blankets hung from the rafters. The families were small, so small, and broken: a married couple who had watched their children die in a bombing; nearby, an orphaned teenage girl whose family had been murdered. Some survivors were missing limbs. All were malnourished. Tuberculosis was a constant threat. They tried to regain their strength, eating meager relief-package meals of Spam and dried peas.

Almost as if in recognition of the devastation, it rained all the time that summer. In winter, some children had no coats or shoes. If you looked into the refugees' faces, you saw confusion and despair. You'd hear people screaming late at night, woken up by nightmares. But the camp offered a roof over Jarema's head, food—and a high school, where he completed his junior year. "In school, we had nothing," one of his classmates, Olga Sawchuk, recalled. "A lot of people had no coats. Some of us had no pencils. We had no books, we had no heat in the classrooms. Until this day I think about those teachers, and I admire them."

Relief workers considered Karlsfeld's conditions so inhumane that it was closed within a year. Jarema, along with other school-children, was transferred to another refugee camp, this one in

Berchtesgaden, a bucolic haven in the Bavarian Alps. As the train pulled into the scenic mountain town, the crisp air infiltrating the cabins and sunlight streaming over snow-topped mountains, the students stared in awe and disbelief. It was as if, one of them told me years later, they had been transferred to heaven.

Jarema would lead a scout troop at Berchtesgaden, and write poetry again, and eye pretty girls with his friends—including Ihor, who made it there as well. Most of all, he climbed mountains. He scrambled across mountain paths and up the highest peaks, reveling in the freedom of the sky and the trees and the great cliffs around him that made him feel as if he were soaring through the air, like a bird. He loved those mountains and the exhilaration that he felt every time he climbed higher and higher, with no one shooting from below. In the mountains, there was no looking back. Only looking forward.

At Berchtesgaden, Jarema revived, though he didn't fully recover. He would never again eat rare meat; even a hint of pink reminded him of the bloodied corpses he saw during the war. He would never sit with his back to a door, either. He always had to sit with a view of the entire room, to make sure no one could sneak up on him and surprise him with an attack.

Still, he and the other Ukrainian children at Berchtesgaden would look on their time there as the happiest in their young lives. Jarema finished high school with highest honors. He became a scout leader, experiencing "my first opportunity at teaching, and became seriously interested in educating young people," he later wrote in Ukrainian. "I felt great satisfaction when my small scouts chased me, shouting, 'Brother Jarema!' Later, it changed to, 'Mr. K, what's up?' Another language, but carrying the same sentiment, same responsibility, same obligations, and same pitfalls ... Teachers have a unique opportunity to build a better world."

On December 9, 1946, Jarema finally rejoined his mother, this time for good, aboard the SS *Marine Marlin*, bound for America, to stay with relatives in New Jersey. He still didn't speak English. He never had learned to play the violin. The war had stolen his childhood. His dreams of a life in music had been shattered. But he had survived. In the years to come, he would almost never speak of that time in his life during the war. "I did not want ... to look into the eyes of the might-have-been dreams and past youth," he wrote in Ukrainian decades later. "I decided that it is dangerous to release such intense feelings. They need to be kept prisoner behind the strong walls of the past."

In New Jersey, his relatives invited some other Ukrainian families to meet the new immigrants. One of the guests was a Ukrainian-born professor who taught at Murray State University in Kentucky. The professor was impressed by the earnest young man, who introduced himself as "Please to call me Jerry" and who, through an interpreter, told a reporter just two weeks after his boat landed: "Now—as for the girls, I am very sorry I can't talk much with them, but you don't have to speak English to dance with them. Man, do I like to dance with them!"

The professor invited the teenager to come back to Kentucky with him. He could learn English there and then go to college. The professor said he would begin teaching Jerry himself, immediately.

The professor's name was Roman Prydatkevitch. He was, as it happened, an instructor in the music department.

Professor Prydatkevitch taught the violin.

FROM POLISH UKRAINE displaced persons camp, Jarema ("If you would, please to call me Jerry") Kupchynsky, 20, right, came to U. S. and Murray State college. Cellist at his side is Miss Betty Anderson, Huntsville, Ala.

Jarema performs with the student orchestra at Murray State in Kentucky shortly after arriving in the United States.

17

The Gift

MELANIE

Back in New Jersey, my father preserves Steph's lilac-colored bedroom exactly as she left it, in anticipation of her return. Late at night, when the anxiety becomes too much to bear—*Where is she now? Is someone holding her hostage in some dank cellar? Is she calling out for him?*—he pads down the hall and turns on her light.

He lives alone in the faded red house now. My mother, in the hospital, is too weak to travel. As the weeks stretch into months, my dad, who seemed so numb when Steph first went missing, is succumbing to a grief he couldn't begin to fathom. He is very private and very controlled. He rarely talks about his despair even with me. But he confides to me that in the middle of the night, long after he's sent his last student home, he will restlessly wander the house, up and down the hall and through the empty rooms, until inevitably he is drawn to the room where he used to read Stephanie bedtime stories and tuck her in, safe and warm, with a good-night kiss. He hasn't touched a thing in her cluttered bedroom. It is a shrine, like the wedding banquet in *Great Expectations*, all laid out and waiting for her, gathering dust.

Kneeling by her bed, my father closes his eyes, folds his hands, and prays. Out loud. The words escape his lips in English, in Ukrainian, in a mix of both.

"I tried so hard all her life to protect her, but I failed," he sobs. "I couldn't keep her safe."

In her hospital room, my mother has now decided that Steph ran off to clear her head. Of course she'll be back. With utter, uncompromising certainty, my mother is sure that no harm has come to my sister. As summer turns to fall, she funnels her worries into practical matters, like the snow and rain.

"The weather is getting colder," she tells me on the phone a few months after Steph's disappearance. "I hope she has enough warm clothes."

Ed and I have to return to Chicago eventually. We've spent almost a month sleeping in Stephanie's bed and eating off her plates, leaving all other responsibilities behind. The atmosphere in Rochester is bleak. We've run out of ideas, the trail is growing cold, and the odds of finding her are shrinking. As time wears on, and we realize that we've run out of steps to take, we have to make the difficult decision to pack up her belongings and leave her apartment.

I can't bear the feeling that I'm giving up on my sister, that I'm letting her down. Surely she must be counting on me to figure out what happened, to stay nearby, searching until I find her, to think of her and pray for her and hold her close in my heart so she doesn't have to suffer alone. Even if the worst has happened, how could I abandon her body to be torn apart by wild animals or rot in a Dumpster? She needs me to find her and bring her home to safety, to the place where she is loved. Late at night, the thought that she may be alive somewhere, held against her will, perhaps tortured in unspeakable ways, drives me to the brink of insanity. I have always been there for her. How can I be failing her now, when she needs me the most?

There is so much raw pain, so much guilt, such a terrible sense of loss. The grief strikes your whole body—a throbbing pain that burrows deeper and deeper, in layers. There is the utter sense of powerlessness and frustration, the terror of not knowing—and even worse, the dread of finding out. There is the pain of seeing my parents' sadness, after they have already suffered so much more than their share. There is the sudden void left by my best friend, my partner, my soul mate, our whole shared past and our dreams for the future together. There is the grief and rage associated with a life interrupted; the music she owns but hasn't yet played, the books unread, the knitting projects half done, the little string players still works in progress, the children of her own she hopes for someday. I have no way to cope with the magnitude of the shock and suddenness of events. There can be no peace, no closure. There is no way to say good-bye—no way to know if we *should* say good-bye—and so no way to heal.

Finally we pack all her things. We return her borrowed furniture and donate her TV set to the Ukrainian club she had joined. Most everything else we box up and move in a U-Haul to our house in Chicago. Ed and I keep Steph's two parakeets and give her cockatiel, Choobie, to Ken. I force myself not to give up hope that she will come back to us. When she does, she'll want her books and papers and music and violin. I will keep them all safe for her.

Ed and I go back to Chicago, back to our new little house that has not yet become our home. We store all of Steph's boxes un-opened in our garage and basement, and try to figure out how life for us can go on.

It turns out that we have some time on our hands: just after we get back, the Chicago Symphony goes on strike. Despite our new status as homeowners, with looming mortgage payments and de-pleted savings, I don't care. Money has never been that important to me, and never less so than now. I withdraw into a private world, with Ed as my only human contact for weeks. I speak on the phone to each of my parents almost every day, searching fruitlessly for something encouraging to say. Our grief is like a wall around each of us, a form of solitary confinement.

When I'm awake, I alternate between crying and praying. I cry thousands of tears, mostly alone. I pray aloud or in my head con-stantly. I scrub and clean obsessively in rhythm to long-forgotten hymns and prayers. I splurge on hundreds of bulbs for the garden and sob as I dig my sadness into the ground. I pray formal prayers and made-up prayers and chanting prayers like "please God please God please God" over and over again.

Nights are unbearable. The horror of the unknown is a black hole that sucks me toward it, its gravitational pull overpowering. I literally cannot close my eyes. Hideous scenarios play in my mind, and nightmares torment my sleep. The ache never leaves, not even when I drift off toward dawn. The grief is like a sound track to a movie, rising and falling in volume but always there. Often I sing aloud just to drive away the thoughts of what may have happened to Stephanie. I get up in the middle of the night and come down-stairs and mop the already clean kitchen floor, singing the Lord's Prayer at full volume. Ed comes stumbling from our room into the light looking for me, worried and sleepless himself. Our house is immaculate, and we are both exhausted.

*   *   *

Ed and I don't consider ourselves especially religious, and we seldom go to church. But we become convinced that if Stephanie's soul is out floating around somewhere, we want to grab it before it's too late. When our baby is born the following June, my sister has been missing for almost a year. We name him Nicholas Stephen, after Stephanie, of course. We make Steph his godmother.

Not long afterward, my dad comes to visit. I hurry out the front door to greet him, carrying Nicky sleeping soundly in a basket. Daddy looks years older and frail. He's lost weight. The bobbling of his chin is more pronounced now, and I notice his hands are shaking, too.

My father's former students rallied when Steph went missing, and that has helped get him this far. Joanne has connected him with newspaper reporters and TV shows, bringing more publicity for Steph's case. He draws strength from the letters of support that have come in since. Miriam, now a music teacher herself, treats him as part of her own family in New Jersey. When Nick is born, she comes to Chicago, stepping into the void that otherwise would have been filled by my mother or my little sister. She cooks, cleans, rocks, sings lullabies, and holds the flashlight as I change diapers during yet another days-long power outage.

But the strain is weighing on my father. His health is suffering.

He peers into the basket in my arms. "Oh my God," he gasps, and it sounds like a prayer. The sadness and loss drain out of his face for a moment as he gazes at his sleeping grandson. "Oh my God," he says again, and it is a prayer—of thanks for the renewal of life and for the sight of the family red hair and chubby little cheeks handed down to another generation.

Stephanie is still missing two years later, when our twins, Gregory and Laura, are born. It has been three years, almost to the day. The private detective my dad hired to keep on the case has run out of leads. We never talk aloud about giving up hope; hope just slips away on its own.

My dad visits us in Chicago that December. He doesn't leave the house much these days, other than to see his grandchildren.

"When I come home, I half expect to find Steph waiting on the doorstep," he confesses, in a rare moment when his iron grip on his emotions falters. "I'm afraid to stay out too late, een case she might be there, locked out and cold."

I worry about my dad. It seems as if, with each day that passes with her still missing, a little piece of him is lost, too. His eyes have begun to lose their focus, his head bobs and weaves, his hand shakes when he holds a fork. I try to ask him about it, but he waves me off, making it clear that questions aren't welcome. But during my next visit to him in New Jersey, I find a bottle of prescription pills in his medicine cabinet. It's a medication used to treat Parkinson's disease.

We still have no news of Steph. The police have settled on a "person of interest": a maintenance man who worked at Steph's apartment complex. He was arrested and jailed after Steph's disappearance, after being caught trying to abduct a teenage girl. It turns out, astonishingly, that he had a long history of felonies, including rape.

But the police have no evidence. My dad and I have no emotional reserves to press them. We need every ounce of energy we have to try to heal our family. We don't want to divert a drop of it into rage or hatred or revenge. We take what little comfort we can in knowing the man is now in prison, unable to harm anyone else.

My dad is in Chicago not just to see us but also to accept a lifetime achievement award from the National School Orchestra Association. I watch proudly as he receives an ovation from the crowd of educators in attendance. Afterward, one of them takes me aside and hands me a tape from her video camera.

"I taped your father's acceptance speech, but I want you to decide if you think he ought to see it," she says softly.

I raise an eyebrow. "What do you mean?"

"I'm afraid it will upset him. When he sees himself. You know, the swaying and shaking…"

While he's still in Chicago, my dad announces his retirement after thirty-seven years of teaching in East Brunswick. "That's great, Daddy!" I say. "You can spend more time with us, tour with me, teach violin to your grandchildren. I think you're doing the right thing."

"I guess so," he says. But he doesn't look happy, just wistful.

The retirement party that spring is held in East Brunswick. It's just one day after I get back from a Chicago Symphony tour to Japan, and I am discombobulated and jet-lagged. Our little family's first airplane trip with all three children, including the infant twins, has been an epic disaster, culminating in an airline worker being dispatched to unbolt and replace the seat that Nicky has ruined with his projectile vomiting.

My mother arrives by ambulance to attend the dinner. My ninety-one-year-old grandmother Baba is there, too, in a big shapeless dress, to all appearances heartier and healthier than either one of my parents. Enough former students and colleagues have shown up with their instruments that we're able to form a small string orchestra.

After the speeches, during which my father speaks tenderly about the "babies born under my supervision," we give an impromptu performance, my dad conducting. It is the last time he will take the podium in front of a group of East Brunswick musicians. He is funny, and as tough as always on the group of middle-aged performers he's known since they were kids.

"Watch intonation! A leetle beet off. Don't be stubborn!" he disciplines the orchestra as we do a bit of rehearsing before the opening number.

Turning to the audience, my father announces the first piece: *Eine Kleine Nachtmusik* by Mozart. He raises his arms dramatically, and the orchestra leaps to attention, just like the well-trained beginners we once were under his baton. Then my father brings down his arms to signal the first note, and the orchestra launches into the piece. But it isn't *Eine Kleine Nachtmusik*. As my dad looks on, at first perplexed, then smiling, then laughing along with the audience, the orchestra pours itself wholeheartedly into his beginner orchestra classic: "Reuben and Rachel."

The other pieces are sentimental favorites of my dad's. *Katahdin Sunrise* had been written for him by composer Philip Gordon years ago, a nod to the mountain that he loved to climb in Maine, whose peak is said to be the first place the morning sun reaches in the United States. "We deedn't have a chance to rehearse thees piece," he explains to the audience before we start, in a tone that signals he is about to issue an order, not an apology: "So eef we fall apart: don't mind."

After the piece is over, he rewards the players with his ultimate compliment. "Hey," he says, sounding surprised. "Not bad."

Then he turns again to the audience. "Thees concert would not be complete without some raw, Slavic sentimentality," he announces, and we launch into "Lara's Theme" from *Doctor Zhivago*. I smile at the memory of our train trip in the Soviet Union before Steph went missing.

Finally, we play his own arrangement of Ukrainian folk dances. "I want to dedicate thees to my mother," he announces, his voice catching with emotion. But Baba has left the room. In the middle of her son's final concert, at the culmination of his four-decade-long career, she decides it's a good time for a bathroom break.

He sighs, and you can see he is willing away a lifetime of disappointment. "Maybe we could play eet a second time for her, something like that."

The Baba moment aside, I am moved to see my dad gathering strength from the crowd, looking more robust than he has in a long time. But another guest, my old violinist classmate Ted Kesler, has perhaps a more clear-eyed view. Ted hasn't seen my dad since we graduated from high school. When he returns home that night, he describes my father this way in his journal:

> I was stunned when I introduced myself to Jerry Kupchynsky. Is this what 17 years does to a person? He was gaunt, three inches shorter than me, his head bobbled uncontrollably, and his eyes were glazed over. It seemed that only his left eye worked. I thought maybe he had had a stroke. Later I found out that he has Parkinson's Disease . . . His wife was contorted in a wheelchair at a table by the windows.
>
> An alumni orchestra played . . . Jerry barked the same commands "Watch me!" "Watch your intonation!" "Stop at no. 4 or answer to me!" Arms flailing, body hunched and rocking: no subtlety whatsoever. Everyone smiling at his bullish charm, making [it] through the piece despite the conductor. It was a throwback to H.S., struggling with the music, following him, intimidated.

During our annual summer visit to New Jersey a few months later, one of the staff at my mom's nursing home pulls Ed and me aside.

"Your mother isn't doing well," the nurse says in a hushed voice in the corridor. "We're concerned that her health is failing."

I turn that thought over and around in my mind. She has been ill and frail for so long that it almost seems as if she can carry on that way forever. Her illness itself is a constant that in a way has lulled us into complacency. Besides, she has so frequently declined, then rallied again over the years. It's a permanent cycle, in its own way oddly static.

This time the nurses want us to be prepared: the next dip in my mother's condition could put her past the point of no return.

In September, I make an impromptu visit back East, bringing two-year-old Laura with me for company. When we get to the nursing home, I am shocked by the changes since just a few weeks earlier. My mother's body is so twisted and crooked in her wheelchair that it makes my neck ache just to look at her. She falls asleep more than once in mid-conversation.

As I watch her doze, it strikes me that my mother has always seemed invincible to me. She's made the best of her situation, keeping up with her music as long as she could, writing for the hospital newsletter, and creating mosaic tables and trivets with the help of the occupational therapists. Her mind is still as active as ever. From eight hundred miles away she keeps track of everything that's going on in our lives in Chicago.

"How did Ed's performance of that weird modern piece go?" she'll ask during our near-daily calls. "What did the doctor say, does Greg have an ear infection?"

Ever since Steph has gone missing, from her wheelchair, my mom is the one who lifts my spirits. She never stops hoping for a miracle, that Steph will come home. My dad and I have long ago given up trying to convince her otherwise. When we're with her, we can almost believe it, too.

Now, my dad and I sit side by side in her room as she tries to rally enough energy for our visit. Though my parents' marriage was frayed even before she became ill, they are approaching their fortieth wedding anniversary. I know he's painfully lonely at home. He takes solace in his career, his students, and music. But he also visits faithfully with my mother, sharing news of their grandchildren and his trips to see us in Chicago.

While we talk, Laura busies herself trying on my mother's necklaces. I always bring my mom costume jewelry from our overseas tours, and Laura is happily running her fingers along the shiny coils of amber and jade and colorful seashells. Conversation is difficult. My mom is having trouble holding up her end, nodding off occasionally while we speak. After a while, she gives up trying. Instead, softly, my mom begins to sing.

"You made me love you . . . ," she starts, as she smiles at me and then at Laura.

"I didn't want to do it. I didn't want to do it," I join her, just as I did when I was a little girl.

And so we sing together, like Steph and I used to do when we were barely older than my own daughter is now. My mother's voice is weak, but in my mind I can still hear her, singing out clear and strong from her wheelchair by the living room window, patiently teaching us the words, the melody, the harmony. Laura watches us, transfixed.

Before we leave, my mom directs me to her bookshelf, where I find a wrapped package.

"For your birthday," she says.

"Mom, my birthday is months away!"

She shrugs a little and looks at me with her beautiful blue eyes, the same eyes I see when I look at my daughter's face. I swallow hard, sensing that there is more to be said. But she doesn't speak. Finally, I do, telling her I'll wait to open the gift until my birthday, and we'll talk about it then. After I leave the room, we've almost reached the elevator when I tell my dad to wait just a minute. I run back to her room and throw my arms around her once more. "Please be around for my birthday," I whisper.

274 • JOANNE LIPMAN AND MELANIE KUPCHYNSKY

"I'll try," she says.

A few weeks later, my father calls to tell me my mother is dead.

When I fly back to New Jersey, Miriam and her mother, Charlotte, help me plan my mother's funeral. She has left detailed instructions, so there are not many decisions to be made. At her request, I will play the "Méditation" from *Thaïs* on my violin at the service. It's the soulful, heartbreaking piece that my dad taught me for my first solo recital when I was a little girl, when I was too young to appreciate the meaning behind it. Now I fear I understand it much too well.

After we go over the details, I make my way to the nursing home, picking through my mother's shower-stall-turned-closet to choose her prettiest outfit for burial. But shoes are a problem. Ever since her fall, back when I was four years old, my mother had stopped buying the beautiful shoes she once collected. They seemed a useless taunt to her, once her feet could no longer carry her.

At home, I go digging around in my dad's basement to see if she has left any footwear behind. I open a little-used closet at the bottom of the stairs and push my way through my mother's wedding gown and the green gingham dress I wore for the ninth grade production of *Bye Bye Birdie*. I pull out old Halloween costumes and the devil mask my dad used when his orchestra performed *Orpheus in the Underworld*. I'm about to give up when I notice, on the floor in the back, a stack of shoeboxes. I reach for them, eagerly tearing off the lids.

There they are: my mother's old high-heeled shoes, the ones I used to stomp around in when I was just a little girl and she was still able to walk. Somehow they have stayed here in the bottom of the closet for all these years, waiting to be rediscovered.

Searching through the stack, I pick out the highest heels I can find. They are in a mouthwatering shade of blue that just matches my mother's eyes.

"Okay, guys, time to clean up! What do you want for dinner? Oh my gosh, look at the time ... let's go!"

The years following my mother's death pass in a blur of concerts and tours interspersed with potty training, playdates, and trips to the zoo. Our children have taken over our lives, and Ed and I love every minute of it. We see more of my dad, too. His solitary life is transformed when he meets his new next-door neighbor, Joan, an avid gardener like him who has three grown daughters of her own. Their friendship flourishes, and after a brief courtship they marry. In their new house, just down the street from his old one, my father teaches a few private students, plants flowers and vegetables, and starts working on a project with the help of Miriam's father: compiling a book of poetry that he has written, in Ukrainian, over the past fifty years. My dad and Joan break away as often as they can to visit us.

Late one afternoon, two years after my mother's death, the kids and I are ankle-deep in toys. Legos, dollhouse furniture, blocks, and books are scattered across the floor. The four-year-old twins, Laura and Gregory, are tumbling around, laughing and speaking a secret language that no one else, including me, can decipher. Nick, a solemn six-year-old, is trying to make his Lego tower stand up straight.

I glance at my watch, wondering if I can fit in Nick's violin practicing before dinner. I signed him up for lessons a year ago, when he turned five, around the same age Steph and I had been when we began lessons. I've given him my own first pint-size violin, dependable old Violet. It's a perfect fit for his little fingers. I figure that between my own music education background and watching my dad all those years, I can teach a monkey to play the violin.

But I didn't count on Nick.

Getting Nick to practice in the few hours after school and before dinner and my evening concert schedule is an exercise in futility. He squirms and wiggles and can't stand still. He never walks in a straight line but flings himself from one spot to the next. He's so hard to pin down, much less to teach, that I draw paper shoe prints on the floor for him to stand on and load marbles on top of his feet, bribing him with candy if he can get through a lesson without them rolling off.

I try to make it fun, exhausting my ingenuity as I attempt ever more creative ways to get him to focus. I use all my dad's tricks, too—they work remarkably well—and like him, I insist on perfect form and intonation. But I don't use a timer, and neither Ed nor I would ever spank our kids. Even so, I find myself yelling, saying all the things my dad said that I vowed I never would, like "What is wrong with you?!" until Ed says, "You should hear yourself screaming. It's not good for him and not good for you, either. You sound just like your father!"

Now the kids are flinging their toys around the living room, dinner isn't ready, Nick hasn't practiced, and my concert is coming up in just a couple of hours. In the confusion, the telephone chooses that moment to ring.

"Is this Melanie Koop-a-chinsky?"

"That's Kupchynsky, yes."

The caller identifies herself as a newspaper reporter from Rochester. Then she asks, with brisk efficiency: "Can you comment on the news that the remains of a woman were discovered in the woods today near Greece, New York?"

Somehow I manage to turn on *The Lion King* to distract the kids and get out of the room in the space of a heartbeat. It takes another beat for me to start to understand what she's said.

"Do they know who it is? Why are you calling me?" My heart has started up again and, shot through with adrenaline, is now pounding audibly in my chest.

"Yes, they have identified the remains as Stephanie Kupchynsky, the music teacher. Have the police not called you?"

I am stunned into silence.

"I'm so sorry," the reporter says. "I thought you would have heard by now. Can I get a reaction? Are you surprised?"

That is how I learn that the seven-year-long search for my sister is over.

JOANNE

Our apartment was chaos. The living room was engulfed in giant, primary-colored plastic toys. Five-year-old Andrew loved sports. There was the red plastic T-ball. The blue-and-orange plastic slide. Various sizes of plastic basketballs and soccer balls that left black scuff marks when he threw them against the walls.

Andrew's room was a shrine to Thomas the Tank Engine. Curtains, rug, pillows—all paid tribute to Thomas, as did the little wooden trains that were constantly underfoot on his bedroom floor. Rebecca's room, befitting a budding ballerina, was pink, a color she recently decided she hated. Her floor was littered with bobby pins and hairnets and ballet shoes that needed the ribbons sewn on. She was dancing around, practicing her party scene role in *The Nutcracker*.

I didn't have the luxury of worrying about housekeeping. I had become an editor at the *Wall Street Journal*, first working on Page One and most recently creating a new section called Weekend Journal as its editor in chief. The seven-days-a-week crush of launch mode crowded out brain space for anything else. My work hours were a scrim of meetings. My nights were spent immersed in page proofs that I marked up with red felt-tipped pens in between reading the kids their bedtime stories.

Now I flopped on my bed, surrounded by catalogs, comparing girls' pink fleece anoraks from a half-a-dozen stores, brainstorming a new weekly feature that would be called Catalog Critic. "Remember to practice!" I called out absently to Rebecca.

There were two activities that I required of our children: going to Hebrew school and taking music lessons. Both qualified as religion, I guess you could say.

We had started both kids on piano, and Rebecca studied violin as well, but they were indifferent students. For Rebecca, ballet held much more appeal, which to my mind was just as good: She danced in ballets composed by Tchaikovsky and Stravinsky. She studied at the School of American Ballet, the training school of the New York City Ballet, where her fierce old Russian teacher poked at her feet with a cane. I found it oddly comforting.

Andrew, meanwhile, had just discovered the French horn. He was inspired by Ronni's horn-playing son, Steven. In fact, between my sisters and me, all seven of our children played instruments, and Steven would go on to become a professional musician. Mr. K's influence had extended to the next generation.

Of course, insisting that my kids play an instrument was one thing; doing it myself was another. My children had never even seen my old viola, much less heard me play it. That was long ago and far away. I was far too preoccupied with other things. Like the six pink anoraks I was studying in six different catalogs, all spread out across my rumpled bedspread.

That's when the phone rang.

"It's Miriam."

The cellist from our old quartet! I hadn't heard from her in years.

"Miriam! How are you?"

"Stephanie's remains have been found."

That stopped me short.

I stood, sinking my bare toes into the bedroom carpet as she told me the details. A couple of brothers, eleven and thirteen years old, were fishing in a shallow stream in upstate New York. They were chasing the fish, sloshing through foot-high water. They stumbled over something and bent down to take a look. Turned out they had run right into human bones.

How long had it been since Stephanie's disappearance? I thought back, back to when I first heard the news from Mr. K, when Rebecca was a baby and Andrew hadn't yet been born. *Seven years.*

A memory tugged at the base of my brain, coming into focus like something out of a long-forgotten dream. Stephanie as a little girl, eight years old, perched on the arm of my chair, her thin arm thrown casually around my neck, her breath gently tickling my ear as she laughed. Her hair, brushing my cheek as she bent to look more closely at the book we were reading together while I waited for my lesson. Her hand, pointing to the pictures as we screeched in delight. The book, *The Bog People*. The photos, of murder victims discovered by fishermen sloshing through the shallows.

I shook off a chill. Miriam was saying something about a memorial service.

"We've picked out the church, in East Brunswick," she said. "So we're all set. See you then."

My thoughts snapped back to work, to looming deadlines. Certainly I wanted to go—how could I miss it? I furiously calculated article assignments and deadline timetables in my head, trying to see how I could squeeze in some time away from the office.

"If I can get out of work, I'll be there," I said.

"Of course you'll be there," Miriam snapped. "You're playing in it."

"What are you talking about?" I asked, confused.

"Our quartet is performing for the service. Darlene Brandt is playing Stephanie's part."

"But Miriam, I don't play anymore!"

"You do now."

A few weeks later, I found myself standing nervously on the doorstep of Mr. K's house. He had remarried by now, and he and his new wife, Joan, had moved to a newly built home down the street. I hadn't seen him in fifteen years.

I was a boss back at work, but here I was a cowering kid again. My mother drove me. On the doorstep, as I heard the door creak open, I edged uneasily behind her, like I did when I was five years old.

As the door swung open, for a split-second I got a glimpse of Mr. K, reassuringly familiar with his combed-over hair and trim little mustache. Then he was on the steps with me, throwing his arms around me and holding me tight in a bear hug. "My baby!" he said, hugging me tighter. "My baby! You're back." We stayed that way for a long time, arms wrapped around each other, not wanting to let go.

It was only after he finally stepped back that I got a good look at him. He was shorter than I remembered, and frail. His hair had thinned. He had an unmistakable wobble to his head. But he was most recognizably my old Mr. K, now grabbing me by the hand to lead me inside.

I had never been happier to see anyone.

Melanie and Miriam were already in the house, warming up on their instruments. Miriam, who had become a music teacher herself, looked the same as she had in high school, with her thick long hair and warm smile, except she was pregnant. Her husband sat on the couch with their infant daughter. Melanie was practicing behind a closed door. Listening to her spectacular riffs, I was intimidated all over again.

Darlene Brandt, who had started out as Mr. K's frightened student and had gone on to become one of our teachers, was there, too. She would be playing second violin, filling in the position Stephanie had played in our quartet. Darlene's own father had died before her wedding. Mr. K had walked her down the aisle.

I unpacked my viola while listening to Melanie behind that door. We had barely been in touch for the last twenty years, aside from trading birth announcements. I couldn't remember the last time we'd seen each other. She sounded so confident, her playing strong and powerful, the music soaring to emotional heights that reminded me of when I used to sit in the audience listening to her when we were kids. I imagined her striding out of the room, self-assured, a world traveler now, maybe a little arrogant. She could afford to swagger, after all, being at the top of her profession. I looked down at my viola, now unfamiliarly cradled under one elbow. It felt like an alien, and I like a musical imposter.

Finally, the door opened and Melanie emerged, violin in one hand. The thoughts racing through my head came to a halt. As powerful as her playing was, her demeanor was as shy as ever. She barely looked up. It was almost as if we were meeting for the first time again, when we were ten and she peeked through the lesson-room door while her dad was yelling at her for his tea and simultaneously yelling at me to play it "Again!"

After an awkward greeting, we settled down to rehearse, setting up in formation in Mr. K's finished basement. As we tuned our instruments, I was so nervous that my right hand clutched the bow in a death grip. When we first turned to play Bach's beautiful, solemn Air from Orchestral Suite No. 3, my bow skittered across the strings. But then something happened. It was like we were kids again. All the years in between disappeared. We were all breathing together. We had such different lives now, but somehow it was as if we were all thinking with one brain. And it felt as if Stephanie was right there with us. The memory of that old connection between us kicked in, and I realized that it had never gone away. It was inside us all the time.

The basement had a big stereo, so that Mr. K could blast his classical music, and a bar at one end. That's where Mr. K was now. I noticed his hands shaking alarmingly as he poured drinks, while the wobbling of his head marked a different rhythm all its own. Still, he was smiling as he looked out at us, watching us play.

"Thees room eez just for me," he said, after insisting we try it "one more time—again." A playful look momentarily wiped away the pain that I had seen on his face earlier. "See? I got my own Black Russian bar."

At the church for the memorial mass the next day, an enormous poster-size photo of Stephanie, propped up on an easel in front of the altar, greeted us. The picture stopped me short. It was difficult to look at but impossible to look away. The photo was the same one that I had seen in my parents' newspaper seven years ago. Stephanie, with her beautiful dark eyes and porcelain skin, with a little smile on her face, ready to break into a giggle. Melanie excused herself and ran from the sanctuary.

When I first saw that photo seven years ago, Steph was still a member of our generation. She looked a lot like the rest of us in our quartet. But since then, I had had a second child, become an editor, fixed up our fixer-upper house. Melanie had had three kids and toured the world. Miriam had married, started a family, and taught too many students to count how to play instruments. We would all be pushing forty before we knew it.

And then there was Stephanie. In the photo, she was in her

midtwenties—almost a generation younger than we were now. With each day, that gap was widening. You could feel it, that she was slipping away from us, receding into the past as we plowed into the future. We would continue to build lives and careers, to collect wrinkles and gray hairs, and to watch our children grow. She would stay that age forever. She was beautiful, but she was in amber. No—she was gone.

Mr. K, accustomed to an audience, seemed to be more collected than any of us as he greeted the crowd. I was too rattled to notice that the church had filled to capacity. The four of us in the quartet unpacked our instruments and sat in formation, to the side of the altar, listening to the service. We performed our Bach Air, and I saw a few people in the front rows dabbing at their eyes.

At one point, Melanie got up to perform a solo in Steph's memory. It was "Méditation" from *Thaïs*, by Massenet, and it was the most heartbreaking piece I've ever heard. I wiped my eyes, smearing my makeup across my cheeks, and as she sat back down, I said something dumb and hopelessly inadequate like, "What a beautiful tribute to Steph." Melanie didn't look at me. She was somewhere far away, far from everyone else.

Afterward, I was surprised by the size of the crowd, which overflowed into the lobby. Mr. K's old students and their parents had converged in force. Some still lived in town, but many had traveled a far distance. My old friend Jonathan, the smartest boy in our class, was there. Now he was a doctor; he had driven in from Boston with his glamorous Italian neurobiologist wife.

Miriam's family was there, too. Of the seven kids in her family—all of them students of Mr. K—four of them had become either teachers or musicians. Her parents were there as well, along with many other parents I recognized, older now, their children long grown, but determined to be there to support Mr. K.

But mostly, there were Mr. K's former students—younger

students, older students, from dewy twentysomethings to graying near-retirees. At the reception afterward, throngs of the now-grown pupils greeted one another, introducing their spouses, trading addresses, and running after toddlers. The room was rippling with happy shrieks of recognition. Children ran around with cookies and punch.

I was talking with Jonathan's mother when Mr. K approached me. He gathered me in one more hug, and I saw tears in his eyes.

He motioned to the crowd circulating around him. "Thees was Stephanie's last gift," he told me. "To bring us all back together again."

18

Meditation

MELANIE

At the church for the memorial service, there is a large portrait of my beautiful sister. When I arrive, the organist, a family friend whose two sons studied with my father, is playing. The portrait and the music together overwhelm me, and I break down, retreating into the ladies' room to recover.

Somehow I manage to play "Méditation" from *Thaïs*, the mournful piece that I played at my mother's funeral, the one my father taught me as a little girl. It is my father's favorite piece of music. There is no better way to say good-bye to our Stephanie.

The last note of the "Méditation" quivers to an end. Still trembling, half blinded by tears, I make my way to my seat in the front pew next to Joanne. She reaches over and squeezes my hand reassuringly.

"That was such a beautiful tribute to Steph," she whispers.

"It was so hard not to cry . . . my bow was shaking . . ." Even though I am accustomed to performing onstage in front of thousands of people several times a week, this was infinitely more difficult. The emotion was overwhelming. "That was one of the hardest things I've ever done."

Then it's time for our quartet to play. Miriam, Joanne, Darlene, and I perform Bach's Air from Orchestral Suite No. 3, the piece Steph had played at my wedding.

Our old quartet is reunited one last time. Minus one.

In Miriam's very large, wonderful family there is a sensitive, kind funeral director named Joe. He drives us to the cemetery in the limousine, and I sit in front next to him. On the seat between us is a little box. I ride the whole way, more than an hour, with my hand on that box of my sister's ashes. It is our last ride together, and it is as close as I can get to holding her hand.

When we get to the cemetery, we are each given a rose to place beside the little box, which is to be buried next to my mother. I hold tight to my father's hand. I bend down to kiss the little box and have the sensation that I could just keep falling down down down until I am next to her, and then I could stay with her forever.

But Daddy needs me, and Ed needs me, and Nicholas, Gregory, and Laura need me. As my father has been all these years, I must be strong. So I stand up and walk back to the limousine and back to my family, back to my life.

My grandmother Baba makes it to the church for Stephanie's service, but she is too frail to go with us to the cemetery. She is closing in on her one hundredth birthday and is finally starting to slow down. By the time my family makes our next visit to New Jersey, she is in the hospital. When we arrive there, she is lying on a gurney in the chilly hospital corridor, awaiting a scan, berating everyone within earshot. We can hear her shrill voice even before we turn the corner and see her.

"Mother, look who eez here!" my dad says. "Malanka and Ed haf brought the children to see you."

My dad looks anxiously at the nurse standing nearby, who nods encouragingly. We file up to her bedside, murmuring our greetings. An explosion of Ukrainian erupts from my supine grandmother, her arms waving wildly. My father responds in soothing tones, clearly trying his best to placate her, while the six-year-old twins edge behind me nervously. After a few minutes, she seems a bit calmer and my dad gestures to Nicky.

"Nick? Why don't you play a leetle of your Vivaldi for Baba? Eez okay eef he plays violin for her here?" my father asks the nurse.

"Of course! That would be lovely! Mrs. DeBaylo, you never told us you had a musician in the family!" The nurse gratefully grabs the lifeline we've thrown her.

Baba snarls a response, but you can tell that some of the fight has already started to go out of her. Eight-year-old Nicky obediently unpacks and I tune him up quickly. A small crowd gathers as Nick energetically plunges into his concerto. The nurses and wandering patients who have stood by listening break into applause when he's done.

"That's mine grand-grandson," Baba says triumphantly.

My father and I exchange a smile.

I fight with myself for a long while about whether to insist that the twins learn violin, too. At first I assume they will play, just as Steph and I had. But my struggles with Nick give me pause. Maybe I should let them decide for themselves, when they are old enough to make a decision.

Having twins, so soon after Nick was born, was overwhelming enough. The thought of teaching them both—when it's a difficult proposition just to raise them while maintaining some semblance of control over the house—is terrifying.

Besides, I want my own children to be able to participate in all the activities that I had not. As they get older, the boys play ice hockey, and Laura takes figure skating lessons. Over the years there are very few activities that one or another of my kids doesn't try. There's Irish dancing and Tae Kwon Do, theater and soccer, baseball and art lessons and tennis and lacrosse and Spanish classes and chess club. I don't want to relive my own childhood. I don't want to prevent them from trying other activities, or playing with their friends. I don't want to burden them with endless practicing.

Still, I can't imagine life without music. This is my special gift. How can I not share it with them? I've learned from my father that music truly is meant to be given away, to be shared with others, even if it has to be delivered to their bedside. He didn't just teach me to play the violin; he taught me that it is necessary for people to have music in their lives.

It's a huge commitment of time and energy to hold daily practice sessions with each child. I've enrolled them in outside music lessons. But as my father did with me, I supervise each of them as they practice. Squeezing the violin into our already packed days is monumentally difficult. When a child is tired, hungry, distracted, or just plain not in the mood, practicing is unproductive, and achieving optimal conditions is almost as rare as a total eclipse of the sun.

Every day I ask myself if it's worth it: the cajoling, the yelling, the tears. If they want to quit, so be it. More than once I offer—but the answer is always no. So every time we travel to the East Coast to visit the extended family, three little violins are stowed in our van among the suitcases, camera bag, carsick bag, the telescope for moon gazing at Aunt Pat's, the buckets of worms and bags of horse manure fertilizer we collect at Aunt Jane's, snacks, pillows, and plenty of CDs ranging from jazz and musicals to the kids' Suzuki practice tapes.

Like my father, I take my children to nursing homes with our violins to play for the elderly and infirm. When Christmas rolls around, we put together a program of carols and cheerful classics that we perform at local hospitals with family friends. We become regulars on the hospital–nursing home circuit, stopping with our violins at my old aunt Titka's nursing home in Ohio before heading to Ed's mother in a home in Warwick, New York, where, though I don't realize it, Joanne spends weekends at her house just down the road.

"Well, that needs a lot of work."

My dad is listening over the phone as the twins play Bach's Double Violin Concerto, the piece Steph and I performed at her last recital.

It is always with some trepidation that I have my children play for my dad. Often, when they play for him in person, he'll pull them into a hug, murmuring, "That was beautiful," into their soft red-gold hair. When he goes back home to New Jersey, he learns how to use Skype on his computer to watch them perform, the better for him to keep an eye on their technique and posture.

But when he thinks there's room for improvement, he can be brutal. He's dismissive of their Suzuki training, which teaches young children to memorize tunes rather than to read notes. "I had you reading notes before you could read words!" he harrumphs. He instructs them to use "More bow!" or to make "Beeg sound!"

It is hard for me not to take his criticisms personally. I always want my children to play well, to show my father that I'm guiding them properly and that the legacy of music in the Kupchynsky family lives on. My dad likes to grade me. Not long ago when he came to visit, I drove him to a Chicago Symphony concert to watch me perform. As we got out of the car in the parking garage next to Symphony Center, he looked back with a frown: "I'd geev you parking job a B-plus."

My children don't seem nearly as rattled by his criticism as I am, but I explain his reaction just in case.

"Grandpa used to be a teacher," I say to Laura and Greg after they finish their piece. "He was a teacher for so long, he enjoys fixing the music, making it better. It's part of the fun for him."

The day he stops criticizing is the day I start worrying.

JOANNE

Rebecca's eleventh birthday was the next day. She had asked for refrigerator magnets to decorate her school locker. That's why I was inside the World Trade Center at 8:46 A.M. I had stopped there on my way to work at the *Wall Street Journal* office, across the street. I had found the perfect magnet, shaped like a violin, in one of the concourse-level shops. The magnet had a button in the middle, and when you pushed it, it played a little tune. I hoped it would be a gentle reminder to Rebecca to practice for her violin lessons. I pressed it idly while waiting at the cash register.

"Everybody's running!" the young woman at the counter suddenly said, looking out at a crowd of people being shooed toward the exit by a security guard. "Maybe we should get out of here."

I pushed the magnet firmly toward her.

She looked anxiously toward the door. "We've got to leave."

I rolled my eyes. Please. People in this town overreact. We hadn't heard anything. The commuters being herded past the store looked more annoyed than worried. It was probably a false alarm.

"Ring this up first. I'm not leaving until I pay."

Hastily, she rang up the purchase.

The receipt read 8:55 A.M., SEPTEMBER 11, 2001.

When I emerged from the building onto Church Street a minute later, blinking in the sunlight, it was snowing. At least it looked like snow, as pulverized plaster drifted down from a brilliant blue sky, pinging metallically when the flakes hit the sunglasses perched on top of my head. Hundreds of papers—blank financial order forms—were wafting through the air. Above us was the unimaginable sight of the World Trade Center on fire, smoke billowing out of an ugly gash in the upper floors. In front of us, cars were pulled up at crazy angles on the sidewalk, abandoned. One was crushed by a giant chunk of concrete. There must have been sirens, and maybe there was shouting, but it was as if it were a dream: every sound was muffled and every action in slow motion.

For a moment I stood with my colleague Joe, who was at the store with me, staring upward, trying to comprehend what appeared to be one of the worst aviation accidents in history. Then we made a dash for the office, for this would clearly be a huge news day.

Turning the corner, trying to get to our building, we were plunged into a war zone. The force of the crash had thrown the debris forward onto Liberty Street, where we now stood. Everything was on fire. Rows of flaming seats were sprawled in the middle of the road, along with what looked like a jet engine. We detoured to avoid the flames and found ourselves fleeing through a side street that was infinitely worse. Human carnage, raw and red, was splattered thickly across the pavement and the sidewalks. We picked our way through an indescribable hell, our heads down, stepping gingerly and trying not to look at the gruesome vista spread out in front of us. When we reached the West Side Highway, across from our building, we swerved to avoid a headless corpse on the sidewalk that someone had inadequately covered with a restaurant napkin. Waiting at a red light, we stood next to a businessman with a head wound streaming blood onto his white shirt collar.

That's where we were when the second plane came in, so loud it sounded as if it were only inches above our heads. The crash was a sonic boom, a deep, deafening, cataclysmic eruption that went on and on, layer after sickening layer of destruction. Animal instinct took over. Everyone on the street ran, diving for cover. Bags, briefcases, and shoes were scattered, abandoned in the middle of the road. I found myself flattened against the back wall of the *Journal* building. Like everyone else there, I assumed I was about to die. In that moment, I felt strangely calm.

It was only afterward, with the explosion still echoing, that the group of dazed people hugging the walls slowly pulled away, realizing this was no accident. The building was now locked, so Joe and I joined the exodus trying to escape, making our way on foot underneath both burning towers as people jumped from the top floors. Minutes later, when the towers collapsed, the *Journal* building was severely damaged, too. I walked uptown to a colleague's apartment that had been hastily transformed into a newsroom.

For the next ten months, with the *Journal* building uninhabitable, much of the newspaper's staff would all but live in a makeshift office in New Jersey. Tom took over at home. On that first night of September 11, I had gotten back to our apartment close to midnight. At home, trying to drive away the day's grisly images, I baked a birthday cake for Rebecca. By the time she woke up the next morning I was gone, back to work.

*   *   *

I ended up missing Rebecca's birthday that day, and Andrew's a month later, and most other major events that year. I also missed doctors' appointments. By the time I got around to the mammogram appointment I was supposed to have had on my fortieth birthday, a year had passed. It was the summer of 2002, and the doctor kept me in the office for hours, kept sending me back in to that god-awful machine for retakes of the pictures. Finally, she ushered me into her office.

"You've got a lump. I don't know what it is, but I don't like it."

A surgical biopsy a few weeks later confirmed her suspicions: I had breast cancer.

The disease was caught early, the doctor told me, and hadn't spread. My prognosis was good. Still, given that I was relatively young and my kids were still in grade school, we decided to treat it aggressively. Lumpectomy, six months of chemotherapy, two months of radiation. Can I do both treatments at once? I asked of the doctor.

"Not a good idea."

"Why not?"

"You won't be able to work if you do chemo and radiation at the same time." Usually those two treatments are given consecutively, the doctor said. The punch of both together is debilitating. You'll be too weak to do both. Your body can't handle it.

Try me, I said.

It didn't occur to me to take off time for the treatments. Of course I would work through it. What else could I do? I would keep working because I had to; I didn't have the luxury to take off, or so I told myself. What would I have done other than wallow if I did? Work was a tonic; there really is no such thing as happiness without hard work. Someone told me that once, I thought.

The treatments made me nauseated and dizzy and bone-tired,

and my head often felt stuffed with cotton. I could get through the workday but had no energy for anything else. I withdrew from social engagements; I didn't have the bandwidth to see friends, much less keep up with the people I had reconnected with at Steph's memorial service. I lost touch with Mr. K.

I came up with a routine to deal with the side effects. After my chemo sessions on Thursday afternoons, I would take the weekend to recover, waiting for the worst of the nausea and fatigue to pass. Tom would take the kids out for ice cream or to a movie while I sat immobile in a chair with the lights turned down low, unable to focus enough to read or even watch TV.

Nausea medicines didn't seem to help. Closing my eyes didn't help, either; even while sitting still, I was knocked off kilter by vertigo. But there was one thing that eased my symptoms: classical music. Especially Bach. A lifetime ago, I had performed plenty of Bach with Mr. K. There was a wonderful order and restraint to the composer's work that somehow unraveled the cottony mess that was my brain and allowed me to breathe calmly and think straight. I would sit back and let the music fill me, and somehow, it seemed to push the toxins right out of my system. *Strange,* I thought, *how music is the one way to keep myself sane. To cope.*

My parents came to visit and my dad brought me a recording of the Yale Cellos performing an all-Bach program. He figured I would get a kick out of a group based at my alma mater. I flipped through the credits—a roster of the best young cellists in the world, from every country imaginable—to see if any of the performers were college classmates. Several were, but what struck me was another name listed among the brilliant musicians on the recording: Miriam Kling Perkoff, who had been a few years behind me back in East Brunswick. The last time I'd seen her, she was a cute little girl sitting behind the other Miriam, our quartet's cellist. I didn't know she had gone on to become a musician.

On the first anniversary of 9/11, we were woken up at five A.M. by the sound of bagpipers marching down Broadway just in front of our apartment, slowly making their mournful journey down to Ground Zero. I had just come off two cancer surgeries and was about to start chemo treatments. At work, we were immersed in coverage of the anniversary. So was every other news outlet in the country.

A lot of powerful journalism would mark that solemn day. But one of the most moving was a newspaper column that appeared half a continent away, in the *Daily Herald* in Utah. It was a stirring treatise about freedom and patriotism, and about how to teach those values to our kids.

Advocates were calling for "classes to specifically teach children to have love for their country...," the writer noted. "Those people should take lessons from a teacher I had who gave eloquent lessons on the liberty guaranteed by this country."

This teacher, the author explained, didn't "overtly [teach] us about patriotism or liberty. He didn't even teach us about civics or the Constitution. [He] was not a social studies teacher. He was a music teacher..."

The teacher was Mr. K.

The columnist was Donald Meyers, the incorrigible kid whom Mr. K never gave up trying to teach to play the violin, whom Mr. K chose to play the devil in *Orpheus in the Underworld*. "He could be tough," Donald wrote about Mr. K. "One of the first things he would tell beginners was, 'Orchestra is not democracy. It is benign dictatorship.' And some days we wondered about the benign part."

But Donald was struck by the fact that for the finale of every annual concert, Mr. K chose a piece "that either celebrated liberty or was by a composer who fought tyranny with music. He encouraged us to learn on our own about these people and their work as a way to better appreciate the music."

It was a lesson Donald had carried with him through his career.

Years later, I asked him about it. "He taught me you really can't say the word *impossible*," Donald told me. "One thing I learned from Mr. K was don't let somebody say you can't do something. He pushed us, but you could sense that he believed in us. He pushed everybody to do better than they thought they could."

Despite Mr. K's best efforts, Donald never did advance very far on the violin. But in the end, he was one of Mr. K's best students after all.

19

Finale

MELANIE

My dad is visiting us in Chicago. His hair, or what little is left of it, has turned white, and he's sporting a goatee. He's finally given up on his trim mustache and comb-over hairstyle, both of which require too much maintenance. He's always despised being bald—the Ukrainian phrase for bald translates to "half a rear end on your head." But in the end, practicality trumps vanity.

At dinner, he slumps down in his chair, his legs and head bobbing involuntarily. His eyes are unfocused. He seems to be shrinking, getting shorter and weaker. I've cooked his favorite meal of chicken and potatoes with green beans. His wife, Joan, who seldom leaves his side, cuts his meat for him.

We have another dinner guest: one of his old students, Miriam

Perkoff, who is in town from California. My dad had spotted her as a little girl and decided she was a perfect fit for the cello. Quiet and shy, by high school Miriam had become a superb musician. She was named principal cellist of All-State Orchestra, then of All-Eastern Orchestra. She went on to study at the Yale School of Music and perform with the Yale Cellos under legendary teacher Aldo Parisot. She is now a professional musician in San Francisco. She's come to Chicago to work on a project with the violinist Itzhak Perlman.

At dinner, my dad's head droops while Miriam and I catch up and compare notes about the music scenes in Chicago and San Francisco. But I can tell she's distracted, glancing across the table at my father, who doesn't speak much. As I set out dessert—homemade walnut cake, my dad's favorite—Miriam fixes her gaze on him.

"Mr. K," she starts out, quietly, uncertainly, looking again like the shy teenager she had been decades ago. She takes a breath. "Mr. K, I've waited too long to do this." She tries unsuccessfully to catch my father's eye. Her own eyes are brimming with tears, and she dabs at them with her napkin.

"Actually, I've wanted to do it for years," she says, and by now she's full-on crying. "I've been wanting to thank you for all these years. I've had this wonderful career. Ever since that day when you told me I had 'cello hands,' so my parents let me choose the cello . . . well, you changed my life. Everything I've done since then has been shaped by that moment. I guess what I'm trying to say is thank you. Thank you for my life."

My dad looks at Miriam blankly.

At my front door later that evening, as I hug her good-bye, Miriam drops her voice to a whisper. "I'm not sure he heard me, or understood what I was trying to say. He looks so different. "

I glance over my shoulder at my dad, still sitting at the table, eating a second piece of cake, paying no attention to us. Then I turn back toward Miriam and give her another hug, promising her that

An outdoor lesson with Grandpa: Twins Greg and Laura serenade
their grandfather with Bach's Concerto for Two Violins in 2006.
Melanie and Stephanie played the same piece together as children.

of course he has been following her career for all these years, always with great pride.

"Don't worry," I tell her as she disappears into the night. "He understood."

My father is seventy-nine years old when what I've been afraid would happen happens. Too stubborn to allow grab bars to be installed in his home, he suffers a fall in the shower and has to be hospitalized. It's more than just a fall; it seems as if he has tumbled right off the edge of the earth. Maybe it was some sort of stroke, the doctor tells me, but it's hard to be sure where the Parkinson's leaves off and the other problems begin.

Until that moment, I have been able to convince myself that my father is still there for me to depend on, to go to for advice, to offer support. We still speak regularly on the phone. But deep in my heart, I am coming to terms with the realization that, for a while now, that feeling that my daddy is still there for me is mostly a figment of my imagination.

In the hospital, my dad tosses in his bed, hallucinating. "Thees cellblock eez where they're keeping the Ukrainians!" he yells at the orderlies who try to restrain him.

Days later, he's transferred to a nursing home, but he's confused about where he is and why. Phone calls are no longer possible, which I realize when I attempt to play our usual game of "Name That Tune" and find myself humming *Scheherazade* to the nurse, who has retrieved the telephone because it had fallen out of my father's weakened grasp. He can no longer hold the phone.

As often as I can break free of my life in Chicago, I fly to New Jersey to be with him. He still enjoys music and food, both of which I can provide. Usually, I stay with my oldest friend Miriam—now Miriam Cotter—and borrow a violin from her so I won't have to carry one on the plane. I bring an insulated bag stuffed with ice packs and my dad's favorite dinner, pyrohy and kielbasa, just like Baba used to make. Baba has only recently died, at 103 years old. She lived at home until the end, mostly because she didn't have a choice: she got kicked out of a series of nursing homes for attacking the patients and staff.

When school lets out that summer, I take fifteen-year-old Laura with me to visit. We squeeze into a tiny rental car and head from Newark down the Garden State Parkway toward the nursing home near the Jersey Shore. We open the windows wide, allowing our lungs to fill with the moist scent of the ocean mixed with exhaust.

I can't help but remember my long ago summer trips along this same road to Long Beach Island. The radio is cranked up all the way, tuned as always to Stephanie's favorite classic rock station.

"*Nostalgia.* Do you know what that word means?" I ask. Laura is preparing for her SATs, keeping a list of new words taped to her mirror so she can study them while she does her hair each morning.

"I've heard it before, but I'm not sure exactly..."

"This is nostalgia. It's a feeling, of remembering times gone by, things from the past, this drive, the smell of the air. It's missing my family..."

The smells and sounds wash over me, bringing back feelings and memories from when I was a little girl. I remember how it was when my father piled Stephanie and me into the big white Pontiac, when my mother could still walk, and when we would all laugh and listen to classical music that was still brand new to us as we drove down to the shore for a weekend at the beach.

It reminds me, too, of a more recent, bittersweet memory of visiting my father some months ago, when his health had first started its precipitous decline. It was a misty May night, and the lilacs were blooming as I rounded the ramp off Exit 9 of the New Jersey Turnpike. Driving down Route 18 through East Brunswick, I felt a pang of nostalgia. This town had been my home, the center of my childhood, the place where I shared so many memories with Stephanie and the rest of my family. Now the connection was severed. None of my family members lived here anymore. In fact, there was no reason for me to have even exited the turnpike here, except force of habit.

On the car radio, song titles slid by on the digital display one after another. As the rain began to fall, the DJ came back on the air, his voice shaking me from my reverie and filling the air. "This next song was requested by Stephanie," he said.

A Bon Jovi tune began to play. One of my sister's favorite groups. A coincidence, surely, I told myself. Still, for some reason that day, long after the song ended, after the next one had already begun, its title remained illuminated on the radio display screen: THANK YOU FOR LOVING ME.

Thinking back on that day, and on Steph, my father, my mother, and all that was gone, I pause. Then I grab Laura's hand and press it to my lips. "I'm just so glad I have you, and that you're here with me now."

At the nursing home, my father is agitated. He won't eat. He keeps trying to get up out of his wheelchair, where he is now confined just as my mother had been for most of her life. "I want to lie down with Stephanie," he says.

Laura unpacks her violin and starts to play some Bach for him, which helps a little.

I hold him and try to soothe him.

"I haf to get home," he says, looking at me without recognition. "I haf a sick wife and two leetle girls to take care of! Doesn't anyone take care of their families anymore?"

"Daddy, it's me, Melanie!" I plead. "Don't you remember Melanie?"

"Of *course* I remember Melanie," he wails. "I just can't remember the stuff around Melanie."

We sit with him for a long time, Laura and I, taking turns playing her violin. Études, Bach, show tunes, Ukrainian folk songs, we play whatever our fingers can remember.

Slowly, the music calms him. It brings him back.

Before we leave, I promise to bring back my whole family the next month. "Daddy, next time we come to see you, we'll all bring our violins. Nicky and Laura and Greg will play, too, and we'll give a concert for everyone here. How does that sound?"

"What weel you play?"

"I don't know yet. Let's plan it now."

My father is silent for a minute.

"Just don't make eet too long," he says finally, decisively. "You always want to leave your audience wanting more."

A month later the whole family comes back with four violins and a viola in tow. We set up in the cafeteria of the dementia ward to perform for the patients, as promised, and to have a small party for my dad, whose eighty-first birthday is approaching. The music soothes some of the patients in the audience, though it agitates almost as many.

"Hey! Can you turn that goddamn thing down!" an elderly man shouts while we play.

"When are we gonna eat? I'm hungry!" comes the voice of a woman.

My three children, accustomed to performing for all sorts of audiences—trained, much as my dad's students were years ago, to reach out and connect through their music—don't break stride. After we finish our performance, they circulate through the crowd, letting the sick and elderly touch them and hug them, just as my dad instructed his own students forty years ago.

"I played one of those when I was young," one woman says.

An elderly man in a wheelchair laughs. "My wife always used to drag me to the symphony!"

One of the old ladies attaches herself to Ed and won't leave his side, clinging to his arm possessively and giving me an evil look as I whisper in his ear that it's time to go.

Leaving the group of patients behind, we wheel my dad down the corridor, to a private room where Ed and the kids have set up a cake. The helium-filled birthday balloons we've tied to the back of the wheelchair bob under the fluorescent lights. My dad's chin sags onto his chest.

I look at his crippled form, trying to conjure the father who taught me everything I know that's worth knowing: How to plant a garden, how to choose a hiking stick, how to ride a bike, swim, drive a car, listen to and love music, and play the violin. How to be a caring parent. How to be strong. Together, we faced life's deepest sorrows and its greatest joys. I can still see us standing next to each other on the highest mountain peaks in the northeast, Mount Katahdin and Mount Washington. I smile as I think of how he used to boil water on the campfire so that I could wash my hair.

Steph and I used to laugh about how Daddy, who was so over-protective of us at home, would scamper ahead up the sheer rock cliffs like a mountain goat, shouting, "Come on, girls! No turning back, only going forward!" We knew that a mistake could end in death, yet he seemed so unconcerned. I realize now that on those trails he knew he had done all he could to get us ready, that there was nothing more he could do for us short of carrying us piggyback up that mountain, and that he had faith in us and our abilities to do what we had to do without his help. I didn't understand it then, but it strikes me with sudden clarity now: This was preparation for things to come. He did all he could to get me ready for my life journey, but I alone must make the climb.

I have so much I want to say to him. But conversation is impossible; he is simply too ill. So instead, I take out my violin and begin to play.

I have lots of pieces "in my fingers," so to speak, and could play any one of them. But the piece I choose is "Méditation" from *Thaïs*, the same mournful composition that he had taught me when I was a little girl and that I had played at my mother's funeral, then at Stephanie's memorial. I fear it might disturb him, might bring back painful memories. But I play it because it says everything I somehow cannot: That I love him, and mourn him, and miss him. That I'm grateful for everything he taught me, grateful he has passed along this incredible gift to me that I can now pass along to my own children.

That he was right: I would thank him someday. That day is today.

Forcing everything else from my mind, I give myself over to the music and play from my heart, the way my father taught me, letting the music speak for us both.

As the last harmonic fades away, in the stillness I look over at my father. His head is bent, his eyes closed. For a moment I think he has fallen asleep. But then his eyes flutter open and my father gazes at me, inhaling deeply. It's as if he is breathing in the music itself.

Then, softly, gently, my father utters one of the last words he will ever speak to me: "Again."

20

Coda

JOANNE

Just before Thanksgiving, en route home from a World Economic Forum meeting, I checked my e-mail at the Dubai airport and saw an urgent message from our quartet's old cellist Miriam, half a world away. She had sent it at almost four o'clock in the morning her time.

The subject line read: "The time has arrived . . ."

Her message said that Mr. K had lost his battle with Parkinson's disease. He had died a few hours before. He was eighty-one. Miriam, a devout mother of five who homeschooled her kids, noted the significance of the date: in the Catholic religion, it was the Feast Day of Saint Cecilia, patron saint of music. "Could there be any more appropriate send-off for a man who brought the gift of music to hundreds, if not thousands of lives?" she asked.

I didn't know anything about saints. But I did know there was something I had to do. After I landed in New York the next day, still bleary and jet-lagged, I tossed my suitcase, unopened, onto my bed and started digging through my closets. I couldn't remember where I had last stashed my old viola. But I needed to find out.

I wasn't the only one. In the days and weeks that followed, the news of Mr. K's passing traveled from student to student, from one generation to the next, from state to state and across the oceans. The tech executive in Virginia. The musician in San Francisco. The writer in Utah. Through Facebook and texts and e-mail came the call: it was time for us—Mr. K's students and colleagues—to play one final concert together, this time for him.

The outpouring took me by surprise. Mr. K was the toughest teacher we ever had. He could be downright mean. If he was teaching today, he wouldn't stand a chance. Parents would be outraged. They'd be calling and complaining. They'd yell at the principal if he singled out their kid for playing out of tune. They'd call a lawyer if he suggested their child was "deaf" or an "*idyot.*" Administrators would be pressured to fire him. Almost surely they would.

In the end, the fact is, Mr. K did push us hard: harder than our parents, harder than our other teachers. He scared the daylights out of us. Through sheer force of will, he made us better than we had any right to be.

It didn't hit me, until then, how much we loved him for it.

I finally found my instrument, squeezed behind some old business suits that should have been given away ages ago. The case was cracked and coated with dust, untouched for more than a decade, since the day of Steph's memorial service. The hinges creaked when I opened it. I was greeted by a cascade of loose horsehair—my bow a victim of mites, the repairman would later explain. It was pure agony to twist my fingers into position. But to my astonishment—and that of my teenage children—I could still manage a credible sound.

It turned out that there were one hundred people just like me. When I showed up at Hammarskjold Middle School to rehearse before that afternoon's concert, there they were: four decades' worth of former students and colleagues. There were lawyers and accountants, engineers and executives. There were people who hadn't played in decades sitting alongside professional musicians like Melanie, who had flown in from Chicago with her musician husband and their three violinist children. There were multiple generations of music teachers. They flew in from California and Oregon, from Virginia and Massachusetts. They came with siblings and children; Miriam Cotter took her seat with thirteen other family members.

Across the room I spotted my old classmate Ted Kesler, the boy whom Mr. K picked on so relentlessly, who sat at the back of the first violin section. When I thought back to Mr. K at his toughest, Ted always came to mind. I could still see Mr. K forcing him to play alone—"Again! Again!"—while the rest of the kids in the orchestra watched. Ted was a college professor of education now. We greeted each other warmly, but I was puzzled. Why show up for a teacher who tortured him so?

"In some ways, Mr. K was a terrible match for me," he readily conceded.

But then Ted told me something I didn't know when we were kids. His mother had died when he was in grade school, before he moved to East Brunswick. His father was a Holocaust survivor who was raising four children on his own; other family members had perished in concentration camps. Mr. K showed his father a respect, a deference, that you didn't see with the other parents. "Mr. K was hard on me in part because I was lost and aimless and unguided," Ted said. "You know, he wanted more from me." What's more, "the orchestra kept me connected within a community," he said. "It sustained me. All of those musicians in the group effort kept pushing me forward ... That kept me going: the collaborative energy."

I settled into my seat in the viola section beside Miriam's younger brother Joe, now a music teacher, and looked around at old friends laughing and hugging and pulling out dusty student instruments they hadn't touched in years. Music teacher Darlene Brandt, who Mr. K had taught in the 1950s, stood in a corner chatting with Melanie's children, who he instructed fifty years later. In between were musicians of all ages and every conceivable level of ability, mixing easily with one another, comparing tales about our fearsome teacher.

Ted was right. Mr. K understood better than anyone the bond music creates among people who play it together. Beyond his bluster—and behind his wicked sense of humor and taste for Black Russians—perhaps that was his lesson all along.

He surely learned it the hard way. He had every reason to be bitter and self-pitying. The nightmarish childhood, the years in refugee camps, the heartbreak of his wife struck down by multiple sclerosis. All those years while we whined that he was riding us too hard, he was raising his daughters and caring for his sick wife on his own. Then there was Stephanie, murdered. There were the seven years, after she went missing, that he spent searching for her, never giving up hope until her remains were found.

Yet on that day, as all of us crowded onto the stage, we saw that the legacy he had left behind was pure joy. You could see it in the faces of the audience when the curtain rose for the performance that afternoon. You could hear it as Melanie, her three children, and her husband performed as a family. You could feel it when the full orchestra, led by Mr. K's onetime protégé Dr. Sandra Dackow, poured itself into his favorite Tchaikovsky and Bach. It powered us through the lost years, the lack of rehearsal time, and the stray notes from us rustier alums.

When Sandy lifted her baton and we began to play, you have heard more polished performers in your life. You have heard more difficult music. But you have never heard any concert as heartfelt as this one. It was plain as could be to everyone in that concert hall, whether on the stage or in the audience: at the close of his life, Mr. K's dreams—forged as a child, when he stood amid the rubble and listened to a German soldier play the violin—were fulfilled. His orchestra played on.

"We succeeded at first because we were afraid not to—and later because we knew this man believed we could play brilliantly, so we believed it ourselves," Darlene told the crowd.

Afterward, Melanie took the stage to describe the proud father who waved like a maniac from a Lincoln Center balcony the first time she played there. Then she introduced her own performance, of his favorite piece, "Méditation" from *Thaïs*. "The last few times I visited my dad, I brought my violin and played for him for hours on end. I played because I knew he loved it," she said softly.

"I'm really glad I had the chance to make music for him while he was still here to enjoy it. And now I would like to play for him just one last time, to say good-bye."

Before the concert, half a dozen old friends had gathered for brunch at a local restaurant. Most of us hadn't seen each other in decades. Melanie and her husband, Ed, were there, and so was Miriam Cotter. John Stine—the strapping cellist whose music-teacher mother was Mr. K's best friend—was now a tech executive who sat on the board of his local symphony. Our old friend Michael Grossman was a professional violinist and teacher in Oregon. Miriam Perkoff was a professional cellist in San Francisco. Jonathan, who went on to Princeton and Yale Medical School, was a doctor in Boston.

Over heaping plates of scrambled eggs and pancakes, we reminisced about the old days, and compared notes about children and jobs and the cities in which we lived. Then the conversation shifted to Mr. K.

I put a question to the others, because I wasn't sure of the answer myself: Why did we all feel drawn to come back? What was it about this one teacher?

The answers flew thick and fast.

"He taught me what discipline was," Miriam Perkoff said.

"Self-confidence."

"How to fail. The experience of having to pick yourself up afterward and move on."

"Resilience."

"My livelihood for the last thirty years. It was a gift from my teenage years with Jerry," Michael said. "If I had to make a choice between performing and teaching, it's so obvious it would be teaching. It's really cool, this gift that keeps on giving."

To those answers, I said, I would add one more: optimism.

If you wanted to, you could have looked around the table that day and seen a catalog of woe: Death. Divorce. Illness. Melanie's parents and sister, gone. Michael's wife, struck by cancer, had died barely a month before. But instead, as we pushed away the remnants of our scrambled eggs and pancakes, reluctant to leave, not wanting the moment to pass, our table was animated by laughter and warmth and hopefulness. There was a bond that decades of separation and a few gray hairs couldn't break.

In a way, that was what Mr. K had been trying to teach us since we were children. I thought back to that day in high school, when Mr. K arranged for Melanie and our quartet to play at the funeral of the boy who had died in a horrific car crash. The boy had doted on his sister, a beginner violinist. We performed "Yesterday," as a reminder of how much he loved to listen to her play.

After brunch, slowly pushing back our chairs, we gathered our instruments and headed to our old junior high school, where the orchestra would be gathering. In the cafeteria, we unpacked our instruments as the far-flung students arrived for Mr. K's final concert.

That's when suddenly we saw her, that little girl, now grown, a professional musician herself. She had never stopped thinking about her brother's funeral, she told me. When she heard about this concert, she flew from Denver in the hope that she might find the musicians who played in his honor.

For thirty years, she told me, she had just wanted the chance to say thank you.

As did we all.

ACKNOWLEDGEMENTS

This book wouldn't have happened if Joanne's husband, Tom Distler, hadn't insisted that she write an article about Mr. K's remarkable memorial concert. For Joanne, the memorial was deeply personal. But Tom realized that Mr. K's story deserved to be shared, first in the article and then in this book. Thank you, Tom.

The fact is, neither one of us set out to write a book. For years, Melanie found it too painful to even speak about her sister, Stephanie. But encouraged by her husband, Ed Harrison, she started writing privately about Stephanie in 2009 while on a sabbatical to spend time with her father. After his death, in 2011, Melanie got a call from the Greece, New York, police, with the news that Stephanie's murderer had confessed. He was, as the police suspected, the handyman at her apartment building, who was now in prison serving two life sentences for other crimes. His murder trial is set for 2013 and he has pleaded not guilty. For Melanie, that phone call and the resolution of the case after so many years seemed like a sign that Stephanie was ready for her story to be told as well.

So many people helped make this book possible. On one of Mr. K's last visits to Miriam Cotter's home, he hugged her and whispered in her ear, "You are my third daughter." Without Miriam holding her hand through the most difficult moments, Melanie might never have found the courage to go on. To list all of Miriam's contributions would require a volume of its own. Suffice to say that even though Stephanie is gone, Melanie still has a "sister" in the truest sense of the word. Thanks also to Miriam's husband, Hilary, her parents, Charlotte and Albert Simon, and the entire Simon and Cotter families.

Nor could we have written this book without Joanne's sisters, Michele Fusillo and Rhonda Slaff, who in the writing process—as in life—have been invaluable guides. Joanne's mom, Diane Lipman, was a font of memories, of inspiration—and of photos taken by Joanne's late father, Burton Lipman, whose spirit of adventure lives on in this book. We are grateful to them all.

Dr. Sandra Dackow provided insights, anecdotes, and decades-old recordings. Darlene Morrow Brandt offered up a trove of "Mr. K stories," and kept us laughing throughout. We are grateful as well to Joan Kupchynsky, who helped reconstruct Mr. K's story and who cared for him so lovingly when he was ill.

Thanks, too, to Mr. K's other former students and colleagues, including: Anna Braun, Peggy Brighton, Paul Fried, Jonathan Friedes, John Gnassi, Michael Grossman, Diane Kerslake, Ted Kesler, Ken Langley, Donald W. Meyers, Kelly Reid McLaughlin, John Stine, LouAnn Stine, Marge Stine, Gordon Tedeschi, Miriam Kling Perkoff, and Andrew Woodruff. Thanks also to Walter Drone and Kappy Scates, who brought to life Mr. K's experiences in Shawneetown.

Charlie Lyons was irresistibly persuasive in urging us to tell this story publicly. Jeffrey Zaslow gave us the final push we needed to embark on the book. We are so grateful to them both. Tragically, Jeff passed away before the manuscript was completed.

The mystery of Mr. K's childhood history required tracking

down numerous Ukrainian and German documents. Thanks to United States Holocaust Memorial Museum Chairman Tom Bernstein as well as to Sara J. Bloomfield and Neal Guthrie. Our appreciation also to Timothy Snyder, Katia Davydenko, Olha Aleksic, Ksenya Kiebuzinski, Phillip Neumann, Kathrin Flor, Nick Kupensky, and Anika Ohm.

We are humbled by, and in awe of, refugee camp survivors Ihor Hayda, Olga Sawchuk, and Helena Melnitchenko. A special thanks to Taras Hunczak, Rutgers University history professor emeritus, who shared his knowledge plus checked the accuracy of our historical descriptions and Ukrainian spellings.

Joe Dizney, Edward Felsenthal, and Amy Stevens were early readers whose suggestions improved this book immeasurably. For their insights and encouragement, thank you as well to: Katie Couric, Kevin Goldman, Jeff Greenfield, Andrew Heyward, Karen Lyons, Inge Reichenbach, Bruce Rockwell, Tony Schwartz, Bob Scully, Ivan Selin, David Shipley, Phyllis Strong, and Barbara Walters. Thanks also to Maestro Riccardo Muti, Deborah Rutter, Vanessa Moss, Martha Gilmer, Rachelle Roe, John Deverman, Anne MacQuarrie, Frank Villella, Ann Smelser, Benjamin Zander, and the Ladies of the CSO Locker Room, especially Catherine Brubaker, Rachel Goldstein, Florence Schwartz, and Susan Synnestvedt.

Books take a village, and we are lucky to live in ours. Kerri Kolen and Elisabeth Dyssegaard are brilliantly talented editors who helped shape this book in ways both big and small—and made every step a pleasure. The Black Russians are on us! We are enormously grateful to Ellen Archer for her passion, support, and vision, and to her Hyperion colleagues, including Diane Aronson, Shubhani Sarkar, Laura Klynstra, Maha Khalil, Kristin Kiser, Nancy Tan, Theresa Karle, Christine Ragasa, Bryan Christian, Elizabeth Hulsebosch, and Jonathan Bernstein. Special thanks to Allyson Rudolph and Sam O'Brien for their assistance and attention to detail.

The incomparable Suzanne Gluck has been our partner

throughout this process. She saw the potential of this book right at its inception, and she has been a tireless advocate and critical reader all along the way. She is simply the best, and so are her colleagues at William Morris Endeavor: Cathryn Summerhayes, Tracy Fisher, Claudia Ballard, Anna DeRoy, and Eve Attermann.

Most of all, we are grateful to our husbands for their sound advice, encouragement, sympathetic ears, and willingness to pick up the slack at home. And to our children, who are an endless source of inspiration and love.

The reunion brunch before Mr. K's memorial concert. Standing, left to right: Miriam Simon Cotter, John Stine, Miriam Perkoff, Michael Grossman, Joanne Lipman, Jonathan Friedes. Seated: Melanie Kupchynsky and Edward Harrison.

MR. K'S BLACK RUSSIANS

Mr. K's signature cocktail was the ultimate gesture of affection, best when shared with one (or many!) friends. He often mixed up a batch and poured it into his oversize flask, which he packed into his suitcase before a concert tour to share postperformance with fellow teachers—and in later years, with Melanie's Chicago Symphony Orchestra colleagues.

Serves eight—or fewer. Depends on your crowd.
Na Zdorovya!

> 4 shots Kahlua
> 8 shots vodka
> Flask or pitcher
> Secret Ukrainian incantations

1. Combine ingredients in a measuring cup. Stir.
2. Pour contents into large flask or pitcher.
3. Serve over ice.
4. Don't forget the secret Ukrainian incantations—but be careful: one wrong accent could curse your entire family for generations.

BIBLIOGRAPHICAL NOTES

FOREWORD

Stanford psychology professor Carol Dweck has written extensively about over-praising children. See Carol S. Dweck, "The Perils and Promises of Praise," *Educational Leadership*, 65, no. 2 (October 2007): 34–39, available electronically at http://www.ascd.org/publications/educational-leadership/oct07/vol65/num02/The-Perils-and-Promises-of-Praise.aspx.

In addition, researchers have found that people who experience moderate stress in childhood are more resilient and better able to cope with stress as adults. Linda J. Luecken of Arizona State University has published several studies of resilience in children. Other studies include: David M. Lyons, Karen J. Parker, Maor Katz, and Alan F. Schatzberg, "Developmental Cascades Linking Stress Inoculation, Arousal Regulation, and Resilience," *Frontiers in Behavioral Neuroscience*, 3, 32 (2009). Prepublished electronically July 10, 2009. Published electronically September 18, 2009. doi: 10.3389/neuro.08.032.2009 PMCID: PMC2759374; and Mark D. Seery, "Resilience: A Silver Lining to Experiencing Adverse Life Events?," *Current Directions in Psychological Science*, n. page (2011). Accessed October 6, 2012, http://seery.socialpsychology.org.

Malcolm Gladwell popularized the concept of 10,000 hours of practice required for true expertise: Malcolm Gladwell, *Outliers: The Story of Success* (New York: Little, Brown and Company, 2008).

Gladwell cited research by K. Anders Ericsson. For Ericsson's early research, which focused on violinists at the Music Academy of West Berlin, see K. Anders Ericsson, R. T. Krampe, and Clemens Tesch-Romer, "The Role of Deliberate Practice in the Acquisition of Expert Performance," *Psychological Review* 100.3 (1993): 363–406.

For Ericsson's later work applying his research to business success, see K. Anders Ericsson, Michael J. Prietula, and Edward T. Cokely, "The Making of an Expert," *Harvard Business Review.* Available online at http://www.uvm.edu/~pdodds/files/papers/others/2007/ericsson2007a.pdf.

CHAPTER 5

British composer and musicologist Cecil Forsyth was witty as well as erudite in his description of the viola, and his observations still ring true almost a century later: Cecil Forsyth, *Orchestration* (1914 edition) 395–396, Cornell University Library. Available online at http://books.google.com/books?id=m9_CTe8qNWIC & pg=PA395 & lpg=PA395 & dq=forsyth+viola+anxiety & source=bl & ots=gkP3wxsypz & sig=XilDJ9HQebJcnb2Y-lNVAmwoaCM&hl=en&sa=X&ei=-AoST5riHIH 20gHY9cX5DA&ved=0CCcQ6AEwAQ#v=onepage&q=anxiety&f=false.

A good overview of the viola's history can be found at viola-in-music.com: http://www.viola-in-music.com/history-of-the<Bi-viola.html.

For additional background on the school reform movement, please see: Maureen Stout, *The Feel-good Curriculum: The Dumbing-down of America's Kids in the Name of Self-esteem* (Cambridge, Massachusetts: Perseus, 2000).

CHAPTER 8

Soyuzivka's colorful history is described in Roma Lisovich's "Soyuzivka: A Look at Its Beginnings as Nonkanahwa," *The Ukrainian Weekly*, LXXVIII, no. 27 (July 4, 2010). Lisovich recounts how the property was purchased by John Foord, who was editor in chief of the *New York Times* from 1876 to 1883. The property was turned into a sanitarium by Foord's son, Andrew, a psychiatrist and society figure, and it grew to greater fame under one of Andrew's sons, Federick "Fritz" Foord, a landscape painter and industrial designer who was a member of the famed Algonquin Round Table in New York City. According to Lisovich, the sanitarium "offered treatment for depression, 'neurasthenia' (a popular nervousness condition of the 1900s), alcoholism and post-operative recuperation."

James Thurber wrote a number of letters from and about Foord's Sanitarium, collected in *The Thurber Letters*, edited by Harrison Kinney with Rosemary A. Thurber (Simon & Schuster 2003). The editors describe Foord's as "a popular drying-out place for *New Yorker* writers and editors."

CHAPTER 9

Theresa Chen writes about peer pressure on adolescent student musicians in her "The 6 Stages of Piano Students: Why and When Piano Students Quit Lessons," *Private Music Lessons*, Opus Music Education Blog, August 19, 2011. Accessed electronically October 6, 2012, http://www .opusmusiceducation.com/blog/2011/08/the-6-stages-of-piano-students -why-and-when-piano-students-quit-lessons. Her work draws on research by Sidney J. Lawrence, who specialized in the psychology of music education. See "This Business of Music Practicing: Or How Six Words Prevented a Drop-Out"; to access this article, see: http://www.amazon.com /This-business-music-practicing-prevented/dp/B0007EWSLS.

CHAPTER 16

Timothy Snyder's *Bloodlands: Europe between Hitler and Stalin* (New York: Basic, 2010) is an indispensable resource for understanding Ukraine before and during World War II. The author, a history professor at Yale University, generously provided additional insights in an interview.

Mr. K recounted his early years in several essays published in Ukrainian in conjunction with school reunions of the Berchtesgaden refugee-camp gymnasium. He also wrote Ukrainian-language articles about his youth for *Svoboda* (Ukrainian for "Liberty"), a newspaper for émigrés published in the United States. See "Dyvnym i neperedbachenym ruslom: spomyny pro Berkhtesgaden z pryvodu 50-ykh rokovyn taboru 'Orlyk,' "*Svoboda* (July 23, 1996): 2; *Svoboda* (July 24, 1996): 2–3; and "Spomyny pro

'Ridnu Shkolu,' " *Svoboda* (June 30, 1998): 2, 5. To access these articles, see: http://www.svoboda-news.com/arxiv.htm.

He also described his wartime experience in several English-language newspaper interviews, including the following:

"Recent DP Now College Student Here," *The Ukrainian Weekly*, XV (January 27, 1947): 2.

Marie Kidd, "Shawneetown Director Is Hero of Metropolis Festival," *Paducah Sun-Democrat*, April 14, 1957.

Pat Ordovensky, "The Old World and the New," *The Town Crier*, XII, no. 3 (March 1960). Published by the Sentinel Publishing Co., New Brunswick, New Jersey.

Additional descriptions of Mr. K's teenage years and/or life in the refugee camps were provided by Ihor Hayda, Olga Sawchuk, and Helena Melnitchenko. Taras Hunczak, history professor emeritus at Rutgers University and a native-born Ukrainian, shared both his knowledge of Ukrainian history and firsthand descriptions of life during the war.

For additional information about the Holodomor and its effects, see Steven Bela Vardy and Agnes Huszar Vardy, "Cannibalism in Stalin's Russia and Mao's China," *East European Quarterly*, XLI, no 2 (2007) Duquesne University.

The lives of forced laborers are vividly documented in *Forced Labor: The Germans, the Forced Laborers, and the War*, a companion volume to an exhibition produced by the Buchenwald and Mittelbau-Dora Memorials Foundation.

Other valuable resources that were indispensable in tracking down original documents and providing historical context include the International Tracing Service in Bad Arolsen, Germany; the U.S. Holocaust Museum; the Ukrainian Research Institute at Harvard; the Shevchenko Scientific Society in New York City; the Ukrainian Canadian Research & Documentation Centre in Toronto; and the Petro Jacyk Central and East European Resource Centre at the University of Toronto.

PHOTOGRAPH CREDITS

Grateful acknowledgment is made to the following for permission to reproduce the illustrations in the text: Pages ii, 51, 92, 114: photographs courtesy of Arthur Montzka. Pages 16, 31: clippings courtesy of the *East Brunswick Sentinel*. Pages 43, 209, 318: photographs courtesy of the Lipman family. Pages 23, 54, 148, 174, 216, 220, 262, 299: photographs courtesy of the Kupchynsky family. Page 164: photograph courtesy of Albert M. Simon, aka "Papa." Page 218: photograph courtesy of Miriam Simon Cotter.

Grateful acknowledgment is made to the following for permission to reproduce the illustrations in the photo inserts.

Photo insert one: Pages 1–2: photographs courtesy of the Kupchynsky family. Page 3 top: photograph courtesy of the Kupchynsky family; bottom: photograph courtesy of Arthur Montzka. Page 4 top and bottom: photograph courtesy of Arthur Montzka; page 4 center: photograph courtesy of the Kupchynsky family. Page 5 top: photograph courtesy of the Lipman family; page 5 center and bottom: photographs by Burton E. Lipman, courtesy of the Lipman family. Page 6 top: photograph courtesy of the Kupchynsky family; page 6 bottom: photograph courtesy of Arthur Montzka. Page 7: photographs courtesy of Arthur Montzka. Page 8 top:

photograph by Kwok Ying Fung; page 8 bottom: clipping courtesy of the *East Brunswick Sentinel.*

Photo insert two: Page 1 top: photograph courtesy of the Kupchynsky family; page 1 bottom: photograph courtesy of the Lipman family. Page 2 top left: photograph courtesy of the Lipman family; page 2 top right and bottom: photographs courtesy of Arthur Montzka. Page 3 top left: photograph courtesy of the Kupchynsky family; page 3 top right: photograph courtesy of the Lipman family; page 3 bottom: photograph by Kwok Ying Fung. Page 4 top: photograph courtesy of Carol A. Turrentine; page 4 bottom: photograph courtesy of Miriam Simon Cotter. Page 5 top: Reprinted with permission of *The Wall Street Journal,* Copyright © 1983 Dow Jones & Company, Inc. All Rights Reserved Worldwide.; page 5 bottom: photograph courtesy of the Rosenthal Archives, Chicago Symphony Orchestra, photo by Jim Steere. Page 6 top: photograph courtesy of Miriam Simon Cotter; page 6 bottom: flyer courtesy of the Kupchynsky family. Page 7 top left: photograph courtesy of the Lipman family; page 7 top right: photograph courtesy of John Henry; page 7 bottom: photograph courtesy of the Kupchynsky family. Page 8 top: photograph courtesy of Leslie A. Foodim; page 8 center: photograph courtesy of Albert M. Simon; page 8 bottom: photograph courtesy of Darius J. Cotter.